BLAISE PASCAL

BLAISE PASCAL

THE LIFE AND WORK
OF A REALIST

Ernest Mortimer

HARPER & BROTHERS

PUBLISHERS · NEW YORK

Library of Congress catalog card number: 59-7155

9

TO MY WIFE

CONTENTS

ILLUSTRATIONS

PREFACE

Like most writers on Pascal I write to a theme though not, I hope, to a brief. Pascal's writings offer a wide variety of interests: devotional, theological, scientific, polemical, literary and mystical. Men have written books on his political theory, but there the material is more slender. His mind was such that when he turned his attention to a subject, that subject came into focus. Its bearing on human welfare was illuminated in words that remain valid beyond the seventeenth century. It is hardly surprising that books on Pascal continue to be written.

My own starting point is the wish that modern thought might be more ready to admit quality as belonging to the realm of fact. On this, Pascal had something to say which was not casual or incidental but integral to his own thought and important for the present day. It comes to a point in his contact with Descartes, of whom accordingly a small picture occupies the opening chapter.

I began, then, with the intention of writing an essay on this subject, and what remains of this intention will be found in Chapter 11; but in the course of writing it seemed impossible to separate Pascal's thought from his person, or his person from his career, so this became yet another telling of a story familiar to many; I can only hope it will be found an interpretation rather than a mere recital.

The Bibliography will enable fellow-debtors to recognize my main obligations, and my limitations. The Provincial Letters and the *Pensées* have been bedside books for years and have accompanied me to the sites of Port Royal and to Saint-Etienne-du-Mont, though not yet to Clermont.

Through great courtesy at the Bibliothèque Nationale in Paris I have enjoyed the privilege of inspecting Louis Périer's album of the manuscript fragments, but shortness of time made it an occasion of piety rather than learning. I have spent hours (where weeks might be necessary for real results) upon the first folio edition of *Augustinus*, in an unrewarded attempt to find the Five Propositions. Bossuet said they were the soul of the book which could explain their invisibility in its body. Its inclusion in my Bibliography is therefore vanity, but I have read the other books.

It seems almost impossible to avoid attaching labels to Blaise Pascal, yet he does shed them as he comes into clearer view. The style, the character, the content of the thinking are stamped with individuality. Even in the *Entretien avec M. de Saci*, an edited version of an account of a conversation, remembered and recorded years afterward by Fontaine, the masterful idiomatic ring of Pascal's voice breaks through. He is bigger than his century. Even in matters purely external and, as it were, accidental, his anticipations are striking.

A modern man, starting out for the office, may glance at his wrist-watch, tap the barometer, slip into the nearest tobacconist's shop for a purchase and receive his change from the cash machine, board an omnibus and presently settle at his desk. How remote might seem the French geometer who got mixed up with Jansenism before Versailles was built! Yet Pascal originated that barometer, invented that calculating machine, was the first man to think of an omnibus and to organize a line of public vehicles, and was perhaps the only man before the twentieth century habitually to wear a wrist-watch.

In more abstract matters his refusal to 'date' is impressive. I have already hinted that he had an answer to a riddle which troubles many today, how to relate the world of commonsense experience with the world as presented by science. But also, he was at least a hundred years ahead of his time in the ability to entertain simultaneously propositions which appeared incompatible. Pascal's interest was in facts, or in sense-data if that term is better. If they contradicted each other, then one must wait for an explanation but meanwhile retain them as facts, since they had been observed. Comment (he might have anticipated C. P. Scott in saying) was free, but facts were sacred. Long afterwards, Hegel would exalt this to a philosophical principle in the sphere of history, where an established thesis would be confronted by an antithesis; and both would simply have to await the appearance of a synthesis. The modern physicist has often to adopt a similar patience.

Or consider that particular method of arguing which he outlines in the *Pensées* and which would have made such a wonderful book of his Defence of Religion if he had lived to complete it. The standard pattern for proving anything is that of Euclid. Pascal saw that that method when applied to the truths of human life (as for instance it was used by Jansen and Arnauld) left men cold. Men were persuaded of such truths not by any single-line chain of reasoning but by the centripetal and simultaneous influence of different sorts of testimony, supporting each other and converging upon the central truth to which they pointed. This is the essence of Cardinal Newman's *Grammar of Assent.*

The whole of the modern Existentialist movement may be considered to stem from Kierkegaard's blunt protest against the Hegelian Absolute: 'Put me in a system and you negate me. I am not a mathematical symbol. I *am*.' There is something peculiarly modern in the very ring of this appeal from abstraction to experience. We should hardly expect to find any parallel to it from a century earlier than the nineteenth, and it would seem especially unlikely from the age of Descartes and Spinoza. But listen to Pascal: 'Man is full of needs. He will only turn where they can *all* be satisfied. Someone may say of me, "He is a good mathematician", but I do other things. He is taking me for a proposition' (36). Jean-Paul Sartre cries today: 'L'homme est une passion inutile!' Pascal was before him with 'Quelle chimère est donc que l'homme!' and his conception of the *néant* is precisely echoed in the most sombre passages of the French existentialists; but Pascal has something to put beside it, or rather inside it.

He was not a pessimist; unless a pessimist is one who cries 'Wolf' when wolves are about, one who has a particular insight into human pain and a profound concern for it. The man who wrote, 'If the whole universe were to combine to crush man, he would still be greater than that which destroyed him', did not take a low view of our nature or a dim view of our destiny.

His was a curiously disjointed career. The short but not simple annals of his life had their discords resolved only in the final chords. In art he regarded symmetry as falsification, and he did not expect life or truth to be simple. 'Que de natures en celle de l'homme! Que de vacations! *Et par quel hasard!*' (116).

The hazards of life bestowed on him genius and pain; gave him an ideal family life and separated him from it; brought him an earnestly desired celebrity which turned to dust in his mouth; opened to him coveted doors of social honour which, for a while at least, inflicted on him an intolerable ennui; flashed upon him a Damascus Road vision and decreed that his 'What wouldest thou have me to do?' should be addressed to a doctrinaire controversialist; flung him into a religious quarrel not of his making but only too vividly to his liking; compounded him of deep compassion and acute contentiousness; enabled him to write like Thomas à Kempis and Euclid and Juvenal and finally like only himself. A loyal monarchist and upholder of lawful authority, he spent a period flouting and dodging the government agents and enjoying it. A Catholic equally by conviction and convention, hardly even interested in the doctrines or polities of the Reformers, he uttered at one crisis S. Bernard's defiance of Rome: 'Ad Tuam Domine Jesu tribunal apello' (920).

It would give a neat picture if we could show that the great turning-point of 1654 meant that from then he abjured science and society; but in 1658 he made his most brilliant contribution to mathematics, and in 1660 he wrote to Fermat that the company and conversation of such men as he, not as scientists but as men of culture, gave him keen enjoyment. He then made his soul and died, but the story was not ended. There were all the manuscript fragments in his room to be disentangled, assorted, explained; a task at which men still work fruitfully.

He did not reach the age of forty. All of his main written works, the Treatise on the Vacuum, the Provincial Letters, the Apology for Religion, tail off uncompleted. It was a rough-hewn life, but a divinity shaped it. For Pascal himself, with his distrust of symmetry, the mutations of life were powerless to ruffle the abiding springs of character and truth. This servant of the Logos gives his message in his person.

The reader will come upon many quotations in the text which are only explained by a number in parenthesis. These are from Pascal's *Pensées* as numbered in Brunschvicg's edition, which is adopted here (in preference to Dr Stewart's excellent arrangement) to help the reader who possesses the Everyman's Library edition, who should note that the translator-editor dropped *Pensée* 514 and renumbered the remainder. Any number above 514 in the present book should be reduced by one to find the *Pensée* in 'Everyman'.

In the narrative section I have cut one Gordian knot. The affairs of Port Royal and those of Pascal's personal life coincide at a moment when it would be impossible to do simultaneous justice to both of them; and when the biographer defers his introduction of Port Royal until that moment he must either sketch it much too rapidly or interrupt the personal theme at a crisis. I have devoted an early chapter to Port Royal, believing that Pascal's story can afford the break in the narrative at that stage, and that in retrospect it will not be regarded as a digression.

The period of Pascal's life of which least is known is 1649–54, which occupies Chapters 5 and 6. Research has defined the outline and established a fair amount of detail. Drawing upon the studies chiefly of MM. Strowski and Mesnard I have, so far as I know, put nothing into this section which presents conjecture as fact. The exploration of Pascal's psychological state is of course subjective, but here also I have tried to draw only plain inferences from known facts. If it may seem a revival of the romantic Pascal of

Chateaubriand and others, let me say clearly that I regard that Byronic dreamer, brooding on his own anguish, wrestling with demonic doubts, as a figment. Pascal was not that sort of man.

But I agree with M. Fortunat Strowski that the contrasting picture drawn by M. Émile Boutroux (in one of the best books on Pascal) is equally unacceptable. Of Pascal in the summer of 1654 Boutroux writes: 'Pascal est loin maintenant de cet état de fluctuation qui avait suivi sa conversion aux idées de Jansénius. Il a retrouvé l'équilibre et l'accord avec lui-même.' The indications lead me, further perhaps than Strowski or Mesnard, to the conviction that at this particular moment of his life Pascal had reached a state for which the only adequate word is despair. His own words seem to confirm it, and the night of vision requires and implies it.

My many obligations to other writers on Pascal are indicated as they arise in the text. In addition I would thank: Mr Evelyn Tisdall who read the first draft and whose experience in authorship was of great value; Miss Shirley Chubb and my sister Miss Winifred Mortimer, who gave great help over the illustrations; Mrs J. G. Stewart and Miss Patience Burne (Librarian of Newnham College, Cambridge) for their great kindness in securing the photograph of the cast left by the late Professor Stewart to Newnham College; and Sir Harold Scott for most generously revising the proofs. Among Pascal's links with the present day I had not foreseen Scotland Yard!

NOTE

The Appendix on pp. 237 ff. includes translations by the author of most of the foreign language passages which occur in the text.

PART I

CHAPTER I

THE WATERSHED

'We see things not only from different sides but with different eyes.'

PASCAL, Pensée 124

———

In September 1647 Descartes made one of his infrequent returns to France and used the opportunity to visit Pascal in Paris. Their interest in each other's theories and achievements had begun at least eight years before but this seems to have been the only occasion when they met. It was hardly two years before Descartes' death; Pascal, at the age of twenty-four, was at one of the turning-points of his short life. He was a very sick man. He had recently acquired that sudden interest in religion which is commonly called his First Conversion. He was working hard, not only upon the perfecting of a calculating machine, but upon experiments in the equilibrium of gases and liquids which would presently make his name resound through Europe.

The Pascal family were good correspondents and we know how the visit went. It took place in the house in the Rue Brisemiche to which Blaise and his sister Jacqueline had returned, from Rouen, in the previous May. For Pascal the visit must have seemed momentous. His visitor was the intellectual leader of a generation that included Fermat, Galileo, Torricelli, Huyghens and Harvey (and we may suppose that Pascal would already assume that his own name was on this list). Descartes was regarded as the navigator who had discovered a new and shorter passage into the little-charted ocean of knowledge. Descartes had first heard of Pascal eight years before, when the boy of sixteen had produced a treatise on conic sections which Descartes had declined to take very seriously. The older man was now more keenly interested, and vaguely disturbed, about the advances in physics which were bringing Pascal's name to the fore.

They had much in common. Each possessed a genius for mathematics, a passion for ordered knowledge, a clear and flexible style of exposition, a high sense of the aristocracy of intellect with something of the infirmity which goes with it, a restless desire to be first in the field. Their differences were no less marked. This was an encounter between a mature celebrity and a young aspirant; between a philosopher who had scientific talents and a scientist with philosophic leanings; between a thinker whose attention was given to principles and what might be deduced from them, and a laboratory student who concentrated upon observed data. But there was a point of difference more profound and significant than these.

It was at 10.30 a.m. on Monday, September 23, 1647, that Descartes presented himself with a few friends at Pascal's house. Waiting for him with Blaise were Jacqueline Pascal, his younger sister, who kept house for him, M. de Roberval, an eminent professor of science of the College of France who had crossed swords with Descartes more than once and was on the way to becoming his *bête noir*; and the poet Dalibray seems to have made up the party of nine or ten people. Clearly it was regarded as an occasion. Jacqueline described it in her letter of two days later to her married sister Gilberte Périer, writing with the observant intelligence and sedate humour which distinguished all that family. Jacqueline at twenty-two had great beauty of character and appearance, the latter marred by an early attack of small-pox. She was accustomed to celebrities. Richelieu had joked with her; she had attended the Queen, acted for Mondory, entertained Corneille. At present she was testing her vocation to the religious life. She was respectfully aware of the high compliment implied by the coming of M. Descartes but able to take it calmly; her brother was also a great man!

There is no known portrait of Jacqueline. We are fortunate in the existence of excellent portraits of Descartes and Blaise Pascal of about this period. Franz Hals' picture of Descartes in the Louvre gives (and how rarely this happens) the very appearance one might expect. It is the solitary independent thinker conscious of power and superiority. The nose and chin are strong and jutting; the thin lips are compressed with the habitual need for stillness in concentration. The raised eyebrows keep the heavy-lidded eyes wide open to gaze at the world of things. Jacques Maritain reads pride in this portrait: 'Tête superbement lourde et violente, front bas, œil pendant, obstiné, chimérique, bouche d'orgueil et de terre.' It may be so. There is no doubt about the thinking. If this man had taken to chess he would have found few rivals.

There are two undoubtedly authentic portraits of Pascal, Domat's charcoal drawing and the death-mask. The former shows him as a young man and must have been drawn at about the time of the meeting with Descartes. The distinguished lawyer (Domat was France's 'Blackstone') displays artistic power in his beautiful sketch, made amongst the entries in a page of his notebook. This eager, confident youth with the firm mouth and the wide open eyes, has not yet crossed any spiritual Rubicon, but if we did not know who he was, we should wish to find out.

After suitable greetings and civilities they settled to business; but here human nature took a hand. Roberval was highly aware that this was an historic occasion, but he saw it as an encounter not of two great men but of three, himself being the link between his brilliant young protégé and his sparring partner of many years of slightly acerbated correspondence. Roberval, then, took charge of the proceedings, performed the introductions, displayed and explained to Descartes 'the instrument', that is the syringe (the first syringe made) which Pascal had recently designed for experiments upon the vacuum, and led the discussion. This suited Pascal well, as he was slightly overawed and reserved, and was too ill to play the host.

Descartes was less docile. For a while he put his questions and argued about the replies, but he was inwardly fuming at Roberval's condescension and at last the fire kindled. According to

Jacqueline's entertaining letter 'il riposte avec un peu d'aigreur', saying that he 'would discuss with Pascal as long as he might, since he talked sense, but not with Roberval who spoke with prejudice'. Jacqueline does not tell us to whom this was addressed; possibly the ceiling. Soon afterwards Descartes pulled out his watch, noted it was nearly noon and excused himself for a luncheon engagement in the Faubourg Saint-Germain. Roberval went with him and climbed into his carriage. Jacqueline saw them depart down the street continuing the argument with gesticulations.

Descartes was resolved to have an interview with Pascal without the risks which had spoiled this one, so he came back early next morning, at eight o'clock, and stayed till half-past ten. Jacqueline was again present for some of the time, during which Descartes (a qualified physician) advised Pascal about his health, saying that he should rely more on soups than solid food, and should stay in bed every day until he felt really inclined to get up. Pascal's sense of irony may have been touched by this counsel from one who paid a social call at eight in the morning; but the philosopher's concern is a gracious detail in a man reputed to have been deficient in sympathies and jealous of young rivals.

For the rest, they almost certainly continued the discussion about the Void but all they seemed to have achieved was a minor misunderstanding.

Two years previously Italy had the honour of hitting upon a small and curious phenomenon fraught with large consequences. Evangelista Torricelli had found that if a tube is filled with mercury, inverted into a basin of mercury with the lower end then opened, the mercury in the tube falls a certain distance, thus facing the scientific world with two questions. What, if anything, was in the apparent empty space at the top of the tube? Why did the mercury fall so far and no farther?

News and details of this experiment had been brought to France by Père Mersenne, the old leader of the scientific group in Paris to which Pascal belonged. In 1646 it had been brought to Rouen from Paris by M. Pierre Petit, a keen and practical member of the same group. He, with Pascal's father and with Blaise himself, had then carried out a series of important experiments which Pascal had embodied in a treatise not yet published when Descartes called upon him. All good scientists pool their information, and in fact that was the practice in France at this time. Père Mersenne corresponded regularly with Descartes but by some oversight he had never told him about the Italian experiment, nor of the Rouen developments. Descartes was almost completely in the dark, and the two brief interviews with Pascal were hardly sufficient to put him *au courant*. Still, he applied himself to the two questions.

What was in the 'empty' part of the tube? To Pascal this was hardly a problem at all. It looked empty; why should it not be empty? It was the other question that interested Pascal. But for Descartes the first question was crucial. The tube could not contain even a few cubic millimetres of nothingness, since nothingness is outside nature and therefore cannot be inside a tube. Nature's intolerance of a vacuum was as universally accepted as the force of gravity, and by Descartes as firmly as in the Aristotelian physics; he had scrapped many dogmas and recast others, but not this one. Various guesses were made as to the contents of the top of the tube: rarefied air drawn through the 'pores' of the glass, or a distillation from the mercury, or, more vaguely, 'subtle spirits'. The last of these was Descartes' consistent reply.

Why did the mercury rest in the tube at a higher level than that in the basin to which it had access? Torricelli had made a brilliant guess that the air above the basin was pressing from the sky downwards. Pascal provisionally believed this to be the truth; it would have to be rigorously demonstrated. Roberval rejected it out of hand; Père Mersenne favoured it, and Descartes was favourably impressed. Jacqueline's letter contains the puzzling sentence: 'Il (Descartes) la croit fort (the theory of the weight of air) mais par une raison que mon frère n'approuve pas.' We suppose the explanation to be that the whole thing was new to Descartes who was trying to sort out his ideas, while Pascal had lived with it for months, made experiments, planned further experiments and formed provisional hypotheses. The height of the mercury could be explained either by the dogma of nature's refusal to allow a vacuum or by the weight of air. Pascal doubted the dogma so was free to entertain the alternative. Descartes seemed to be approving two adequate causes for one effect. This confusion led to another. Descartes (as he claimed later and there is not the slightest reason to doubt his word) suggested to Pascal that tests taken at different heights on a mountainside would give valuable data. Pascal had his programme for such tests already cut and dried. He probably agreed politely that it would be the right line of action. Later, Descartes complained (mildly, and paying compliments to Pascal) that he was not given credit for the original idea which resulted in the great experiment of the Puy de Dôme.

Pascal has been studied in a variety of moods, and both his admirers and his critics have differed in the choice of the characteristic they have regarded as pivotal. Our reason for describing his encounter with Descartes, so casual in itself, so inconclusive in results, is to state the key and indicate the main theme of this study. We see him at the moment when a line was drawn between past and future, and in the presence of the man who drew the line.

There are rivers to which Descartes' contribution to human thought and activity may be likened. They grow as they flow, full in view, irrigating great tracts, serving hamlets, villages and towns, increased by tributaries, becoming navigable and carrying cargoes, ministering to many needs of many people.

And there is more rarely a river of another sort. It trickles a short way from its source and disappears underground, into the side of the mountain from which it appeared. Many miles from that spot, perhaps on the other side of the mountain, and probably unrecognized, it reappears in power and fertilizes a province. I do not say this is a picture of Pascal the Christian or of Pascal the literary artist or of Pascal the scientist. He has never disappeared. But of Pascal the thinker, corrective of what was missing in Descartes, there may be something in the picture.

CHAPTER 2

THE GENIUS

*'By labour and intent study (which I take to be my portion in this life) joined
with the strong propensity of nature, I might perhaps leave something so written
to after times, as they would not willingly let die.'*

MILTON, The Reason of Church Government

Blaise Pascal was born at Clermont in Auvergne on June 19,
1623, and christened eight days later. His father Étienne
Pascal was a high public official in the Department, being Con-
seiller Élu pour le Roi in the electorate of Bas-Auvergne at Clermont, and about to be (from 1624) President of the Cour des
Aides. Blaise's mother, Antoinette Bégon, also came of a local
stock of substantial merchants who aspired to public service and
position. She died at the age of thirty, leaving Blaise aged three
with an elder sister Gilberte and a younger sister Jacqueline.

The story of the Pascal family gains in fragrance and interest
from the affection which bound them. It was undemonstrative and
even formal in expression (in their letters the 'vous' becomes 'tu'
only occasionally and as if by accident) and it was free from excessive emotional demands and from excessive mutual admiration.
There was nothing stuffy about it but it was warm and enduring
beyond the custom of that time.

The people of the Auvergne show a sort of spiritual parallel to
the volcanic character of their soil. Typical Auvergnats like the
Arnaulds, the Domats, the Pascals, have that combination of external sobriety and toughness with the suggestion of hidden fires.
Étienne respected and taught his children to respect the sound
formalities of social life, and it was within a decorous frame that
each of the four attained unmistakable distinction.

In some ways Gilberte furnishes the best, because the least expected, example of this. There would be some excuse for regarding her as the worthy but dull member of the family. Strowski rightly calls her the Martha of that household. When Blaise was the talk of Paris for his cleverness and Jacqueline was being fêted for her beauty and charm, Gilberte was absorbed in the housekeeping. Later she became an estimable wife and mother, and adopted a deep but rather narrow form of piety which seemed to extinguish finally any prospect of her shining. When Blaise died it fell to her to write some account of him, and she did this as she did everything, dutifully and methodically. Even for a born writer, the memoir of a near relation is notoriously a difficult form of literary exercise. Gilberte's short biography, which is our first source of knowledge about Blaise, is extraordinarily well done. There are some stilted phrases in the centre of it where conventional piety veils the sentiment and seriously warps the record of facts, but her accounts of the infancy and education and then of her brother's last years glow with perception and inspire confidence. No writer on Pascal can ignore, or is likely to surpass, her unassuming portrait.

Blaise was one of those fortunate children who are encouraged rather than forbidden to stare. Among the things at which he must have stared daily were two abrupt and surprising heights—Clermont Cathedral, which soared (like the choir of Beauvais) not many yards from the back windows of the Pascals' home, and the Puy de Dôme rising some miles from the town. Fancies may be out of place for so matter-of-fact a mind as Pascal's, but we allow ourselves to reflect that the kindred worlds of grace and of nature first presented themselves as heights to be scaled.

He was born into a post-war society, even though the Thirty Years' War had begun five years before. To the people of France, Richelieu's foreign battles meant little, except in the growing burden of taxation, compared with the internal religious wars which had agonized recent generations. The militant cause of the Protestant reformers had already been lost long before Richelieu crushed the remaining Huguenots at La Rochelle in 1628. Indeed the process of unification and reconstruction under Henry IV had begun about the time when Blaise's father was born; but the misery, weakness and poverty had required at least a generation for recovery. Blaise was born into a France on its way up from the depths, and already some way up.

The victory of Catholicism had been (to abridge the Duke of Wellington's verdict on Waterloo) a near thing; and it had been more than a reaction. No one had the intention of establishing the *status quo*. The Counter Reformation perhaps touched deeper springs in France than in Italy or Spain. The deepest roots of the Protestant revolution had been ethical, and all awakened consciences admitted the need for amendment of life. The real question had been whether a more genuinely Christian spirit would necessitate new forms or could be reinfused into the forms of the historic Church. The private history of many a good and notable Frenchman of the sixteenth century would, if fully known (and we do know some of them), be a story of perplexed conscience and vacillating loyalties, as such a man would try to reckon where his duty lay, would throw in his lot sometimes with one party and sometimes with the other, would hear the voice of religion sinking to a whisper under the din of conflict and realize at last simply that his country was bleeding to death. Something like a universal sigh of relief went up when the leader of the Protestant forces embraced Catholicism, became king as Henry IV, and brought peace.

France could breathe again. A political and social order could be rebuilt within which the Church could repent and do the first works. The typical figure of this revival is that winning and gracious character, S. Francis de Sales, who died some months before Blaise Pascal was born. His successor was S. Vincent de Paul who carried the Church's Gospel and works of mercy to the most ignorant and needy, rather as in the English Church revival of the nineteenth century the generation of Pusey and Keble was followed by that of Dolling and Lowder.

This post-war France could take its due part in what may be called the second chapter of the Renaissance, the expansion of natural science. Blaise Pascal's life covers the second quarter of the 'century of genius' which had begun with the almost simultaneous publication, in 1605, of Cervantes' *Don Quixote* and Bacon's *Advancement of Learning*; a backward and a forward glance, as Professor Whitehead points out. Towards the middle of the century only a few months separated the publication of Descartes' *Meditations*, Galileo's death, Newton's birth and the appearance of Descartes' *Principia Philosophia* with its preface, the *Discours sur la Méthode*.

But there were two clouds in the sky.

One was spiritual exhaustion. Wars of religion are not religious events. We do not equate Christianity with pacifism if we note as a fact of history that peoples emerge from wars less spiritual than they went in, even after making full allowance for signal examples of endurance unto death and for the general response of human nature to the call to self-sacrifice. Large sections of the French population had lost their sympathies or convictions, whether Catholic or Protestant: 'a plague on both your houses'. There had been a flight from religion in various directions.

With the masses of the poor it had been perhaps not so much a case of their dropping religion as of religion dropping them. A country given over to banditry, looting, sporadic forays and political anarchy cannot maintain the regular supply of sacrament and teaching of a Christian country at peace. Shepherds were few and flocks were scattered. But there were many who left the fold with more or less of deliberation, tired of the whole business. Passion is only one of the characteristic fruits of controversy, which can also generate tedium. Men had somehow, by courage or cunning or luck, survived a brutalizing period when life and rights were held cheap and it was every man for himself. In saying goodbye to all that, they felt that life should have something more entertaining to offer than Calvin's arid disquisitions or the counter-arguments of the schools. If there was now some real prospect that the world's great age should begin anew, such men had no intention that it should begin with theological formulae, of whatever complexion. Libertinism in all its types and a wide choice of shades was one legacy of the struggle.

Another effect, apparently clean contrary to libertinism but not without a deep-lying kinship, was an appeal to certain pre-Christian ideals of public and private virtue. There was a considerable and honourable section of the nation, of whom Étienne Pascal perfectly represents the type. They were responsible, public-minded men, mostly officials with a taste for learning, a devotion for law and order, a sincere acceptance of (rather than a fervid attachment to) the religion of the State; non-mystical men of solid worth, believing in God, sustained by self-respect. Such men would have formed their own opinion of the chicaneries and fripperies which had come to disfigure the Church. In many cases they had been moved to support the Protestant cause but changed their mind on concluding that Reform seemed to mean an alliance of a grim theology with social anarchy. Such men constituted the floating vote which kept France Catholic; but Catholicism as they saw it needed stiffening, and that stiffening was sought from pagan sources with full confidence that the teachings of the Stoics, especially as expounded by Epictetus, would bring no harm to Christian theology and much benefit to the Christian ethic. We shall see that the penetration of Blaise Pascal was required to expose a danger here.

That was one cloud in the sky. Christian France had large arrears to make up in evangelization and pastoral care. The other cloud was smaller but more heavily charged with electricity. A disastrous and disruptive storm was brewing.

The Renaissance in one aspect was a bid for freedom, a breaking of the shell of the medieval polity; and in that aspect the Protestant Revolution was simply one manifestation of the general breakaway. But to another aspect of the Renaissance, that is, its pride and confidence in human achievement, the Reformers were directly opposed. The typical Renaissance artist, poet, savant or builder, would be very unlikely to say, 'Nothing in my hand I bring'; whereas to Calvin you had no merit whoever you might be. Your best works and most admirable qualities were as septic with sin as your worst. By grace you were saved if you had that fortune at all, and that not of yourself. You might be among the few saved or the many damned; and in this decision you not only had no voice whatever but no clue whatever as to God's reason for His choice. You only knew that deserts did not enter into the matter since the best of men deserved only hell.

This was heresy, but like most heresies it was an over-emphasis to the point of perversion of an element in Catholic belief; for the Christian Gospel is offered not as a course in self-improvement for good people who would like to be better but as a seeking and saving of men who have lost their way. There is here an unresolved tension in the Christian account of man's condition. Jesus Christ could recognize and hail natural virtue in an untaught pagan centurion while He could seem to ignore its presence in an instructed and sincere spiritual seeker like Nicodemus. 'Except a man be born again he cannot enter the Kingdom.' The problem has been usually latent but always present in the Church. Christian humanism which recognizes the natural virtues and encourages their development has contrived to exist side by side with more radical insistence upon detachment from the world and reliance on supernatural grace alone. Usually the Church has felt large enough to contain the two elements without being forced to define their relation to each other, but the tension has at some periods been dragged into the foreground. The seventeenth century was to be such a period. The issue was not yet, it never would be exclusively, a clash between Jansenist and Jesuit, but it would take that form; and in it Blaise Pascal was destined to play a part.

'As soon as my brother was old enough for talk he gave tokens of an extraordinary mind by the extremely apt little replies he made to questions, and still more by his own questions on the nature of things, which surprised everyone. . . . He was always far ahead of his age.'*

We shall omit some picturesque details of Blaise's infancy which appear in nearly all biographies and are derived from the memoirs of Marguerite Périer, Gilberte's daughter and Blaise's niece. This will deprive students of the occult of a fine case of exorcism, and students of Freud of material for conjecture from Blaise's attitude to his parents while his mother lived. But Marguerite, unlike her mother, was inaccurate and haphazard, and we shall take from her only the intimation that Blaise showed early signs of a serious malady.

This illness is usually treated as a mystery but it seems that a large part of the explanation was made clear after his death. Of the two apertures in the skull of every baby, which should knit up in the early weeks of life, it was found that in Pascal's case one of them had never properly joined up at all, and the other had clamped or overlapped so as to form a bony ridge. The wonder is not that he suffered from headaches but that he was ever free from them.

Marguerite Périer tells us that Étienne in his student days at Paris had come into close association with the great barrister Antoine Arnauld, and this we can accept from her. Arnauld, himself from Auvergne, would not have ignored a promising law student from Clermont, and real life has no artistic scruples about avoiding coincidences. This was a coincidence, for Arnauld founded the family which reformed and largely populated the religious community of Port Royal which we must describe in the next chapter.

Étienne Pascal, on the death of his young wife, made and kept a resolve almost unique in those days. He would be father, mother and tutor to his children. A governess was installed, Louise Defaulte, who remained attached to the family throughout her life. But the formal education of Gilberte, Blaise and

---

* Gilberte Périer, *Vie de Blaise Pascal.*

Jacqueline was undertaken and carried out single-handed by their father.

Already we can see some of the moulding influences of Blaise's character. A motherless only son between two affectionate sisters, a child whose health gave anxiety and whose quick intelligence extorted admiration, a small boy whose only companion of his own sex was a father serious by nature and saddened by loss; such a boy explains much in the man whom he grew to be. For one thing, all the great masters of dialogue from Plato onwards probably had the pattern of their thinking formed by long imaginary arguments in childhood. On the natural level he would always be sensitive, imperious, quick-tempered, impulsively affectionate, over-ready to score a point or to claim a point. Such qualities are neither of the surface nor of the depths. Blaise had deeper attributes than these which will emerge with the story.

In 1631 Étienne Pascal moved with his family to live in Paris, renting a house in a quarter which would have delighted the late Hilaire Belloc with its street-names. It was in the Rue de Tisseranderie which was intersected by the Street of the Two Doors, the Street of the Bad Boys, Cock Street and the Street of the Devilish Wind. Here near the newly-built Hôtel de Ville they lived for three years and then moved to the left bank to the aristocratic Saint-Germain quarter, occupying a house near the Luxembourg. Another move in 1636 brought them finally to a house in the Rue Brisemiche which Étienne would hold (though absent in Rouen for a number of these years) until 1648. Here, adjoining the Church of Saint-Merry, they were very near the Friary of Père Mersenne and the town house of the Arnaulds in the Rue du Regnard-qui-Prêche (or Pêche; it seems not quite certain whether this fox went preaching or fishing).

The removal to Paris had involved apparently the ending of Étienne's quite eminent professional career at the age of forty-six, and it is natural to wonder why he decided on this. Domestic loneliness may have had much to do with it, but a sufficient answer is really indicated by what the life in Paris actually brought

BLAISE PASCAL

Crayon drawing by his friend Jean Domat, sketched on a page of Domat's legal notebook

him. A royal patent of two generations previously made him a member of a modest stratum of the nobility. He possessed a competent fortune and invested it in the Hôtel de Ville, which looked (but was not) a gilt-edged security. He could now, in the most stimulating surroundings, give up the greater part of each day to the education of his children. He could give free rein to his own taste and considerable talent for natural science through those informal learned groups which would presently develop into Societies and Academies. And being a more sociable man than he is sometimes pictured, he could enter and enjoy a wider, more varied and, frankly, more cultured social life than Clermont afforded. Finally, there might be, as there proved to be, opportunity in Paris for advancement if he should wish to resume practice. Étienne Pascal was to be a Counsellor of State before he died.

The link with Auvergne was never broken, but for Blaise from the age of eight years Paris was either his home or the base of his work, the centre of his chief interests and friendships.

Étienne's education of his children was remarkable for its paternal self-denial, its eccentricity, rigour, patience, and success where failure might almost have been predicted. He had a just scorn for the sort of pedagogy which he had suffered himself, but the Jesuit schools were introducing better methods and an altogether higher standard. They could claim S. Francis de Sales and René Descartes among their products. Étienne Pascal was an obstinate lay theorist who thought he could do better on his own lines. It is tempting to dwell in imagination on a Prize Day speech referring to Blaise as an ex-pupil: 'Two years before he left school he wrote a mathematical essay which marked a great advance in higher mathematics and laid the foundations of the integral calculus. At the age of twenty he invented, constructed and afterwards patented the calculating machine. In his early twenties he solved the problem upon which European students of physics were chiefly engaged. In his early thirties he revived the literature of his country with a book which created a new standard of excellence in prose. Soon afterwards he solved the outstanding mathematical problem of the time. In his late thirties he assembled notes which he never fashioned into a book, but in their scattered state they rank as an abiding religious and philosophical classic.' Étienne's educational method aimed at results and these were his results. As to this method, Gilberte is our informant:

'His principal maxim in this education was to hold the child always above his work' (that is, not to let the work get him down; not to rush him or overload him with knowledge), 'and that is why he did not wish the boy to learn Latin until he was twelve, when he could do it more easily.' (Schoolchildren were started at Latin much earlier than that.) 'Meanwhile he taught him the things he saw the child able to take in. He gave him a general picture of languages, and showed him how these followed certain grammatical rules which allowed of exceptions that had to be noted; and that thus one could render languages communicable from one country to another. This general idea clarified his mind and showed him the reasons for grammatical rules. . . . After these studies my father gave him others. He spoke often to him of unusual natural effects like gunpowder and other things which surprise when one reflects on them. My brother was delighted with these conversations, but he wanted to know the reasons for everything; and as some of these reasons are not known, whenever my father gave no reason, or gave some conventional reply (which was in fact no explanation) he would not be satisfied; for he always had an astonishing sharpness for detecting anything spurious. Always and in everything the truth was the one goal of his mind and nothing short of it contented him. From his childhood he would give himself only to what seemed to him plainly true, so that when people failed to supply him with sound reasons for things he sought them himself, and when he was on the trail of a reason he would not stop until he had tracked it down. On one occasion someone at table accidentally struck a porcelain plate with a knife and it made a sound. My brother noticed this and that when the plate was touched the sound stopped. At once he wanted to know why, and this led him to make other experiments in sound. He noticed many things, which he assembled in an essay (at the age of eleven) which was thought very carefully reasoned.'

As a postscript to this let us see Blaise Pascal's own mature verdict on his education in a letter to his friend Le Pailleur*: 'Par un bonheur que je ne puis assez reconnaitre j'ai toujours été élevé avec une méthode singulière et des soins plus que paternels.'

Gilberte describes a famous incident of which too much and too little has been made. The father's own bent for mathematics decided him to make that subject the coping stone of his plan. Up to twelve years of age Blaise should learn general knowledge; from twelve to sixteen, Latin, Greek, other languages, history and geography; and at sixteen he should be introduced to the joys of geometry. Meanwhile books on mathematics were not allowed in the house, and the subject took no place in the daily conversational instructions. One day when Blaise was twelve years old his father came upon him surrounded with diagrams and so absorbed that he still thought himself alone. Inquiry proved that he had been trying to work out for himself the principles of geometry, calling straight lines 'bars' and circles 'rounds', and was now trying to find some method of proving his guess or conviction that the three angles of a triangle must add up to two right angles. This, be it noticed (as Prof. Mesnard makes clear), is what Gilberte says, and is a long way short of the usual version of the story, which practically claims that Blaise had rediscovered the whole of Euclid independently, up to the thirty-second proposition of the first book.

On the other hand it cannot be dismissed in favour of the alternative version of Tallemont des Reaux (contemporary as that is) that Étienne merely found Blaise studying a volume of Euclid. This version is sometimes preferred, by Brunschvicg among others, as being less 'marvellous', but it would be a great deal

* *Oeuvres Complètes*, edit. Lahure, tome III, p, 61

more mysterious. It would leave quite unexplained Étienne's outburst of paternal pride and joy. At the age of twelve Mozart had composed symphonies, Capablanca had won the chess championship of his State. We are here concerned with a twelve-year-old boy who four years later would formulate Pascal's Theorem. If the average little boy does not pore over Euclid it is because he does not want to, not necessarily because it is beyond his power. Moreover if Blaise had read Euclid he would have called lines and circles by their right names, and Gilberte would be convicted of an inventiveness quite out of character.

The education had been devised on broad humanistic lines but there were gaps in Étienne's interests and knowledge. Blaise's introduction to history must have been sketchy and slight. Languages were studied probably more for the principles of syntax than for their fruits in literature, though Blaise quickly mastered Latin to read it easily, and probably read a lot of it in these years, with rather less Greek. Theology was limited to the elementary religious teaching open to every child.

Perhaps the most notable limitation was in regard to the natural sciences, which were studied as a system of abstract rules applying to inanimate substances, or at most to bodies regarded as mechanisms. This accorded not only with Étienne's mind but with the mood of the century. The living sciences—organic chemistry, biology, physiology, psychology—were as yet waiting their turn, broadly speaking. There was indeed at this time a strong school of biology in Padua, and in England Harvey had already discovered the circulation of the blood, and Blaise himself would show no mean ability in psychology, but the broad character of seventeenth-century science relied upon automatism and mathematics. Here, indeed, will be the real drama of Blaise's achievement. Born with a driving passion for the 'clear ideas' noted by Descartes and an exceptional gift for handling them, he would develop later an even greater interest in the lives and lot of his fellow men and would find that, to borrow a book-title of the late A. E. W. Mason, they wouldn't be chessmen. This geometrical approach would not suffice for the study of men. He must find, and in the little time that Providence allowed him he did find, other principles and other methods.

For a man who wished for himself and his family a life of independent activity and varied interests, ex-President Pascal had chosen a good moment to come to Paris. Centralization had brought new importance to the capital. Always the focus of learning, it was now drawing in from the provinces the great families of nobility and fashion and commerce. The Hôtel de Ville and the Luxembourg were splendid witnesses not only to the revival of building but to advances in administrative power and social brilliance. In concentric rings around the Court, France was relearning its culture. Étienne renewed old friendships and formed new ones.

An old friend of student days, Le Pailleur, was perhaps the first link between Étienne and the two worlds of society and of scientific research. The leading actor of the day, Mondory, was a fellow Auvergnat and a very good friend, who brought contact not only (presumably) with his own new theatre of the Marais but with the great family of the Seigneur de Morangis, Counsellor of State and Director of Finances. He and his wife were enchanted with the child Jacqueline and took her in 1638 to the Court at Saint-Germain to present her to the Queen, Anne of Austria.

Le Pailleur was a strange but typical figure in that scene. A man of fundamental integrity (Étienne Pascal paid high testimony to his worth) and serious intellectual attainments, he seemed to live for the fun of it, a diner-out of the first water, excelling at light verse and light conversation. A great friend of his became perhaps the Pascals' closest friend, Dalibray the poet, brother of Madame Sainctot at whose house Gilberte and Jacqueline found a second home and playmates in the Sainctot children. Madame Sainctot was a widow of very high position by marriage, possessing some wit, great beauty and an accommodating code of ethics. She had been the mistress of Voiture the poet, but during this period he was forming other attachments.

A feature of the time, and not only in Paris, was the formation of sociable groups in which the arts and the sciences could be discussed seriously but outside academic settings, informally and experimentally. They were the seed-beds of later learned societies. M. Strowski has discovered an interesting publication of 1673 (*Conversations de l'Académie de Monsieur l'Abbé Bourdelot*, par le Sr. le Gallois) describing such groups as they were some thirty or forty years previously, and giving the names of the members of Bourdelot's group, mentioning among others Père Mersenne, La Mothe le Vayer, Le Pailleur, Roberval, Petit and Pascal. But long before then the elder Pascal had joined Mersenne's group which includes all these names, and which seems in about 1638 to have transferred its meetings to Bourdelot's house.

Père Mersenne was an ageing Friar Minim of European reputation with a bold, capacious, untidy and extraordinarily vivacious mind, a friend and regular correspondent of Descartes. In the year when Blaise Pascal was born he had published *Questiones Celeberrima in Genesim*, in which he very nobly and courageously took up the cudgels in defence of Galileo and with equal fervour claimed that theology was not hostile to science: 'No! No! If the truth is dear to any man it is dear to Catholics, who fight only what is false; and they know that different passages of Holy Scripture have a variety of senses, and take them in the sense which does not impugn the truth.' He was the strongest individual link between religion and science in Europe. His second book, *The Truth of the Sciences against the Sceptics*, was that of a man who saw the Church and science as allies against a common danger, the unbelievers who would cast doubt equally on religious doctrines and mathematical principles. In 1636 he published his *Universal Harmony*, crammed with profundities and puerilities. He was so sure by now that religion and science were two aspects of one body of truth that he seriously offered the propositions of Euclid as headings for a course of sermons! All was fish that came to his net. As leader and host of the Group he encouraged the widest discussions.

Next in eminence and superior in mental clarity was Gilles Personne de Roberval, the choleric and prosaic Professor of Science at the College of France. He is the original of a story told about several mathematicians. Having seen a performance of *Le Cid* he complained that he could not see what it proved. Members of the legal profession who found recreation in the Group were the lawyer Carcavi and Judge Mydorge, who at his own expense supplied Descartes with optical instruments.

Early in his boyhood Blaise was allowed to accompany his father to these seances and even encouraged to bring his own quota of ideas. Two members who must have attracted him and almost certainly influenced him were Pierre Petit and Gerard Desargues.

Petit is called 'cet Archymède de nostre temps' by Le Gallois in the book referred to above. He was a brilliant young engineer who would later be put in charge of the fortifications of the Channel ports. The transitions from diagram to model and from model to finished construction were things Blaise may have learnt from Petit.

Desargues was a mathematician of the first order but he had something else to impart to Blaise. As an architect of Lyons, dividing his time between there and Paris, he pursued his studies with a strongly humanitarian motive. Having many workmen under him he wished both to lighten their labour by inventions and also to make it possible for that class to share in the new knowledge; so he studied the art of explaining scientific subjects in ways that the less educated could follow. The peerless clarity of Pascal's scientific writings and his concern for the conditions of labouring men owe much, we feel, to Desargues.

The Pascal family practised religion sincerely, regularly and unquestioningly; perhaps without notable fervour. The father had discovered, possibly in the decisions of the Council of Trent, possibly out of his own head, a happy formula which preserved due respect for revealed truth without hampering natural experiment: 'Nothing that has to do with faith can be the concern of the reason.' For a modern person this would beg a number of questions but it satisfied the Pascal father and son and Blaise would make interesting developments of the principle without essentially altering it in his 'Fragment on the Nature of the Vacuum'. It carried the useful implication that there was nothing in the whole field of natural inquiry which ought to trouble the theologians. The only form of conflict between religion and science which Blaise would ever encounter in his own experience would be the struggle between two rival attractions.

Desargues produced an important treatise on Conic Sections based on his own brilliant hypothesis that all three of the characteristic curves might be treated as special cases of one theorem. Blaise, at the age of sixteen, read it with keen interest and himself produced a short essay on the same subject, with respectful admissions of his use of Desargues' work. One might expect, and one would forgive, a boyish pastiche of the work he had admired. Instead, Pascal's essay was at once recognized by Desargues himself, by Roberval and Mersenne, and later by Leibniz, as a startling advance on anything previously written. The young Pascal had isolated and proved (as Desargues had not) the peculiar property which is common to all conic sectional curves, namely, that if any six points on the curve be joined up and the sides of the resulting hexagon be produced beyond the curve, their three pairs of opposite sides will meet at three points which are in one straight line.

Pascal's Theorem, as the books still call it, drew almost universal praise. The exception was Descartes, who wrote in reply to Mersenne's enthusiastic letter: 'He seems to have copied Desargues. I cannot pretend to be interested in the work of a boy.' He was annoyed at the time because Pascal senior had recently collaborated with Roberval in an open letter intervening on the side of Fermat, the Toulouse mathematician, in a discussion on Maxima and Minima which Descartes was waging with that great man.

But at this time the Pascals possessed a star of greater brilliance, though less magnitude than Blaise, in Jacqueline. She had every inducement to become thoroughly spoilt, but resisted such temptations and remained natural in character. The lively pretty child was growing into a lovely girl with spontaneous charm and the gift of happiness. She developed a talent for verse, of which Sainte-Beuve gives some examples. They are mostly clever trifles but at least one of them (on the death of a Huguenot) gives true lyrical form to a feeling which was not very easy, or perhaps even very safe, to express.

Jacqueline was to be instrumental in the fortunes of the family. Towards the end of 1638 Étienne (of all people) got into serious trouble with authority. This man of almost legendary rectitude and loyalty very narrowly escaped the Bastille by timely flight to Clermont. The trouble was over his investments in the Hôtel de Ville. Richelieu in his need for money to wage war marked down the value of these *rentes* by one-third, and Pascal was one of a very angry group who protested vigorously enough to frighten and infuriate Séguier the Chancellor. Richelieu acted, and Étienne fled, leaving his family with Madame Sainctot.

The Pascals were liked, and a friendly conspiracy was hatched to mend the situation. No one cared to risk Richelieu's dangerous temper by direct intervention, but an opportunity offered itself when Richelieu's niece and housekeeper, the Duchesse d'Aiguillon, planned to amuse his guests with a performance of Scudéry's *L'Amour Tyrannique* with a cast of children, under Mondory's direction. Jacqueline was given a leading role and earned an ovation. She gained also the real purpose of the plan, an interview with the Cardinal, and made good use of it; and her pleading was followed up by Mondory and the Duchesse, who said, 'Truly, Sir, you should do something for this man. He has a fine character and is very learned; it is a pity to leave him unused. He has a son of only fifteen who is already famous in mathematics.' But there was no need; Jacqueline had already been promised all she wished. She wrote to her father:

'When I saw him in such a good temper I asked whether he

would allow you to make your reverence to him. He said you would be welcome and added, "Tell your father that when he comes back he must come and see me," and repeated this several times. Then as Madame d'Aiguillon left my sister saluted her, and she asked where my brother was, saying she wanted to see him. My sister brought Blaise to her and she paid him many compliments on his science. Then we were taken to a room where a wonderful feast was spread for us.'

Jacqueline's intervention had a larger result than anyone had foreseen. That same poverty of the Exchequer which had nearly brought about Étienne's imprisonment now gave him high promotion. The taxes were not coming in as they should, especially in Normandy where general rebellion had flared up. Richelieu determined upon a ruthless punitive expedition aimed chiefly at Rouen, to be accompanied or followed by a Commission with orders to restore the collapsed administration. For the latter he wanted one or two men of experience and proved character. It was in the spring of 1639 that Étienne was recalled and paid his respects to the Cardinal. Six months later he was appointed 'Deputy Commissioner to the King for the Imposition and Levying of Taxes on the Commonalty' with authority in Rouen and High Normandy. He joined the Intendant of Rouen at Gisors, where the latter had been forced to retreat; and then followed or accompanied the troops into Rouen, where his family joined him.

The eight years at Paris which had changed Blaise from a child to a youth of sixteen had been intensely formative. They had made him, and at least until Providence breaks and re-makes him, the qualities he will show have already made their appearance. This is a convenient moment to try to read them.

He was much more than a precocious young intellectual and he reserved mathematics, as did his elders, for his leisure moments; yet admittedly they were his keenest interest. 'Il trouvait dans cette science la vérité qu'il avait si évidemment recherchée, il en était si satisfait qu'il y mettait son esprit tout entier,' wrote

Gilberte. But he was mastering Latin, beginning Greek, absorbing paternal disquisitions on philosophy at mealtimes! It was stiff going, for the girls as well as for the boy. Gilberte notes that it was not until he was eighteen that his health showed signs of strain, but that even then it did not prevent him from continuing his ordinary occupations. Indeed, part of the legendary Pascal, the brooding and incapacitated invalid, disappears when we realize that his life in almost all its stages was inordinately busy. Here in his teens he is learning half a dozen subjects, applying himself to original research, going to parties and to Court with his sisters, enjoying a life that was varied, full and even normal in everything except his astonishing promise. Until his last two years this multifarious industry will be almost uninterrupted.

It is, or was, customary to speak of Pascal's First Conversion as happening in the year 1646; his Worldly Period, from about 1649; his Second Conversion in 1654; and thereafter an almost entire renunciation of social enjoyments and scientific pursuits for the remainder of his life. If we do not use these terms in this book it is not that we deny them any appropriateness or criticize the use of them in better books than this. But they can give a misleading impression of the actual curve of Pascal's career. For example, the fact that we have already seen him moving easily in Parisian society from 1632 to 1639 should modify the impression that his first taste of *la vie mondaine* came ten years later.

One trait that has appeared is his passion for the concrete and the actual. It may be objected that there seems no marked taste of that sort in his enthusiasms as yet, Euclid and conic sections; but in fact these do illustrate the point. While Descartes was very brilliantly using and even devising algebraic methods to solve all geometric problems, Pascal insisted on the diagram, and that did indicate his need to be that much nearer the tangible fact. An inscribed circle may not be a very good representation of the globe on which we live, but it is more like it than is $2\pi r$. In the club which Blaise attended there was a down-to-earth feeling which exactly suited him.

There was also, be it admitted, a combativeness to which Blaise was introduced perhaps too soon for his good. They were not a mutual admiration society but a collection of vigorous mutual critics, some of them wedded to ideas and impatient of rival theories, some of them (Roberval especially) over-eager to shine and to be first in the field. Blaise had, as his sister Jacqueline tells us, an 'humeur bouillante', which may be a sisterly euphemism for a fiery temper though the term must also refer to the extraordinary ardency with which he could throw himself into an argument, a friendship, a problem or (later) a spiritual meditation as well as into a quarrel.

Another characteristic point has been seen in his use of Desargues' work on conic sections. His genius, like Shakespeare's, was of that sort that requires material provided by others. The only exception to this that we can think of is his calculating machine, for previous attempts had been feeble. All his great work on the Vacuum followed from Torricelli's experiment. Every one of the Provincial Letters was nourished by data supplied by Nicole and Arnauld. His spiritual counsels were to be modelled on St Cyran. In the *Pensées* the influence of Montaigne is so pervasive that sometimes even in refuting Montaigne, Pascal unconsciously uses Montaigne's own phrases. None of this diminishes Pascal's stature. All his work is stamped indelibly with his signature. He himself was aware of this possible criticism and met it: 'Do you say I use the same words as another? Two tennis players use the same ball; but one of them places it better.'

We have seen already some of the ferocious energy with which his mind will always attack a task, like a terrier at a rat-hole, unappeased until what is sought has been unearthed; but with that went another characteristic, the fecundity of his intellect. Where Descartes' mind was always simplifying, Pascal's was ramifying; a fact once found brought to life a whole family of associated facts. It is said that he followed up his theorem in conic sections with between three and four hundred corollaries deduced from it. This no doubt was boyish extravagance; having started he felt he could not stop. Everything that could be asserted of such curves must be brought into relation with this one common property. But it was characteristic.

One final point, Pascal's peculiar feeling about infinity, has already come into the picture with the essay on Conics, for two of the curves involved go off to infinity and all three of them involve infinitesimals in the calculations to which they give rise. Pascal's application to this subject had two results. Mathematically, it made him one of the pioneers of higher mathematics. 'The period between 1615 and 1688 was dominated by the discovery of the calculus, and in this Frenchmen played the leading part. Two of them stand out pre-eminent. Fermat in leading up to the Differential Calculus, Pascal in preparing the way for the Integral Calculus.'*

And mystically, this feeling for infinity will govern all his thought about human nature and bring him to a point at which he will see and describe all things *sub specie aeternitatis*.

* Moritz Cantor, *Geschichte der Mathematik*, II, p. 543.

CHAPTER 3

PORT ROYAL

'Ma fille, ne vaudrait-il pas mieux ne pas prendre de si grands poissons, et en prendre davantage?'

S. FRANCIS DE SALES (to Mère Angélique)

In the last chapter we mentioned a cloud that loomed over the religious scene. During the Pascals' years in Paris, it hung, scarcely larger than a man's hand, over the religious community of Port Royal which occupied two premises: Port Royal des Champs, some fourteen miles south-west of Paris, and (since 1626) Port Royal de Paris. The first rumbling of the storm had been heard before the Pascals left Paris, for Richelieu in 1638 imprisoned Saint-Cyran, the spiritual director of Port Royal, at Vincennes, but the Pascals' move to Rouen coincided with the first real thunderclap, the publication of Jansen's book, the *Augustinus*.

Pascal's association with that community was destined to have such bearings on his thought and personality that no portrait of him can omit some account of Port Royal. We shall pick up the thread of Pascal's story in the next chapter.

Port Royal is adequately documented. Sainte-Beuve, for one, wrote six large and crowded volumes describing its leaders, inmates and fortunes, and that is little compared with what they wrote about themselves and each other. All that will be attempted here is a summary.

At a time when the Church wished to increase its membership and thus might be tempted, so to speak, to reduce the subscription, a contrary movement presenting Christianity as stark renunciation, disposed to emphasize the cost and concentrate on a select membership, found a centre and an instrument in Port Royal. The difference was accentuated by a quarrel.

The powerful Society of Jesus was active and prominent in the Church's outward movement to the world, and the Jesuits had no love for Port Royal. They disliked the Arnauld family who practically controlled it, Saint-Cyran its spiritual director, and Saint-Cyran's friend Jansen who would write the *Augustinus* against them. In the ensuing conflict the Jesuits would be badly mauled; Port Royal would be extinguished.

In the story of Port Royal three strands cross and intermingle without ever quite merging. One is, of course, Jansenism; another is what M. Fortunat Strowski and Mgr. Ronald Knox call Saint-Cyranism; the third (to coin a phrase ourselves) is Arnauldism. They will appear here in the reverse order. There is no essential connection between any two of them. The Arnauld sisters might have preferred Saint Francis de Sales or someone of his stamp to Saint-Cyran as director; Saint-Cyran would have been a gifted peculiar doctor of souls had he never met Cornelius Jansen; Jansen's connection with Saint-Cyran, and through him with Port Royal, was quite fortuitous. Unfortunately for religion in France, events brought the three together inextricably though still distinguishably.

By Arnauldism we indicate in the first place a sheer weight of numbers. At the date at which we have arrived, 1640, Port Royal contained at least fifteen members of the family. They were the widowed mother of the Arnaulds, Soeur Catherine de Sainte-Félicité; her six daughters, Soeur Catherine de Genes (the only married daughter, now widowed), Mère Angélique, Mère Agnès, Soeur Anne Eugène, Soeur Marie Claire, Soeur Madeleine de Sainte-Christine and four daughters of Soeur Catherine de Genes; and at Port Royal des Champs were three sons of Soeur Catherine de Genes, M. Antoine le Maître, M. de Séricourt and M. de Saci; the eldest member of the Arnauld family, M. Arnauld d'Andilly, had left the Court to join the solitaries, and the youngest member, M. Antoine Arnauld, now completing his studies at the Sorbonne, would soon be the spearhead of the attack on the Jesuits. Moreover, Mère Angélique, now Novice Mistress, had practically recreated the ancient Cistercian community; her sister Mère Agnès was now Abbess, and the le Maître brothers with d'Andilly were leaders of the male solitaries at des Champs. If this family had characteristics then it seems fair to use the term Arnauldism of Port Royal.

In 1597 Jacqueline Arnauld had become Mère Angélique at the age of *seven*, having been jobbed into the post of Co-adjutrix Abbess of Port Royal by her very celebrated but impecunious father. At the same time her younger sister Jeanne became Mère Agnès as Co-adjutrix Abbess of Saint-Cyr, her age being five and a half years. Their parents had twenty children, ten of whom died in infancy. They were Auvergnats of distinguished rank. Angélique's grandfather, de la Mothe Arnauld, a Huguenot, had been Procureur-Général to Catherine de Medicis. Her father Antoine Arnauld was the star of the legal profession in the closing years of the sixteenth century. His most famous oratorical feat was a speech made in 1594 against the Jesuits on the charge of their complicity in the assassination of King Henry IV, a speech which the Jesuits never forgot and never forgave. Some wag has called it the original sin of the Arnaulds.

With a swarming family and limited means, Antoine was glad to get two of his daughters off his hands. The child Mère Angélique had been, according to her own account, disliked and neglected by her parents. Real or imagined, this sense of grievance set up some of its usual effects in a personality which was in any case remarkable. She was a sulky, self-willed child with no wish to be a nun and no intention to keep the rule more closely than she need. Convents had become largely receptacles for redundant daughters for whom no dowry could be found, and as spiritual vocations could not always be fairly expected the standard was eased. Port Royal was one of the many religious houses where the rule had become lax, in manners rather than in morals.

Port Royal was a huddle of old buildings on marshy, misty

48

ground in the pit of a narrow valley, an unattractive and un-
healthy spot, but a valuable property if it were not, as then, in
the hands of a dishonest agent. The farm which supplied it, Les
Granges, was more fortunately situated on the hill-top. The nuns
lived in permanently damp cells and rheumatism was endemic.
Permission from Rome for Mère Angélique's election was delayed
and she spent her novitiate first at Saint-Cyr in the Cistercian
habit, and then as a Benedictine at Maubuisson, a convent needing
more reform than most.

In 1602 the Abbess of Port Royal died and Mère Angélique
was installed, aged eleven. Her father hoped to set the affairs of
the property on a sound basis. Both parents assumed that the
child was still under their tutelage but she had a different view,
and the first years were years of conflict between the parents of
an unruly child and the Abbess fully aware that she was responsible now only to the General of her Order, and otherwise in
charge of all within her walls. With the help of an experienced
Prioress, Angélique learnt the routine of control and exercised it
competently, though with a slack rein as she herself cared little
for the daily Office.

In 1608 during Lent she allowed a wandering Capuchin monk,
Père Basile, to preach in the Church. He spoke about the poverty
of our Lord's birth in the stable and his message permanently
affected Angélique in two ways. It showed her the meaning of
religious austerity and resolved her to bring the Abbey back to
the Cistercian simplicity. Characteristically she overdid this and
condemned herself and many others to squalor. As Miss Margaret
Trouncer points out (in her novel about Angélique, *The Reluctant
Abbess*) there is a difference between the acceptance of poverty
and the pursuit of squalor. But her conversion was sincere and
deep; it made her one of the great reforming Abbesses of the
time. Within a year she had properly enclosed the community,
enforced the rule against personal property, tightened up the
recitation of the daily Office and robed the nuns in a much less
comfortable and attractive habit.

On September 25, 1609, she refused admission to her parents and a number of the family, an act of defiant resolve which is highly dramatized by Sainte-Beuve. While it must be admitted that Mère Angélique originated the fashion of dramatizing her experiences, we feel that behind the stampings and declamations, the tears and swoons of this *Journée du Guichet*, something decisive had been done. Mgr. Knox* asks: 'Was it really necessary to lock every door of the convent, and treat her eminently pious parents as if they were brigands?' Waiving the problem whether, in suitably rare instances, this may not be the last remaining resource for dealing with some eminently pious people, it is still imaginable that if one of the convent doors had been left unlocked they might as well all have been flung open. Until this show-down Port Royal was an Arnauld annexe; from this date it began annexing Arnaulds. One by one, Angélique's sisters found their way to the damp cloisters.

The other effect of Père Basile's sermon was to give her a deep suspicion and dislike of the great religious orders, for Père Basile turned out to be a rogue.

Conventual reform was in the air. Mère Angélique's example put her and Mère Agnès in demand for introducing similar reforms elsewhere. The most startling example was Maubuisson, where the need was not only in manners but in morals.

The lady Abbess of Maubuisson, Madame d'Estrées, had twelve children whom she trained according to their station, that is, the station of their putative fathers. Most of them performed useful functions in the large establishment maintained by the Abbess, who entertained lavishly. The story of her expulsion in 1618 (it required more than one military expedition) calls for the pen of Dumas. She was locked up in a corrective home for prostitutes and Mère Angélique was installed, Mère Agnès, transferred from Saint-Cyr, remaining in charge at Port Royal. Angélique's formidable powers of example and persuasion won only moderate success at Maubuisson. She received encouraging visits from

* *Enthusiasm*, OUP, p. 189.

S. Francis de Sales, who had already visited Port Royal to support Mère Agnès and had called upon the Arnaulds. Even in her own rather vainglorious accounts of these visits, Angélique reveals how accurately her character had been read by the author of *La Vie Dévote*. He appreciated in her a stubborn core of purpose, an unsparing devotion to duty, a genuine if rather imperceptive sympathy. He perceived a certain lack of mystical fervour in this brave young reformer, and did not hesitate to advise her to enlarge her prayers. Most revealing, and most like the man, is the comment he made to her about the austerities she had imposed at Port Royal: 'My daughter, might it not be a good plan to catch fish not quite so large, but more of them?' Angélique felt a profound devotion to M. de Genève and wished to leave her Order and be received into that of the Visitation which had been formed under his guidance. He evaded her entreaties, recognizing in Mère Angélique a bird of a different plumage from those in his aviary at Anneçy.

One September morning in 1619 Maubuisson was thrown into turmoil. Madame d'Estrées, in a beautifully laundered habit, appeared raging before the gates surrounded by a few minor nobles with drawn swords. The porter was wounded and the party forced their way in. The two Abbesses confronted each other at the church door, and an august dialogue followed. Madame d'Estrées begged to thank Mère Angélique for her care of the Abbey during her absence and requested her to be good enough now to return to her own Abbey. Mère Angélique regretted for her part that she was not a free agent in the matter since the Superior of the Order had placed her there as Abbess. 'But, Madame,' retorted d'Estrées, 'I am the Abbess and am here to relieve you.' 'Having been deposed, Madame, you are no longer Abbess,' said Angélique, and went into the choir. Between Terce and Mass she conferred with her nuns and said they must all make their Communion. After Mass the high-level conference was resumed. Mère Angélique maintained a superb dignity even when Madame d'Estrées with her men was forcibly dragging her from the church, while her own nuns held her back by the girdle. Angélique was extruded and walked with her nuns, two by two, to Pontoise. Next day a small army arrived and they were reinstated under an armed guard. Madame d'Estrées had escaped again. The details which we have abridged may be relied upon; they are Mère Angélique's own account.

The contact with S. Francis de Sales shows how uncommitted was Port Royal as yet in character and doctrine. If someone like Camus, Bishop of Belley, friend of S. Francis and like him in gentleness and wisdom, had been found as spiritual director, Port Royal might never have been the victim or the source of trouble.

In 1626 Madame Arnauld, seven years a widow, felt a vocation and took the veil. She had reasonable objections to living in a swamp and brought about the transference of the entire community to new premises in Paris at the rural end of the Faubourg Saint-Jacques, so Port Royal de Paris was created. A chaplain was left at Port Royal des Champs to serve the church. About the same time Mère Angélique requested Zamet, Bishop of Langres, to be spiritual director of Port Royal. Largely through him she secured, in 1627, a papal Brief removing the community from the Cistercian Order and placing it under the Archbishop of Paris. Angélique had been particularly stung by the criticism of the new General of the Cistercian Order, de Nivelle, of the *singularities* of Port Royal. He may have meant merely the new austerities which had come with the reforms, but whether by intent or by accident he had hit a nail on the head.

We have been trying to convey a meaning for the term Arnauldism, and perhaps singularity is the quality which emerges: the itch to be different and to be noticed. There was, as Mgr. Knox has shown in *Enthusiasm*, a potent streak of histrionics in the make-up of the Arnaulds and not least in Mère Angélique. But it is a harmless, even an enviable, quality which enables some people to enrich their lives by acting them out before an admiring imaginary audience. Singularity is akin but has this subtle and serious difference, it insists that the audience be real. One of the banes which contributed to blight so much that was holy and heroic and spiritually timely in Port Royal was this exasperating fact, that ordinary people were never allowed to let their attention drift very long without being nudged. Port Royal was a school for endurance, and it could endure anything except disregard.

We approach the subject of Saint-Cyranism. Mère Angélique about this time was unsettled. Her failure to get transferred to the Visitation made her wish to be dispensed from her profession, but Zamet renewed her sense of vocation. She obtained leave to abdicate from being Abbess and in 1633 became Superior of a new aristocratic religious house established for the perpetual adoration of the Blessed Sacrament, near the Louvre. As Mère Agnès had been sent to the Abbey of Tard, Port Royal for a few years almost ran out of Arnaulds. At the Institute of the Saint-Sacrement a devotion was used called the *Chapelet Secret* compiled by Mère Agnès, not a classic of its kind but sincere, fervent and innocuous. It gave sixteen headings for meditation, one for each century since the Last Supper. Some of its expressions caused a storm in a tea-cup in which Zamet was involved as the director who approved it. Another who openly approved it, even after it had received a censure from the Sorbonne and a frown from Rome, was the Abbé Saint-Cyran. Zamet was pleased at finding an ally and when he left Paris to attend to his diocese he persuaded Saint-Cyran to act as locum tenens.

As Sainte-Beuve pithily suggests, Saint-Cyran was difficult to get in, and impossible (once in) to get out. He directed upon the Saint-Sacrement the full heat of his personality and his brand of spiritual regimentation. Mère Angélique, with intense reluctance, made a general confession, and from then was wax in Saint-Cyran's hands. Zamet took violent offence. Angélique obtained the Archbishop's permission to return to Port Royal, as Novice Mistress. In the same year, 1636, Mère Agnès was brought back from Tard to be Abbess of Port Royal. As the Institute of the Saint-Sacrement lacked funds, its constitution and privileges were merged into Port Royal. Zamet was excluded and Saint-Cyran installed.

His name in the world was Jean du Vergier de Hauranne, but it is as Saint-Cyran that he challenges the historian and the amateur mind-reader. Born at Bayonne in 1581, he won admiration as a scholar from the great Lipsius at Louvain and completed his studies at the Sorbonne. At Louvain he had formed a life-long friendship with a very different but congenial man, Cornelius Jansen. Jansen was poor and spent long periods at the Hauranne home in Bayonne, where they developed their common ideals or hatched their plots (according to the view taken) and grew in their agreement on the decadence of the Church during the past twelve centuries. Like the Arnaulds and the Pascals, they were staunchly Catholic in that they never questioned the Divine authority and necessity of the hierarchy, the sacraments and the creeds. They felt that a regeneration of the Church was needed, more radical and less accommodating than the Counter-Reformation, and that they were called to lead it. De Hauranne would direct souls; Jansen would write books. Thus they spent their holidays, a reading party of two, immersed in patristics. De Hauranne became a Canon at Poitiers and then, in 1616, Abbé of Saint-Cyran-en-Brenne, where he met and impressed Arnauld d'Andilly (the two strands were interwoven thus early) who introduced him to the Arnauld family.

In 1623 Saint-Cyran was living in Paris 'au cloître Notre Dame' directing consciences, writing long and rather cloudy letters (including at least one to Mère Angélique), supporting Berulle the General of the Oratorians, helping S. Vincent de Paul to establish Saint-Lazare, winning high opinions everywhere; everywhere, that is, except in one quarter. Richelieu cast a cold appraising eye, recognizing the force but doubting the direction. 'He is a Basque,' said the Cardinal. 'His entrails are on fire and they send into his head vapours which he mistakes for inspirations.'

Saint-Cyran was credited with the authorship of *Petrus Aurelius*, a collection of pamphlets in one volume published in 1633, which was widely acclaimed. A tug-of-war having arisen in England between certain members of religious orders and the Vicar-Apostolic, this anonymous book maintained episcopal as against monastic authority; an acceptable line to the French hierarchy, especially where the Gallican spirit was strong. Saint-Cyran neither acknowledged nor denied the ascription, which no one doubted.

Opinions on the man vary between Sainte-Beuve's 'The Christian director *par excellence*' and the Abbé Bremond's 'this maniac'. M. Strowski* gives a judicious summing up, with a sting in the tail:

'Il y avait du mystère dans Saint-Cyran; il y avait je ne sais quoi de prophétique et d'étrangement inspiré. Ses paroles venaient de plus loin que lui; il attendait pour les prononcer qu'elles fussent dictées d'ailleurs. Il était impérieux et absolu, tendre cependant et plein de miséricorde; ce dualisme s'harmonisait sans peine en lui. En lui c'était à celui qui était l'inspiré, de commander et de trancher; mais l'homme aussi savait s'attendrir, s'attacher et pleurer. Ses élus n'étaient pas trés nombreux, c'était une élite; c'était un état-major; c'étaient en réalité ses fanatiques.'

If we have to venture our own estimate it would accord with all of M. Strowski's except the opening sentences. There, in regard to the mystery in Saint-Cyran's nature, we feel some doubt. About his solid virtues and moral size there should be little doubt, but he was an odd mixture of disparate qualities. His whole theory of direction turned upon the necessity of standing aside and letting the grace of God operate. He held this theory sincerely and practised it humbly, yet exercised an extraordinary and often ruthless ascendency over his penitents. He was unquestionably a man of God, patient, prayerful, courageous, free from base ambitions; yet some sort of ambition devoured him. Before Richelieu, who

* *Pascal et Son Temps*, Vol. II, p. 199.

not only commanded but freely exercised powers of life and death, he was disinterested.

Saint-Cyran had stature. He cannot be dismissed as the idol of a little clique. He retained the respect of men like Berulle and S. Vincent, and (surely) inspired some fear in Richelieu. It is difficult to reconcile the opinion of such contemporaries with Bremond's estimate of 'un pauvre cerveau incohérent dont les pensées étaient insignificantes'. There was some unaffected profundity in Saint-Cyran.

The strange thing is that there was also an *affected* profundity. Those dramatic silences, those unexplained withdrawals into himself, such remarks as he made to Balzac: 'I see the mysteries of the other world more clearly than you see those of this world,' or his explanation of a break in his discourse to the solitaries at Port Royal: 'It is not that I have nothing more to say. I have so many things to say that I wait for God to show me which of them to choose'—we can be embarrassed by such traits without accepting Bremond's picture of a negligible and muddle-headed charlatan.

Saint-Cyran seems to have been that rare thing, a mystic who was also a mystagogue. Few real mystics bother to waste the time and trouble to act the part. There may or may not be characteristic signs by which spirituality is indicated, but the mystic does not consciously cultivate them. He may resemble, and he will not mind resembling (he may even be, and not mind being) a successful company promoter, a musical-comedy star, a Hanoverian bishop. He will not see himself in the flapping draperies, with the rapt gestures and upcast gaze of a saint sculptured by Bernini. But by some unhappy quirk Saint-Cyran did cultivate these attitudes. He did spread an aura of mystery which was taken seriously by his contemporaries and by later minds as penetrating as M. Strowski. Men continue to ask, what *was* this special source of inspiration, this unspoken and unspeakable message? But apart from his assiduous meditations, his view of Divine grace and his ability to handle souls, was there any? He was perhaps a sphinx without a secret.

If so, if this 'je ne sais quoi de prophétique' was a mannerism, it was an unfortunate one. Potentates like Richelieu can deal with strong men whose cards are on the table. They can use diplomacy or cash or simple firmness to keep such men where they belong; but dictators are allergic to the unpredictable. In 1638 Richelieu sent Saint-Cyran to prison at Vincennes without trial, charge or explanation except the comment made to a friend; 'If Luther and Calvin had been clapped into gaol the moment they started dogmatizing the nations would have been saved a lot of trouble.'

But Saint-Cyran's influence was already beyond the budding stage. His life in the Vincennes cell, whence he was released five years later, after Richelieu's death and just before his own, was not unlike what he would have experienced in the Chartreuse, which happened to be the goal of his desires; and the halo of un-merited suffering canonized him in the eyes of his disciples, with whom he freely corresponded. After his death the Paris chapel where he was buried became a shrine, where commemorative Masses were not of requiem in black, but in white vestments as for a Confessor of the Church. Saint-Cyranism had come to stay.

Saint-Cyranism was single-standard Christianity. It isolated and applied with naked literalness the Dominical saying: 'Ye are not of the world but I have called you out of the world.' It was the counter-argument to the Church's seventeenth-century bid to go out into the world. Berulle at the Oratory, Olier at Saint-Sulpice, S. Vincent at Saint-Lazare were reaching outwards to the people, seeking to touch the courtier, the man in the street, the labourer, the peasant. The Jesuits everywhere were concerned to commend the Church's beliefs and practices to the worlds of science, literature and high society. The attendant risks of such a movement are plain—an adaptable reduced ethic, a secularized Church—and it was salutary that there should be a counter-movement. Neither was Port Royal by any means the only wit-ness against a relaxed discipline. The Catholic religion has never denied or forgotten its need of an absolute standard maintained in the centre, and of souls who would pledge themselves without diminution or reserve to the ideal of perfection. Indeed the leaders of the evangelistic movement were themselves so pledged. There was room, there was need, for an ascetic counter-movement to the world-seeking mission of the Church. Saint-Cyran had plentiful authority in the Scriptures and the Fathers for his view of the Christian life as one of separation from the world, initiated by Divine election and an inrush of supernatural grace, sustained by penitence, contemplation and renunciation. Saint-Cyranism alone, without the Jansenist polemic, might have retained an honoured if rather embarrassed welcome within the Church, in spite of its faults.

For it had grave faults. The Scriptures and the Fathers were never quite so stark in their demands as they appeared to Saint-Cyran. They allow things which he did not contemplate: that the vision of God is offered to all, that all are called to it, that the approach to it is not normally by sudden and final illumination but by stages, in which the duties, relations and interests of ordinary life play a part. Thus S. Basil (addressing monks) could say: 'This is the goal of Christianity, the imitation of Christ in the manner of His humanity *so far as the vocation of each man allows.*' And even Saint Augustine, who seems to make an utter severance between life in grace and life in the world, recognized the function of mundane interests as a stage in the progress of the soul: 'The active life is necessary, not for its own sake but as preparing for contemplation.'[*]

We quote from Dr K. E. Kirk's *Vision of God*[†] his account of the Patristic view of man's condition which he holds to be 'in essence wholly true to the New Testament. It offers the vision of God to all; it calls all to the search for the vision; the ideal is laid upon the married as upon the monk. Purity of heart is still the condition of seeing God. It allows for the rigorist element in the New Testament by insisting that self-discipline and renunciation are of the essence of the active life; but it sets a bar against rigorist

[*] *Contra Faustum Manichaeum*, XXII, c. 53.
[†] Longmans, 1931; p. 252.

excesses by asserting that the Christian cannot become perfect in a moment, and that he must be allowed to progress slowly towards such degree of renunciation as may be necessary for the vision and its fruits.'

Saint-Cyran did not think that the vision was open to all, or that many were called to it, or that the married could fulfil the ideal, or that progress was by stages, or that worldly occupations rightly used could contribute to such stages. He did, with the love of God and of souls in his heart, devote himself to the direction of those of whose election and conversion he saw evidence.

His most original creation was the group of male solitaries who occupied, in growing numbers, the deserted premises of Port Royal des Champs, turning their backs upon the world to devote themselves to penitence, austerities, and contemplation. It hardly needs saying that the first and chief of these were Arnaulds. In 1637 Antoine le Maître, whose mother's maiden name was Catherine Arnauld, retired from the Bar where he was showing brilliant promise at the age of thirty. He was being showered with briefs and his name was down for early promotion to the Bench. He might well have outshone his famous grandfather, but all this was sacrificed suddenly and finally. Antoine made a small hermitage outside the empty convent, where he was soon joined by his youngest brother Isaac, who later, under Saint-Cyran's direction, entered the priesthood and became the solitaries' confessor, contorting his Christian name into Saci. Arnauld d'Andilly's son Luzanci followed, and presently d'Andilly himself forsook the court for the hermitage. Another le Maître, de Séricourt, came out of the army, and gradually the example was followed and the group increased until there were about thirty ex-students, soldiers, doctors, copyists, teachers. They took no vows but lived to rule, observing the day and night hours of prayer. They lived hard, sleeping on planks, taking little food. Times of recreation were permitted but not enjoined. Each of them was directed to some particular work. They drained the marshes, made a garden, managed the estate, transcribed manuscripts, started a printing press, taught in Saint-Cyran's Petites Écoles and ceaselessly studied the Scriptures and the Fathers. The keynote of their existence was penance for sin.

As we shall see in following the Pascals' fortunes at Rouen, Saint-Cyran's spiritual influence was by no means confined to Port Royal.

As yet we have been keeping Cornelius Jansen in the wings though with no intention of understating the closeness of the liaison between him and Saint-Cyran. They certainly shared hopes, if not cut-and-dried intentions, of transforming the Church of their time. For each of them the doctrine of S. Augustine on grace was the backbone of his theology, and each of them was concerned with moral reformation (Jansen wrote a book on the reformation of the interior life).

Yet their aims were no more identical than their personalities. We have felt justified in detaching and following the Saint-Cyranist thread because Port Royal became Saint-Cyranist by a sort of necessity, but became Jansenist almost by accident; and because this is a book on Pascal. We can hardly think of a wider contrast than that between Pascal and Jansen, but Pascal's ideas on religion and morality drew heavily upon Saint-Cyran.

While Saint-Cyran directed souls, organized his Petites Écoles and mustered his solitaries, Cornelius Jansen at Louvain and Ypres was pursuing his own industrious, pedestrian and high-explosive work. For him wisdom had ceased with S. Augustine and the Church could never be renewed until S. Augustine's teachings were assiduously studied. In 1636 Jansen was made Bishop of Ypres; he completed his great book but died in 1638, two years before it was published and fell like a delayed-action bomb.

The *Augustinus* was a massive Latin presentation of the teaching of S. Augustine on grace. Jansen had spent years of study (he read the anti-Pelagian books over thirty times) patiently extracting, systematizing and 'mounting' like botanical specimens everything that S. Augustine had written on his chief subject. Perhaps no writer could be named for whom this sort of treatment would have been less appropriate.

S. Augustine's doctrine of grace is the effect of an ardently religious nature reflecting upon its own miraculous conversion. To remove such reflections from the warm and living context of that nature and that experience was to be left only with the ethical dilemmas which S. Augustine did in fact bequeath to the Church.

We see some men evidently walking in the way of righteousness and making spiritual progress. Is this an effect of Divine grace or of their own moral decision, or a blend of the two? The 'common-sense' reply is that it is a blend, and this reply is orthodox, supported by Scripture and the early Fathers. Indeed the solution looks so obvious that there seems no problem, except perhaps in apportioning the parts of God's aid and man's response. The fact of co-operation seems to have caused the Church no difficulty. S. Clement of Alexandria compared it to the relation between doctor and patient in the effecting of a cure, where the willing collaboration of the patient admittedly plays an important part. S. Augustine's own experience forced him to look closer and to conclude that 'co-operation' was less obvious than it seemed, and even to doubt whether it took place. He was led to attribute to God not only the desire to amend but the decision to do so. He had sinned repeatedly in the flesh and in the intellect and each fall had weakened his resistance to further temptation, which had been inadequate to begin with. *Video meliora proboque; deteriora sequor.* The good life was beyond his reach precisely because the choosing of it was beyond his power. What kept him from God was not inability to see what he ought to do but an inhibition from taking the plunge. The 'common-sense' account of such a man is that God puts the desire for amendment into his heart and then the man makes up his mind; that is co-operation. But Augustine was quite sure that he could never have made up his mind. God wonderfully did His part in persuading Augustine of the truth, but Augustine was as far as ever from being able to grasp it. Then God still more wonderfully made up Augustine's mind for him.

Where was the co-operation in that? The division of functions as between man and God dwindled to a point and almost disappeared. God did it all. A sea-captain who, through bad navigation, has steered his ship on to a reef and then had it floated off by an incoming tide congratulates himself on his fortune, not his seamanship.

Certain inferences arose which Augustine did not hesitate to draw, the first of which was the corruption of human nature. Our nature with all its vestiges of a noble origin is contaminated as universally and as chronically as an area over which there has been a fall-out of radiation from a nuclear explosion. Original sin is of course not S. Augustine's invention but he painted it in darker colours and clearer outline than any predecessor. Fallen man was lost, and S. Augustine seems to hear in the word perdition a ring of doom which is surely absent from our Lord's words about lost sheep and lost coins.

Next, S. Augustine faced the question how it came about that some men, but visibly not all nor indeed a large proportion of men, did turn to God with all their hearts. It could not be through any *merit* of their own, so it must be by Divine decree; and it could not be through any *effort* of their own, so it must be by some form of Divine compulsion. Therefore grace was given to those for whom it was predestined, and when given it was irresistible, not indeed as an external force is irresistible, but as love at last dissolves away all resistance. He did not shrink from the further logical inference that if God predestined some souls to life He predestined others to death, only with the tempering clause that this predestination was consequent upon the fall and therefore linked with man's guilt and moral responsibility. It remained for Calvin to separate God's decree of death against any soul from all contingency and from any ethical standard comprehensible by us.

The Church honours S. Augustine as the Doctor of Grace,

whose experience of God and knowledge of men qualified him to disclose truths hidden from lesser men, certainly hidden from that almost jaunty optimist (and that very good man) the monk Pelagius. But the Church, with the Scriptures in hand, has always been concerned to temper the rigour of some of S. Augustine's conclusions. Predestination can be reconciled with the moral sense if it connotes God's foreknowledge of the conduct, and therefore the fate, of a soul which has given dispositions. There is no coercion in such foreknowledge. The irresistibility of grace also loses the element of external force if it is conceived in terms of spiritual attraction; and always S. Augustine has to be read within the glowing context of his own story.

Jansen lifted it out of the context, concentrated upon its least 'natural' features, and presented the result as the pure doctrine from which the Christian world had declined for nearly twelve centuries. Jansen's death in 1638 frustrated his intention of asking Pope Urban VIII's permission to dedicate the book to him, which would surely have been refused; for the *Augustinus* on its very title-page, by attacking the Jesuit theory of grace, reopened a controversy which had been officially closed in 1607 by Pope Paul V.

Saint-Cyran in prison hailed the book's appearance with the remark that there were three great writers on grace: S. Paul, S. Augustine and Cornelius Jansen. He had some doubts and reservations (and those on the very points which were to earn the condemnation of the *Augustinus*) but he declared that the moment for action had come, and he charged the young Antoine Arnauld to lead the coming campaign for the purity of doctrine and morals. This young and brilliant Arnauld, the baby of the family and the ablest of them all, accepted the charge. His career was in the balance and it promised fame and position, but the call which came from Saint-Cyran, and again from his mother, on her death-bed, seemed a call from God.

The die was cast. Port Royal was committed to defend the *Augustinus* through thick and thin against the Jesuits, against the Sorbonne and the Court, finally against Rome, not because of its own merits (it is very doubtful whether Mère Angélique ever read the book, and virtually certain that the nuns under her charge did not) but because Jansen was a friend of Saint-Cyran and because Antoine Arnauld was an untiring and unceasing controversialist.

It is not to be forgotten that these leaders were not only lovers of God but made love for God the centre of their religion; and Port Royal's works of mercy to the suffering, especially during the Fronde, faithfully reflect this aspect. Yet it was a gloomy version of Christianity that Port Royal adopted. For all the idyllic Arcadian atmosphere with which Sainte-Beuve invests 'le Port-Royal de M. Saint-Cyran'—d'Andilly's pear-trees, the antiphonal singing of solitaries without the walls and nuns within, the chivalrous soldierly protection during the Fronde, there was a chronic joylessness in the movement, a strong ingredient of vinegar in the diet of these heroic Christians. 'Jansenism', writes Mgr. Knox, 'never learnt to smile.'* Even if you were not lost by failure to be among the elect you were condemned to endless spiritual anxiety. You were bound in conscience to suspect natural affections and frown on ordinary interests. You learned to talk of the lost outer world, the perdition of unbaptized children, the worthlessness of non-Christian philosophy and poetry, if not with relish at least without felt regret. The miasmas of the valley of Port Royal des Champs had their counterpart. The beauty of holiness was there and the sweetness of disposition, which belongs to it. Some happy souls were there but the happiness had much to overcome.

Thus fatefully, and thus fortuitously, a haven of peace became an instrument of strife.

* *Enthusiasm*, p. 212.

RENÉ DESCARTES
By Franz Hals. Musée du Louvre

CHAPTER 4

ROUEN

'Philosophia quaeret, theologia invenit, religio possidet.'
PICO DELLA MIRANDOLA

From 1640 Pascal lived at Rouen for seven years and emerged from a precocious boyhood to an early and distinguished maturity. The period brought him much hard work, a religious awakening and the beginnings of a profound spiritual dilemma.

The new home was in the parish of Sainte-Croix 'by the walls of Saint-Ouen' in what might be called Rouen's Whitehall district. As representative of the King in assessing and levying taxes for the city and the province around it, Étienne Pascal honourably discharged an unpopular and unsparingly arduous task. During the revolt the administration had broken down and the finances were in a muddle and almost at a standstill. He had to reorganize, appoint local officials, adjudicate claims for exemption, apportion the tax payable from the well-to-do, and reassess the eighteen townships in the area. 'I am working ten times harder than ever before,' he wrote to Gilberte, 'a little more would break me. I never get to bed before two o'clock.' Blaise helped with the figures and also by making occasional visits to Paris, which kept him in touch with the scientific group.

The spectacle of his father, night after night wearily coping with endless columns of figures, put an idea into Blaise's head. These calculations required a machine-like precision. Why should not a machine do them? Already the clumsy device known as 'Napier's Bones' was used in some counting houses, but the trouble it gave was scarcely less than what it saved. In 1640, their first year in Rouen, Blaise conceived the possibility of a compact mechanism which could add, subtract, multiply and divide, with a device for carrying the correct digits from one column to the next, and another for recording the result. This involved him in applied mathematics and the direction of such craftsmen as Rouen afforded. It was long before the first working model was completed. Within five years of constant application some fifty models had been constructed with a variety of design and material. Blaise then, in 1645, felt able to write an Epistle Dedicatory to the Chancellor Séguier, accompanying the gift of one of the models, which served the treble purpose of staking his claim for a patent, advertising the machine for sale, and placating the Chancellor in case he still remembered Étienne's aggressiveness. The machine to which this letter refers is now (we believe) in private ownership in the south of France. It is the size of a glove-box, simple in appearance, portable and workable. The final standard model as produced in 1652 and placed on sale at one hundred livres is exhibited in the Paris Conservatoire des Arts et Métiers.

Pascal had reasonable hopes of enriching himself by this invention but never did so. He could not market it at an economic price, and the invention of logarithms reduced the need. But '*la Pascaline*' is the true original of all computing machines. Gilberte was perhaps the first to speak in terms of a mechanical brain when she wrote in her *Vie de Blaise Pascal*: 'He reduced to mechanism a science which is wholly in the human mind.' From now, Blaise began to be referred to as *le grand M. Pascal*.

Social life must have been severely limited for father and son by the long hours of work, but Rouen offered cultural opportunities hardly second to those of Paris. As friends of Mondory the Pascals at once found a friend in Corneille, who recognized merit in Jacqueline's verses. In her first year she was awarded a public prize annually given for poetry, and her winning lines were recited by Corneille.

Blaise Pascal's references to natural and artistic beauty are so few, and on the whole so negative, that he is often described as being deficient in the aesthetic sense. We have little material on which to judge, apart from the fact that he was a supreme artist in prose. The fact that his writings contain almost no reference to natural beauties would be more significant if we could find many writings that did so before the latter half of the eighteenth century. Lord St Cyres takes Pascal to task for writing 'The weather and my humours have little to do with one another. I have fogs and sunshine of my own within me'; and describes this as 'perhaps the most unnatural declaration ever made by mortal man'. But it only tells us that Pascal's soul was something more than a barometer. It is similarly risky to argue from Pascal's silence on literary beauties. 'Poète et non honnête homme', writes Pascal (38), and Lord St Cyres is ready with his exegesis: 'Long before his conversion to Port Royal Blaise had adopted the dictum of its leaders that the exigencies of rhyme have turned many a poet into a liar.' But this is mistranslation. *Honnête homme* does not mean an honest man; it means a *man*—whose manhood includes and transcends his occupation whether he be king or soldier, poet or peasant. Even a poet (Pascal means) should prefer the larger label to the smaller.

Certainly he distrusted and disliked the emotional influence of the drama, and was made restless by the poetry of his day, finding it (as it was) artificial and stilted. 'On ne sait que c'est ce modèle naturel qu'il faut imiter; et à faute de cette reconnaissance on a inventé de certains termes bizarres: Siècle d'or, merveille de nos jours, fatal, etc.; et on appelle ce jargon beauté poétique' (33). His artistic code was from the first as austere as his private life. He would cut verbiage to the bone: ' "Éteindre le flambeau de la sedition", trop luxuriant. "L'inquiétude de son génie", trop de deux mots hardis' (59). His own style was formed in a hard school, that of mathematical demonstration. His scientific writings are lucid and cogent to a degree which shows that he worked as hard over the form of his arguments as over their content. When he was called later to use words for wider needs than mathematical demonstration his writing acquired other qualities but it never lost these. That early discipline gave Pascal's style the virtue that will always be present in the art of a colourist who mastered the pencil before he took to the brush. 'Il faut de l'agréable et du réel; mais il faut que cet agréable soit lui-même pris du vrais' (25).

Étienne had brought to Rouen on his staff a young lawyer of Clermont, Florin Périer, to whom Gilberte was married in 1641. The marriage was happy, and when after a few years the Périers returned to Auvergne, a link with their native town was remade for the whole family.

If the life at Rouen robbed Blaise of one thing that Paris had given him, the daily society of men engaged in enlarging the bounds of scientific knowledge, it supplied him in compensation with abundant material for reflection on the condition of man; a branch of knowledge which would later absorb all his interest. He had before his eyes the hardships which had provoked rebellion and the cruelties with which rebellion had been suppressed. He saw the destitution and hunger which, except for the privileged of whom of course he was one, were the common lot. Intellectually Rouen was more humanistic than Paris. It was at Rouen that the books were printed which brought, or attempted to bring, the precepts of ancient Stoicism within the ambit of Christian belief and morale. Blaise's special interest in Epictetus came later but we cannot think that he spent seven years at Rouen without reading du Vair, whose books strongly influenced the class of higher State officials, and supplied the ethical background of Corneille's dramas.

In the religious world events were moving in which as yet the Pascals probably took only a detached interest. The *Augustinus* was published in 1640 at Louvain, in 1641 at Paris, in 1643 at Rouen. It was received with mixed feelings and close attention. Its declared hostility to Jesuit doctrine commended it to the more Gallican-minded clergy and theologians, but all were aware that it broke a religious truce. Someone unkindly noticed that the letters of *Cornelius Jansenius* could be rearranged into *In ore Calvini sensus*. The Jesuits complained at Rome and Pope Urban

VIII promptly reimposed the peace, but his Bull was not accepted at Paris until 1643. Meanwhile there were rumblings suggestive of a coming storm. M. Havert, a canon of Notre Dame, preached three notable sermons against the doctrine of the book and Saint-Cyran, in the last year of his life, launched Antoine Arnauld to the defence.

Arnauld responded principally with his book *La Fréquente Communion*, published in 1643, which enjoyed an immense and prolonged vogue among the devout and was even praised by the Jesuit Cardinal de Lugo at Rome. Like many of Arnauld's writings it was the ponderous result of a slight occasion. Two ladies of high society, desiring to go to a ball on a day when they had received Holy Communion, had received different counsel, one being told by her Jesuit confessor that she could go to the party, the other being forbidden by her Saint-Cyranist director. Arnauld supported the latter in this long treatise on the importance of the right dispositions for Holy Communion. It was a high-minded plea for treating holy things with the reverence they claimed. In Arnauld's inevitable manner it was legalistic, formal and long. It recommended delay of Communion where there was risk of unworthy reception; indeed one may say without irony that a more suitable title might have been *L'Infréquente Communion*. Absolution ought to be deferred if the confessor did not find true contrition in the penitent, that is sorrow for having offended the love of God, but only found attrition, that is sorrow for sin arising from a sense of its consequences to the sinner. The book emphasized the cost of being a Christian, and its popularity shows how many people there were, in all strata of society, who were honourably uneasy at getting their religion too cheaply. It sold edition after edition and, at least in the early days, won golden opinions from bishops and theologians. Père Nouet, S.J., who plunged into premature execration of the book, had to retract in public and in some haste. But it was soon found that *La Fréquente* was scaring people from the altar. S. Vincent de Paul complained in a letter: 'The book drives them from Communion. This Easter at S. Sulpice there were three thousand fewer communicants than usual. No one, or very few, come now on the first Sunday in the month. For a hundred who have profited from the book by greater reverence in using the Sacraments there are at least ten thousand whom it has harmed by putting them off altogether.' The book was creating a religious *élite*. In the metaphor of S. Francis it was catching the big fish and ignoring the little ones. One effect was to populate Port Royal des Champs with more solitaries.

It is unlikely that the family of a highly-placed and hard-worked bureaucrat took much notice of the appearance of these two books, or of the arrival about this time of one Jean Guilleberte to take up, at the direction of Saint-Cyran, his duties as curé of the Rouen suburb of Rouville. The attitude towards religion of public functionaries like Étienne Pascal was one of respectful but watchful conformity. They were the guardians of the common law, which indeed required the sanctions of the Catholic religion but must not be subject to its encroachments. The spirit of Gallicanism was strong among these laity as among the clergy, though it did not go to the lengths attained by Anglicanism. Papal Bulls were not recognized in France until they enjoyed the Royal assent and the formal consent of the clergy. The Pope's infallibility was not yet a defined dogma nor even a very acceptable idea. All the indications suggest that the religion of the Pascal family was dutiful, cautious, conventional and typical. Jacqueline's confirmation was deferred to the age of twenty. To all men of France at this time whose religion might be best expressed by the word rectitude, the current of Stoic teaching made a special appeal, which was enforced by the stoic colour of Maleherbe's poetry and Corneille's plays:

> '*Fortune, quelques maux que ta rigeur m'envoie,*
> *J'ai trouvé les moyens d'en tirer de la joie.*'
> (Sabine in *Horace*)

Even the youngest and most ardent of Corneille's characters intellectualize their emotions. The central tenet of this school was that all passions could be, and ought to be, subdued to the rational judgment and will of the individual, who would thus be raised by his own power above the reach of fate.

The main sources of this influence were the books of Guillaume du Vair, who had been a great man of France (almost *the* great man of France) during Étienne Pascal's younger days. From humble beginnings and precarious fortunes he had won his way upwards, studying the ancient Stoic writings, adapting them to Christian doctrines, basing upon them his own practice, as he made his slow way up to the highest position a commoner could attain, the Chancellorship. His chief works were *La Sainte Philosophie*, an attempt to answer the question how man can make the necessary effort to attain virtue; *Le Traité de la Constance*, a trio of very moving Platonic dialogues intended to stiffen men's fortitude in the presence of great evils such as anarchy or exile; the *Manuel d'Epictetus*, a faithful translation; and his final book, the *Traité de la Philosophie Morale des Stoiciens*, asserting that man's fate is in his own power since he can decline to be cowed or crushed by anything outside his own governance.

It is known that Blaise Pascal spent years over the study of such teachings, and is practically certain that his study began at this time. He conceived a deep admiration for Epictetus which he never quite lost. 'Voilà, Monsieur,' he would say in 1654 to M. de Saci, 'les lumières de ce grand esprit qui a si bien connu le devoir de l'homme.' But even in Epictetus he found a fatal flaw, and for the older Stoics with their lack of a sense of God, their whistling to keep their courage up, their tendency to greet the unseen with a sneer, he can never have felt any regard. They anticipated Swinburne's meaningless rhapsody, 'Glory to Man in the highest, for Man is the master of things', of which G. K. Chesterton observed that only one comment was possible, it was not true.

In 1645 a new interest came to Blaise which would command his attention and talents for years to come.

In August, Pierre Petit, now Intendant of the Fortifications, came to Rouen on his way to inspect the harbour at Dieppe, and brought news of Torricelli's experiment of two years before. Petit and Étienne reconstructed the experiment with Blaise looking on. His account is a good example of his clarity:

'A four-foot tube having one end open, the other end hermetically sealed, is filled with mercury. The open end is closed by a finger or otherwise and the tube disposed perpendicularly with the open end downwards and plunged two or three fingers'-depth into an open vessel which has been half filled with mercury, its upper half then being filled with water. If one then releases the open end, while it is still immersed in the mercury, the mercury in the tube partly descends, leaving at the top of the tube a space apparently empty, the remainder of the tube continuing full of mercury up to a certain height. If then one slightly lifts the tube so that the open end, which was in mercury, is now in water, the mercury in the tube will ascend, and water will mingle with it, but presently the mercury will fall and the tube will contain only water.'

Blaise's imagination caught fire, and he took charge. The ascent of the water seemed to suggest that the apparent emptiness might be a real emptiness, since the water was not obstructed. This in itself would mean a revolution in physics but there were other, more practical, inferences and possibilities which would need many more experiments and much more reflection. Rouen furnished good craftsmen and the best glass-works in France; Étienne had the financial means; Petit had the engineering experience; Blaise had the scientific enthusiasm, the experimental rigour, the power to interpret things seen.

The experiment was repeated many times with as wide a variety of conditions as could be devised; with tubes of different lengths and breadths and shapes (two were so long that forty-foot ships' masts were used to strengthen them), placed at different angles, and filled with different liquids. Blaise resolutely refrained from theorizing until a multide of corroborative data justified a theory. In the course of the experiments he invented the syringe. Wishing

72

to obtain a larger 'vacuum' (if it were a vacuum) than the Torricelli experiment gave, he filled a fifteen-foot tube with a course of wooden cylindrical sections linked by a cord, filled the interstices with water, up-ended the tube under mercury and pulled the cord, obtaining a very large 'void'.

The experiments gave one constant result. Whatever the volume, angle or width of the tube, the height of the liquid in the tube (for any one liquid) was the same. The inference was that this height was not dependent in any way on the 'empty' space at the top. The liquid was not being sucked up from above, or from within; it must be pressed up from below and from outside.

News came from Poland which made it urgent for Pascal to get his experiments completed and published, to establish priority over a learned Capuchin, Père Valerio Magni, who simply performed the Torricelli experiment in Cracovia in 1647 and then, less simply, published a highly metaphysical and rather confused treatise on his inferences: 'Demonstratio ocularis loci sine locato—corporis successive moti in vacuo—luminis nulli corpori adhaerentis'; the style is different from Pascal's, but more to the point was Pascal's fear that this sort of thing might compromise the new chapter in knowledge which he himself was opening. He published in October 1647 an abridgement of his intended treatise on the Vacuum, calling it *Expériences Nouvelles Touchant la Vide*. A month previously his friend Roberval had also published an excellent account of the Rouen experiments. It is a small matter that Pascal's work was prior to Valerio Magni's; the superiority of it is what counts. The experiment was Torricelli's and it rightly goes by his name; moreover Torricelli was the first to give the right reason for the suspension of the mercury in the tube. Yet the fame which accrued to Pascal was merited. He had taken up this novel phenomenon and by a series of exact, thorough and decisive demonstrations had promoted it to an important new branch of scientific knowledge. The way was open for hydrostatics and hydrodynamics.

But not many months after the experiments at Rouen another way had been opened for all the Pascals.

On a night in January 1646, Étienne hastened out of doors to prevent a duel, slipped on ice and dislocated his thigh. First aid was rendered by two reformed characters, brothers of noble birth whose name was Deschamps, the Sieur des Landes and the Sieur de la Bouteillerie. They had been converted by Guillebert of Rouville, and were devoting their lives to good works, especially the good work of bone-setting in which they found themselves adept. They stayed in Étienne's house for three months nursing him. They brought into the Pascal household not only their skill but an example of charity nourished by continual contact with God in prayer and meditation.

Through them a religious awakening came to each member of the family, beginning probably with the father. The usually accepted version, Marguerite Périer's, is that Blaise was first won over; he converted Jacqueline, and the two then persuaded their father. But in 1648 Jacqueline, writing to Gilberte on this subject, said, '. . . tu sais que mon père nous a tous prévenus'. Gilberte was at Clermont with her husband, but when they visited Rouen later in 1646 the same faith and devotion was granted to them.

What they drank in from the Deschamps brothers, or from M. Guillebert (ultimately from Saint-Cyran) was that basic Christianity which places the eternal above the temporal, the unseen above the seen, and inculcates complete detachment from worldly standards of value, and much waiting upon God for His disclosure of vocation. The movement (which affected many notable people at Rouen as well as at Paris) was an evangelistic awakening within the Church which laid stress on the duty of submission to the Church and the importance of the Sacraments.

All the family responded sincerely but in different ways corresponding to their characters. For the father, beginning to age, it was a serious opportunity, taken seriously, to make up leeway in his spiritual progress which the exactions of a busy life had caused him to lose. Gilberte and her husband became a consistently devout couple practising religion in the world for the remainder of their lives. Jacqueline developed a clear vocation to the religious life. Blaise's response was never in doubt or question, but it was more enigmatic in form. He devoured the books lent by the Deschamps brothers, Arnauld's *La Fréquente*, and the spiritual letters of Saint-Cyran. Almost certainly from this date began his serious study of the Bible, which brought him a knowledge of it that few men have equalled. Eventually he could quote from memory any passage he required to support the great argument of his defence of religion, translating it (apparently *ex tempore*) into French worthy to put beside our Authorized Version:

'Et cependant Sion a osé dire: Le Seigneur m'a abandonnée, et n'a plus mémoire de moi. Une mère peut-elle mettre en oubli son enfant, et peut-elle perdre la tendresse pour celui qu'elle a porté dans son sein? mais quand elle en serait capable, je ne t'oublierai pourtant jamais, Sion. Je te porte toujours entre mes mains, et tes murs sont toujours devant mes yeux.'

Among his final papers Pascal left many pages of such citations, currently translated for the immediate purpose but with never a false note and never descending from the heights. This is looking ahead, but his letters of this time begin to show something of the tone, and even something of the inimitable undertone, of the still distant *Pensées*. Thus in the spring of 1646 he is writing to Gilberte: 'Les choses corporelles ne sont qu'une image des spirituelles, et Dieu a représenté les choses invisibles dans les visibles. . . . Nous devons nous considérer comme des criminels dans une prison *toute remplie des images de leur libérateur* et des instructions nécessaires pour sortir de la servitude.'

The enigma arises in connection with his scientific interests, which the Deschamps brothers certainly regarded as morally dangerous (as leading to intellectual pride and distracting the attention from the quest of salvation) and of dubious value. Did Blaise feel any scruple about pursuing his experiments? Here the usually reliable Gilberte fails us. She says positively that the spiritual awakening of 1646 was a decisive turning-point in that 'from this time he renounced every other subject of knowledge to apply himself solely to the one thing that Jesus Christ calls necessary'; whereas in fact the years 1648–54 were his most fruitful and triumphant period of scientific discovery, and of researches into the nature of society and of the human person. The relation of such studies to Pascal's conscience will be a latent problem in our next three chapters. Such a man as Antoine le Maître dropped his legal activities completely and for ever, although they were his *métier*—or more likely because they were that. Blaise will not do anything like that for some years yet, and will never do it with the same finality.

But at this moment in 1646 he is aflame with religious zeal. For him any new living interest demanded action, immediate and (as often as not) contentious action. His nature and all his upbringing made him a Rupert of debate. He and his family had not *thought* their way to this new assurance of God; it had come by grace and God's kindness through the Deschamps brothers, and it had come as a gift. The human reason might play a part, a necessary part, in religious knowledge, but its function would always be ancillary; it could not compete in immediacy, in the quality of conviction it brought, with this irradiation of the soul by faith.

This was therefore an unlucky moment for one Jacques Forton, Sieur de Saint-Ange, to arrive at Rouen glowing with the intention to win disciples for his theory that man's reason was competent, without the crutch of faith, to demonstrate the truth of all the articles of the Creed. He came with a considerable though rather eccentric reputation and with good credentials; a Papal dispensation to leave the Capuchin order, and the somewhat hesitant approval of the Sorbonne of the views he had published in his book *The Conduct of Natural Reasoning*. He had prospects of a benefice near Rouen which might be equivalent to a Chair of religious philosophy. He lodged in the house of the Attorney General of Normandy and was eager to expound his views to all inquirers. Among these were three young men: Du Mesnil, son

of a Rouen judge, Adrien Azout, who would grow to eminence
in astronomy, and Blaise Pascal. They were treated to a queer
mélange of views, some of which they found interesting, some
ludicrous and some definitely alarming. Forton suggested that
our Lord's body was a new creation, not drawn from the blood
of the blessed Virgin, and that her body also was supernaturally
generated (Dr Stewart finds in this the germ of the doctrine of
the Immaculate Conception; v. *The Secret of Pascal*, p. 2).

Pascal and his friends acted with decision but not hastily. They
privately told Forton of their concern. He waved their objections
aside as the difficulties of young students. In a second visit they
made it clear that unless he modified some of his teachings they
must refer the matter to authority, a warning which he dis-
regarded. Then they submitted a list of objections to the acting
Archbishop of Rouen, Jean-Pierre Camus, a good easy-going
prelate who was the reverse of a zealot. He judged that they were
straining at a gnat and dismissed them with reassurances.

They were not reassured, and carried the affair to the Archbishop in person who was cultivating his gardens and his health
at Gaillon. Proceedings were started which led to a retraction.
Gilberte Périer, summing up, leaves a favourable impression of
Forton: 'Il n'a jamais témoigné de fiel contre ceux qui lui avaient
causé cette affaire. . . . Ainsi cette affaire se termine doucement.'

Several characteristics come into clearer view with this episode.
Pascal is formidable. If a truth needs defence he will strike at once,
effectively, without regard for seniority or prestige or (apparently)
for feelings. There is nothing tentative or deprecating about him;
but somehow this does not earn him hostility. Forton is only the
first of a list of individual adversaries or protagonists in debate
with Blaise: Descartes, the Père Noël, Le Méré, de Saci, Arnauld
himself, and most likely there were others. They find themselves
confronted and confuted by this imperious youth. They are not
swept off their feet; they stick to their guns, but with a deference
and even with an affection which, of course, speaks very well for
them, while it also helps to build up the picture of Pascal.

And again we may see Pascal's flair for using and improving what is provided by others. Even Jean Forton, with his extravagant but panoramic mind, gave Blaise something. He held the theory, dear to vague thinkers, that all people are right in what they affirm and only wrong in what they deny: 'Opinions which appear most ridiculous when detached from true principles were none the less true and in line with orthodox belief through the fact that men always recognize truth and only go astray through recognizing only a fragment of truth, or through excluding some fragment of it.' Pascal rejected all the chaff in this and hoarded the grain.* It reappears in Pascalian form in *Pensée* 861:

> 'There are, then, a great number of truths both in faith and morals which seem to conflict, but which hold together in an astonishing order. All heresies spring from the exclusion of some of these truths. The ground of our objection to any heresy is its ignoring of some of our truths. Men fail to imagine any relation between two opposing truths and so they assume that to state one is to deny the other.'

Here the same ball is used, but it is better placed. Pascal is avoiding the absurdity of suggesting that every theory which men care to advance is true. He retains the conception that truth is too rich and complex to avoid the appearance of paradox; he incorporates this into his own thinking and shapes it into clear expression. But the hapless Sieur de Saint-Ange gave it to him.

In 1647 overwork caused Blaise to fall seriously ill. In the summer he retired to Paris with Jacqueline as his housekeeper and secretary, re-occupying the house in the Rue Brisemiche. He was medically advised to avoid all intellectual work and to seek relaxation in society, but does not seem to have followed the first part of this. He was working at his *Nouvelles Expériences Touchant la Vide* and in September he met Descartes, as already related. His moving and beautiful 'Prayer to God for the right use of sickness' may have been written at this time (though we are inclined

* I owe this *trouvaille* to the late Prof. H. F. Stewart.

to accept M. Mesnard's belief that it belongs to the last years of his life). He was giving brotherly encouragement to Jacqueline in her advance to the life of religion. Her response to God's call had been total; she had found God and God had found her. It only remained for M. Singlin, Saint-Cyran's appointed director at Port Royal as well as a great mission preacher, to instruct her towards the novitiate.

Blaise had a clash with Singlin's assistant, de Rebours, who came from Clermont and was a friend of the Pascal family. In discussion he innocently put it to de Rebours that the type of religious awakening in which Port Royal was engaged might reach a wider circle if men of science and letters could be shown that it preached a reasonable faith. De Rebours took strong exception to the idea and charged Pascal with intellectual pride. There was perhaps a touch of poetic justice in this, as de Rebours was regarding Pascal much as Pascal had regarded Forton; but of course the cases were not parallel. Pascal never asserted or entertained the *sufficiency* of reason; he only rejected the Saint-Cyranist idea that human reason was worthless for spiritual convictions. He made some efforts to explain himself but only widened the breach with de Rebours, and desisted.

His physical experiments had been followed with interest by the ageing, urbane and honoured Rector of one of the chief centres of Jesuit education, Père Noël of Clermont College in Paris, who had once been tutor to Descartes. As an Aristotelian he was committed to the dogma that a vacuum was impossible. Having read the *Nouvelles Expériences* he wrote Pascal a letter courteously recognizing the importance of the work but pointing out that an empty space would be a contradiction in nature. The letter lengthened into a dissertation on Aristotelian physics and included a definition of light as 'the luminous movement of trans-lucent bodies contained in transparent bodies', which moved Pascal to give him a lesson in the art of definition. Indeed, Pascal's reply, of October 29, 1647, amounts to a patient instruction in the rudiments of logic and scientific method. Here, as in some other writings, Pascal displays at once his astonishing self-assurance and his power; the letter is a milestone in methodology.

Père Noël replied irreproachably; he admitted that some of his views had been greatly modified by Pascal's arguments. He had heard of Pascal's illness and begged him not to continue the correspondence if it wearied him. Blaise availed himself of this considerate offer. Within a few weeks he was confronted with a new publication over Père Noël's name entitled *Le Plein du Vide* (the fullness of the vacuum), dedicated to the Prince de Condé and making ponderous fun of this new fashion of pretending that there could be gaps in nature. Blaise flared up, in a letter to his friend Le Pailleur, saying what he thought of this double dealing. These Jesuits . . .! His father took up the cudgels and wrote an elephantine rebuke to Père Noël direct.

And all the time Père Noël was innocent. He also had fallen ill, and while he was kept in bed his friends prepared a happy surprise to greet his recovery. They took to the printers the manuscript of a treatise Noël had completed before ever writing to Pascal, and rushed it through the press. Its author was as distressed as the Pascals by the appearance in print of this essay in his 'early bad manner', and he hastened to publish his amended opinions. Honour was satisfied and feelings subsided.

Perhaps the chief fruit of this discussion was the following passage from Pascal's letter to Noël:

'One should never form a decisive judgment for or against a proposition unless one can affirm or deny that it satisfies one of two conditions, namely:

Either, that it presents itself so clearly and distinctly to the sense or to the reason (according as it is the subject of one or the other) that the mind has no means of doubting its certainty —and we should then call it a principle or an axiom.

Or, that it is deducible as an infallible and necessary consequence from such principles or axioms.

Whatever satisfies one of these two conditions is certain

and true. Whatever satisfies neither of them should be regarded as doubtful and uncertain.'

With all its simplicity this is a combination of Francis Bacon with René Descartes. It boldly welds together the Englishman's inductive appeal to experience (that which presents itself to the senses) with the French philosopher's recasting of the deductive argument, the appeal to principles which convince the reason.

Blaise continued to defy spiritual and medical advice by plunging more into scientific activity. Somebody (Père Noël says that it was Pascal himself) broached the interesting question known as the Void within the Void. What would happen if the Torricelli experiment were made, using a very small tube, inside a much larger tube in which the experiment had already been made? If the pressure-of-air theory were correct, then one would expect all the mercury in the smaller tube to fall out, since in this case the space around it would contain no air to exert pressure. It was done, and the mercury did all fall out, and the 'vacuists' were jubilant—all except Pascal. He knew that a result may conform to a theory without confirming it. It was equally open to the opponents of the vacuum to account for the result the other way; nature's hatred of the vacuum is such that the mercury in the small tube was sucked out to try to fill the larger space in the larger tube.

The real proof would be the test already in Pascal's mind. On November 15, 1647, he wrote to his brother-in-law, Florin Périer:

'I have thought of a conclusive experiment. It is to make the usual experiment many times in one day with the same tube, with the same mercury, sometimes at the foot and sometimes at the summit of a mountain, to find whether the level of the mercury will be constant or variable at the two elevations. If the height of the mercury is more at the base of the mountain than at the summit it will necessarily follow that the pressure of the air is the sole cause of the suspension of the mercury.'

The Puy de Dôme was the ideal mountain for the purpose. Unable to move from Paris himself, Blaise asked Périer to make these tests and gave clear and minute directions. The matter was delayed by weather and business but in September 1648, Périer reported complete success. The directions had been scrupulously followed in the presence of responsible witnesses, on a day of variable weather. Two tubes had been used, one of them left at the foot of the mountain, the other taken up and the mercury level tested at five different heights and carefully recorded. The mercury-height varied steadily according to the altitude.

Pascal really cared little for the question which agitated so many minds, whether nature did or did not abhor a vacuum: 'les passions présupposent une âme.' His concern was with the consequences to theory and practice of this proof of the air pressure. Could it perhaps be measured? He lost no time in printing a brochure (a copy of it is preserved in the Public Library at Bordeaux) containing a brief Preface, his letter to Périer, Périer's report and an almost lyrical postscript hailing the new knowledge.

He then rapidly sketched two treatises, one on *La Grande Expérience de l'Équilibre des Liqueurs*, the other *De la Pésanteur et de la Masse de l'Air*, but these were not published till after his death, and they are sections of his larger *Traité du Vide* which has been lost.

The impression created by the Puy de Dôme experiment is faithfully reflected by Robert Boyle some years later: 'Atque ejus modi *experimentum crucis*—ut cum illustri nostro Verulamio loquemur—nobis ex insigni illa observatione Domini Paschalli.'

Science is a communal pursuit. Credit for an advance is rarely due, and was not due here, to one person. But Pascal's reputation from 1648 became European. At Rouen his purposeful elaborations of the Torricelli experiment had resulted in sound hypotheses and incidentally in the important invention of the syringe. His account of them had set a new standard in the presentation of data and conclusions. At the Puy de Dôme the main hypothesis had been confirmed under plain and rigorous conditions set by him. He had achieved an addition to knowledge.

But it was Pascal's nature to use a goal as a stepping-stone. Almost before the Puy de Dôme success was announced he saw that the pressure of the air was a detail, a particular case of some general laws governing the behaviour of 'liquids' (including gases), and to this he turned his attention. Two equal tanks filled with water and joined by a pipe at the base will be in equilibrium, like two equal weights in the pans of a pair of scales. But if one tank is a hundred times as large as the other they are still in equilibrium. Why? In working out the reason, Pascal found that one man, pressing down the surface of the water in the smaller tank, could do the work of a hundred men pressing down the surface of the larger. The hydraulic press was born.

All this period, 1646 to 1648, Pascal was a spiritually awakened man, studying and practising the religion which had cast its spell upon the family. Several encounters, with Forton, with de Rebours and with Père Noël, had raised for him the question of the part played by the reason in gaining religious faith. De Rebours had brushed the reason aside, as being useless and having the nature of sin. On the other hand, Père Noël's disposition to place Aristotle almost among the inspired writers of Holy Writ had offended the principle which Blaise had learnt in boyhood: 'Nothing that has to do with faith can be the concern of the reason.' Characteristically he worked up the paternal formula into greater fullness. His own formula occurs in a remarkable fragment which remains of the *Traité du Vide*.

It does full justice to the other side of the picture, the rights of the human reason. 'Things which fall under the reason and the senses' should be completely unfettered by authority and free from the appeal to antiquity: 'Those whom we call ancient were really new in all things . . . it is in ourselves that we should find the antiquity which we revere in others.' He is almost quoting Francis Bacon's 'The antiquity of history is the youth of the world. It is we who are the ancients' (*De dignitate et augmentis*

Scientiarum). On this side of the argument his fragment offers an account, very remarkable for its time, of the progress of knowledge in matters that 'offer themselves to the senses'. On the other hand: 'In matters in which we only seek to know what the authors have written . . . authority alone can enlighten us. In theology . . . authority is inseparable from truth and we may only know it through her.'

Pascal probably never entertained the idea that the reason could *discover* religious truth; but could not the reason *support* it? Saint-Cyran denied this emphatically: 'Indignissimum et vix tolerandum est doctrinam fidei ad puerilia principia logicae, vel omnino ad humanae mentis captiunculas revocari.' But Pascal refused to be stampeded into this flight from reason. 'It is the way of God, Who does all things gently, to put religion into the mind by reasons, and into the heart by grace' (185). This *Pensée*, which Dr Stewart places as number one in his classification, decisively refutes any charge that Pascal immolated the intellect. Port Royal itself spoke with two voices on this question. For Jansen, for Arnauld and Nicole, philosophy was an important element in the approach to religion, while for Saint-Cyran and Singlin and perhaps de Saci it was anathema. But Pascal's problems, now and later, are all personal ones. We shall not label them. We note that a cleavage is opening between him and such good men as Guilleberte and Singlin. In the next chapter it will widen, and it will never trouble Pascal's conscience. But a more fundamental question, the morality or the wisdom of employing all one's best energies and talents upon 'matters that fall under the senses', perhaps already began to press upon his spirit.

CHAPTER 5

PASCAL'S FRONDE

'Divers men may walke by the Sea side, and the same beames of the Sunne giving light to them all one gathereth by the benefit of that light pebles or speckled shells, for curious Vanitie, and another gathereth precious Pearle or medicinall Ambar by the same light. So the common light of reason illumines us all; but one employes this light upon the Searching of impertinent Vanities, another by a better use of the same light finds out the Mysteries of Religion; and when he hath found them loves them.'

JOHN DONNE, Sermon on Christmas Day, 1621

Richelieu had died in 1642 and King Louis XIII's death followed within a year, leaving the country under the Regency of Anne of Austria with Mazarin as her Minister, while Louis XIV was still a boy. The Thirty Years' War was carried to a victorious conclusion in 1648, but at home there had been a slackening of the rein. Resentments which had been suppressed became vocal and active and during 1648 rebellion broke out, spreading from the capital to the provinces.

The Fronde was a confused affair waged by different sections for different reasons, having no cohesion. The nobility scrambled to recover an importance which Richelieu had reduced; the professional judicature saw a chance of destroying the new executive offices which cut across their authority; the tax-paying property owners tried to check the drain on their resources; the poor fought for bread. The struggle increased the poverty, sharpened the misery and accomplished nothing except to plant a resolve in the mind of the boy king that when his time came to rule he would rule; as he did.

The Fronde lasted from 1648 to 1653. During these same years the mind of Pascal was subject to a growing perplexity, tumult and eventual conflict which we shall try to trace and which may justify the name of this chapter.

Étienne resigned his Rouen post in 1648, just before all such Intendancies were forcibly abolished, and retired with honour. No chief tax-collector could be popular but his fairness and integrity had won general respect; he was made a Counsellor of State.

He joined Blaise and Jacqueline at Paris and was angered to learn for the first time of Jacqueline's desire to become a nun. At first he forbade this, but gave way to the extent of asking her to postpone the step until after his death. She promised this and kept the promise, but lived at home under a voluntary rule as strictly as though she had taken the veil.

Early in the following year Étienne took his family to Clermont, joining the Périers, away from the Fronde and from M. Singlin. So for one year the family were re-united in their native town.

The convent which Jacqueline proposed to enter was enjoying peace and enlargement. Pope Urban VIII's Bull of 1643, prohibiting the *Augustinus* as a breach of the truce, had been quietly received; in fact the Sorbonne ignored it and Antoine Arnauld's prestige was high at this time. Port Royal steadily added to the number of its solitaries and received an almost embarrassing amount of attention from devout people in high society. In 1648 Mère Angélique led back nine of her nuns to Port Royal des Champs after twenty years of exile from her insalubrious spiritual home. The solitaries retired to higher ground at Les Granges, and a converted nobleman, the Duc de Luynes, built his château of Vaumurier a hundred yards from the convent and superintended the enlargement and fortification of the convent buildings.

Antoine Arnauld knew that the Jesuits recognized in him the man upon whom Jansen's mantle had fallen, and he retired from sight, making only fitful appearances at Port Royal. Formal hostilities were reopened in 1649 when Nicolas Cornet, the Syndic of the Sorbonne, compiled seven propositions and laid them before the Sorbonne as being representative of the teaching in the *Augustinus*, and heretical. Arnauld counter-attacked vigorously and with effect. Cornet and his friends reduced the propositions to five and sent them to Rome for scrutiny, where for a while we leave them.

At Clermont, Blaise worked at his *Traité du Vide*, entered into the devout spirit and practices of the Périers' home life, and found a growing enjoyment in being a real uncle to Gilberte's children; he would later undertake the education of the eldest son. But the attitude of Blaise towards Jacqueline's religious vocation gradually changed. Having impetuously encouraged and abetted Jacqueline without consulting their father, he had found that Étienne, whose word had always been law and whose opinion in most things had been accepted as the last word of wisdom, was opposed; and this was not the opposition of a worldling but that of a humble convert who was now putting God first in his own life. *If* perhaps it would serve God's purposes that Jacqueline, like the rest of the family and like so many others touched by the religious movement, should lead the devout life without taking religious vows, Blaise was free to consider what a difference this might make to him personally; and there is no doubt that he did consider it.

Blaise was aged twenty-six, and up to now had never tasted solitary existence. The year in Paris had brought out Jacqueline's qualities as a nurse in his sickness, a secretary to help in his work and correspondence, a hostess for his social contacts, and a most charming companion. Where would he be if his father died and Jacqueline took the veil? He might marry, of course, and his quite normal enjoyment of women's society and his love of children would make this appear a likely prospect; but on the whole Blaise Pascal, like Charles Lamb, may give us the impression of one of nature's bachelors.

Indications of his contemplating marriage are few and slight, but fairly definite, such as they are. There is a report that at Clermont, on this or his next visit to the Périers, he cultivated the society (*papillonait* is Strowski's delightful word for it) of a learned and attractive young lady of Auvergne. We hear no more of it. Marguerite Périer writes that at one time he contemplated an advantageous marriage, and Racine in his Memoirs says much the same. Racine was educated at one of the Petites Écoles of Port Royal in which Pascal became interested. Even if Pascal wrote the *Discours sur les Passions de l'Amour* (which we may presently discuss) it casts little light on his own feelings and none on his plans. In fact Blaise may reasonably have felt dismay at the bleakness of the prospects for him if the father should die and the sister should depart.

They returned from the Périers to Paris, to a new home in the Rue de Touraine, and soon afterwards Étienne did die, on September 24, 1651. Blaise wrote a long letter of consolation to Gilberte, more doctrinal than personal but showing deep feeling kept under control, and revealing, also, how he had been studying and pondering the Bible. It is an essay on the Christian view of death: all life is an oblation to God and death is only the crowning moment of the sacrifice, with all men as it was with our Lord. Our just memorial to the dead is our continued heed to their example and their directions. Blaise adds, 'If he had died six years ago I should have been lost', which seems to support the view that Étienne had been the moving spirit in the spiritual revival of the family.

There followed the necessary business of apportioning the estate. As circumstances brought this on to the small but well-lit stage of Port Royal it comes into this story although it was private, legal and sensible. Their father had enjoyed a good income but had not amassed any large fortune, and what was left was largely tied up at that time in the form of debts owing. The parties to the settlement were, of course, Blaise, Gilberte and Jacqueline. The greater part of Jacqueline's portion was taken over by Blaise in consideration of his undertaking to pay Jacqueline a corresponding annual sum. In effect, she purchased an annuity from her brother. By civil law and canon law, such property in a family estate would, if one member entered a monastery or convent, revert to the remaining legatees, that is to Blaise and Gilberte; and in this case Gilberte waived her claim.

Blaise now hoped with all his heart that Jacqueline would not take the vows. He implored her to stay with him, at least for a few years; but her decision was irrevocable. Gilberte was with them in Paris when the day came for Jacqueline to enter Port Royal as a postulant, on June 4, 1652. On the previous evening Gilberte had tried at Jacqueline's request to give Blaise the impression that at first only a temporary retreat was contemplated, but he guessed the kind intention and the truth, and retired to his room without comment, heavy with grief. Jacqueline slipped away early in the morning without trusting herself to say goodbye even to her sister.

Gilberte went home and Blaise was alone, detached by circumstances and not (as later) by voluntary sacrifice from his human ties. There had already been some evidence of his interior Fronde, if we compare the letter on the death of his father with another letter he wrote less than a month before, to Ribeyre, President of the Court des Aides at Montferrand. This was a resentful and imperious protest against certain remarks to his discredit which had been passed by a Jesuit at Montferrand, accusing him of stealing Torricelli's ideas and presenting them as his own. Ribeyre sent a courteous and moderating reply. No man should be blamed for defending his reputation, especially such a reputation as Pascal had recently earned, but he did it with more bitterness and vigour than the occasion deserved. The two letters show two sides of Pascal's character, and they are coming apart.

In 1651 began an important friendship with the young Duc de Roannez, four years Blaise's junior and a former playmate of his boyhood days, now a nobleman of the highest degree. In this same year Roannez became Governor of Poitou. His deeply religious mother lived at Paris in the Cloître Saint-Merry; two of his sisters were nuns. He was the most eligible bachelor in France but his interests were more in science than in women, and he had some talent in mathematics to match his interest.

Through this friendship Pascal gained an enlarged experience of the fashionable world with its currents of belief and disbelief, its arts of conversation and social conduct, all that which may be summed up as the atmosphere of an aspiring civilization, which Pascal would enter and savour and judge and finally incorporate into his deepest conclusions about human nature. At the same time it furnishes a striking instance of Pascal's dominating magnetism. Morally and intellectually Roannez came under his spell. The etiquette of the age demanded a deference to rank which no doubt Roannez received from Pascal as fully as from others, but beneath the surface the deference was all the other way. One instance will suffice. After Pascal's death there was discussion about the best method of editing his written fragments. One of the suggestions, wisely rejected though seriously made and considered, was that Roannez should reconstitute the whole projected book from his own personal knowledge of Pascal's intentions.

Two months after leaving Blaise, Jacqueline wrote him a letter of singular beauty, the first of a number of letters from which readers can still infer her charm. Grieved by his unhappiness, she tried to show him the road to acceptance:

'Ne m'ôtez pas ce que vous n'êtes pas capable de me donner. Car encore que Dieu se soit servi de vous pour me procurer le progrès des premiers mouvements de sa grace, vous savez assez que c'est de lui seul que procède tout l'amour et toute la joie que nous avons pour le bien, et qu'ainsi vous êtes bien capable de troubler la mienne, mais non pas de me la redonner si une fois je viens à la perdre par votre faute. . . . Si vous n'avez pas la force de me suivre, au moins ne me retenez pas. . . . Fais par vertu ce qu'il faut que tu fasses par nécessité. Donne à Dieu ce qu'il te demande en le prenant. . . . J'attends ce témoignage d'amitié de toi principalement.'

Appealing to his highest instincts, she took care that this should reach him on the feast of the Ascension. The following day he came to Port Royal, much distressed but 'fort adouci', and reduced his plea (that she should defer for two years her vesture as a novice) to a request to wait until All Saints. She could not agree, d'Andilly was brought in to support her case, and Pascal assented to her robing on Trinity Sunday, May 26, 1652.

Within a matter of days after this interview Pascal gave a lecture to a brilliant assembly in the drawing-room of the Duchesse d'Aiguillon, Richelieu's niece. He displayed and demonstrated the calculating machine and spoke further on the recent advances in physics, especially in the field of hydrostatics.

His famous letter to Queen Christina of Sweden is dated at this time, June 1652. It accompanied the gift of one of his calculating machines to this royal patron of the sciences (who had recently caused the death of Descartes by requiring him to expound his theories on cold mornings before breakfast). It was good business to write such a dedication of an invention which Pascal wished to turn to profit by steady sales; but the letter itself is remarkable. Its almost explicit argument is: 'Your Majesty is a very great person by virtue of your sovereign rank. As we may agree, I am a still greater person by virtue of my sovereign intellect.' He just saves himself from this bald statement by conceding to Christina intellect as well as rank. 'I have a particular veneration for those exalted to high degree, whether of power or of knowledge. Unless I am mistaken the latter can be regarded as sovereign equally with the former . . . the power of monarchs over their subjects is only, in my view, a symbol of the power of minds over the minds that are inferior to them, over whom they exercise the right to per-suade, which is for them what the title to command is in the body politic. This second empire seems to me even of a higher order, in that minds are superior to bodies, and even more equitable, since it depends on merit instead of on birth or fortune.'

He had sounded a similar fanfare seven years previously in his Epistle Dedicatory to the Chancellor Séguier:

'Je m'attends bien, Monseigneur, que parmi tant de doctes qui ont pénétrés jusque dans les derniers secrets des mathématiques il s'en pourra trouver qui d'abord estiment mon action téméraire, vu qu'en la jeunesse où je suis, et avec si peu de forces, j'ai osé tenter une route nouvelle dans un champ tout hérissé d'épines et sans avoir de guide. . . .'

We do well to remember that in France *élan* and *la gloire* are not terms of reproach; and that Pascal's chief moral struggle and victory will be over this naïve egotism; also, perhaps, that Pascal had something to crow about. But the chief point of interest in the letter to Queen Christina is the early reference (in a social connection) to Pascal's fundamental doctrine or perception of 'orders'. This concept will come before us as the most powerful and significant of all Pascal's ideas. This apparently trite comparison of worldly rank with intellectual prestige belongs to a way of thinking which entered into his mathematical studies and later into his apprehension of the natural world and the world of men. Meanwhile the letter gives us one superbly Pascalian phrase, 'the right to persuade'. He wrote a treatise later about the *art* of persuading, but *le droit de persuader* asserts that men who can think clearly and accurately are alone entitled to influence others by their words. It is easy to surmise what would have been Pascal's attitude to some 'persuaders' of our era. This chance phrase disenfranchises every form of irrationalism.

He gave up the house in the Rue de Turenne and took lodgings. His father's death had left him somewhat straitened for ready money, which he needed to meet the expenses of continued experiments and to live not only as he had been accustomed but more on the level of his new friends.

In October 1652, he went again to Clermont and stayed with the Périers for seven months. At the end of this time there arose one of those domestic situations in which everybody behaves naturally, nobody behaves perfectly, and each thinks the other has behaved monstrously. Gilberte and Blaise received from Jacqueline a letter which took them aback. It asked them to send her share of the patrimony as a 'dowry', for her to divide between

Port Royal and the poor. It was a most warm-hearted resolve but
—had she forgotten or not understood that the family inheritance
must remain in the family? Blaise and Gilberte replied in separate
but similar letters protesting that the suggestion was not reasonable, and would disinherit her own kin.

The point of these letters was sound but perhaps the tone was
wrong. One gains the impression that they were prompted by the
mistaken idea that the proposal really came from Port Royal.
Jacqueline was immeasurably distressed; indeed her grief and the
difficulty Mère Agnès and Mère Angélique found in consoling or
calming her might seem extravagant if one did not realize the root
of it. Her brother and sister had offended against something more
elemental than conventual regulations, more ancient than Christianity, the code of the nursery. During all her life those three
had stood together. Whatever childish quarrels they may have
had, they stood by each other, in an alliance as unbreakable as it
was indefinable; and Blaise and Gilberte had broken it, on the eve
of what should have been the happiest day of her life.

A long and woeful letter she wrote to the Prioress makes this
clear:

> 'You know that I have had good reason to trust my brother
> and sister owing to the unity and affection which always bound
> us . . . but they wrote, each separately, but in the same style,
> not *saying* they were shocked at my proposal but treating me
> as if they were. I know well that according to the strict letter
> of the law they were right; but we had never been accustomed
> to treat each other like this.'

The incident gives a glimpse of Port Royal at its best and also
its most characteristic. Mère Agnès devoted herself to comforting
Jacqueline, assuring her that the money did not matter at all.
Mère Angélique came up from Port Royal des Champs and
showed herself a true mother, loving and sensible. It brought out
all she had, warm understanding, sturdy advice, and an irresistible
urge to improve the occasion. She begged Jacqueline to note that

her relations, living in the world, could only be expected to behave as they were doing. Lacking grace they could not, at the best, exceed mundane friendship; and Blaise especially (who had lately given disturbing signs of a disposition to enjoy himself) would inevitably prefer his interests to hers. To expect more would be looking for a miracle. The money was nothing. We should allow nothing in life to grieve us except our sins.

At this point M. Singlin threw (if the expression be permitted) a holy spanner into the works. He questioned the morality of refraining from pressing a claim for the money. The convent, in clearing itself of any suspicion of cupidity, could hardly be unaware that it had made a fine gesture, and that awareness would imperil their humility, a more important virtue than disinterestedness. Moreover to condone an injustice would involve complicity in the guilt. But on further reflection he agreed that Port Royal might drop the claim.

Blaise had returned to Paris and had been touched by Jacqueline's distress. He saw that his behaviour had been certainly stiff and possibly shabby; and his pride was touched by Mère Angélique's rather emphatic magnanimity. He insisted on making, in due legal form, a deed of gift of more than was expected in the first place. It was accepted with dignity, and Mère Angélique had her prerogative of the last word: 'Voyez-vous, Monsieur, nous avons appris de feu M. de Saint-Cyran à ne rien recevoir pour la Maison de Dieu, que ne vienne de Dieu.' The dowry was God's gift to Port Royal and Blaise must not walk off with any idea that it was his gift. He did walk off feeling that in spiritual diplomacy he was no match for Port Royal.

A new world was opening for him, a world in which he had already made a name and might make a fortune, and where he might slake a stronger thirst than either of these, his need for facts. Entry into society enlarged his scope for studying human nature. 'Pascal had,' writes Sainte-Beuve, 'in the highest degree of intensity, the feeling of the human person.'* He always gave

* *Port-Royal;* Pléiade ed., Vol. II, p. 121.

his attention to what was in front of him, what was actual; and from now onwards his steady regard is fixed on men, their actions and reasons for acting, their opinions and the chromatic background of desire, imagination and reflection from which opinions emerge; the trend and the fate of the lives he saw being lived.

It may well be that this new awakening of interest in humanity was in part compensatory for that loss of religious fervour which (on his own later admission) he suffered at this time. There was a gap and he filled it. Lectures, drawing-room conversations, new friendships, the study of polite behaviour, games, books, gave him constant and congenial occupation.

If Pascal wrote the *Discours sur les Passions de l'Amour* it was almost certainly about this time, the latter half of 1653. This is a curious piece of writing, with not enough form to be regarded as an essay and too much to be a string of aphorisms. It might well be a series of notes in preparation for a spoken discourse (and we know from the *Pensées* that Pascal did provide himself with extended notes before giving an address). Less probably, though this view is favoured by M. Strowski, it might be a summary of a discourse already given, incorporating the comments made in the discussion. It was discovered in manuscript by Victor Cousin in the nineteenth century at the library of Saint-Germain-des-Prés, where many Port Royalist documents were kept. Under the title someone had written: 'On l'attribua à M. Pascal.' One other copy has been found, without the inscription. The authorship is unsettled though the majority view among scholars is that Pascal wrote it.

We favour this ascription for one external reason and for several internal indications. M. Ernest Havet has cogently argued that no Port Royalist would have attributed it to Pascal if he could have helped it, for although the discourse is quite innocent it is also quite secular, treating of human love without reference to Divine love. The internal evidence concerns some passages which have, so to speak, the same wavelength as Pascal's.

The *Discours* begins at once with 'L'homme est né pour

penser' (cf. 'L'homme est visiblement fait pour penser' (146)). Presently there occurs a paragraph on the difference between two ways of thinking, geometrically and intuitively, which precisely summarizes the very first of the *Pensées* in Brunschvicg's arrangement. There are also passages which, if they cannot be so easily paralleled, are yet deeply characteristic: 'À mesure que l'on a plus d'esprit les passions sont plus grandes . . . dans une grande âme tout est grand.' 'À mesure que l'on a plus d'esprit l'on trouve plus de beautés originales.' There are reminiscent turns of phrase: 'Il y a une éloquence de silence qui pénètre plus que la langue ne saurait faire' (cf. 'Le coeur a ses raisons que la raison ne connait point'. The thought is different but the form is like). 'Néanmoins il faut deviner, mais bien deviner' (cf. '—il n'est question que d'avoir bonne vue, mais il faut l'avoir bonne' (1)). There are sentences of which, without tracing parallels, one can only say that they have Pascal's elevation and energy, his accent: '. . . dont il sent dans son coeur des sources si vives et si profondes' (who but Pascal wrote that?) and: 'Nous naissons avec un caractère d'amour dans nos coeurs'; our hearts are stamped at birth with the very imprint of love.

The *Discours* contains much that is less musical and less exalted than this, though it contains nothing that is not edifying. It is hardly an important document except as an index to Pascal at a transitional moment. If we accept it as his then we know that he entered whole-heartedly into the discussions of this sort which were fashionable in the salons of the *précieuses*; and that he held his own in them; and that he was exploring human nature and motives; and finally that he had rather definitely moved away from Guilleberte, Singlin and 'feu M. Saint-Cyran', for there is not a word in the discourse which acknowledges God as the source or the recipient of love. For the rest, it is a somewhat dispassionate review of the passions. We cannot use it to help us in deciding whether Pascal was ever in love.

To Christian minds an 'interest in human nature' must always have one particular connotation, a fellow-feeling for the poor.

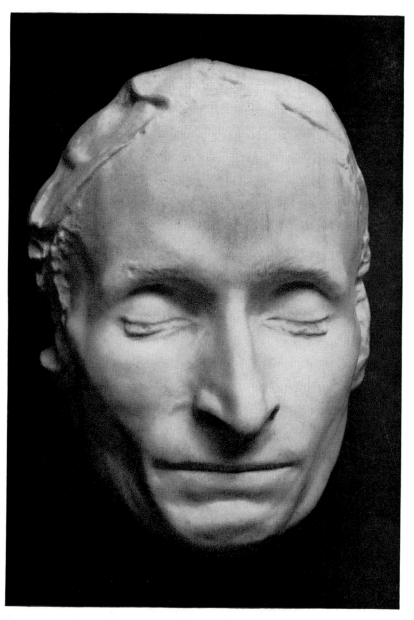

PASCAL'S DEATH MASK
From the cast in the Library of Newnham College, Cambridge

During Pascal's lifetime this spirit was alive in France, preeminently in and through Saint Vincent de Paul. The student of Pascal who looks for its emergence in him will not be disappointed but the time for clear evidence for it is not yet. Gilberte testifies that all his life he was moved by the spectacle of poverty. He had witnessed scenes of great suffering—the Nu-Pieds in Normandy, the victims of the Fronde in Paris; and even without the aggravation of civil strife, the poor of that day were poor indeed. Here we shall only note that he had become deeply convinced that anarchy and sedition inevitably increased the misery of those who resorted to violence to relieve their condition, and with this he acquired, perhaps from Thomas Hobbes, a deep scepticism as to the possibility of founding human rule upon ideal principles of justice, however loudly such rule might invoke such principles. 'Summum jus, summa injuria . . . ainsi on appelle juste ce qu'il est forcé d'observer. De là vient le droit de l'épée, car l'épée donne un véritable droit. . . . De là vient l'injustice de la Fronde, qui élève sa prétendue justice contre la force' (878). 'Pour faire que les membres soient heureux, il faut qu'ils aient une volonté, et qu'ils la conforment au corps' (480).*

In this period, 1653 to 1654, we see him living in his own *milieu*, a man of science, fashion and ambition, and something of a man of business; a man with a deep background of recent but real spiritual experience and faith, which background however is being curtained off. For a while the drama of his life is played between the footlights and the curtain. The human types which claim his interest as he turns to the study of human nature are mostly those of the circles in which he moves.

While Pascal was haunting the salons in Paris, at Rome a Congregation of five cardinals assisted by thirteen consulting theologians had been examining the orthodoxy of the five propositions, said to be drawn from the *Augustinus*, which had been submitted by Cornet and his friends. At the end of May 1653, just

* Pascal's political realism is well discussed in M. Chinard's *En lisant Pascal.*

about the date when Jacqueline Pascal made her profession and took the veil as Soeur Sainte-Euphémie, the five propositions were condemned in the Bull *Cum Occasione* of Innocent X, an event which is not likely to have interested Pascal as yet. But as the Five Propositions will soon come into his story it may be fitting to record them here:

1. Some commandments of God are impossible to good men though they desire and strive to observe them.

2. In the state of fallen nature, resistance to interior grace is impossible.

3. In the state of fallen nature man need not possess inner freedom in order to deserve merit or demerit; it is enough that he be free from external force.

4. The Semi-Pelagians were heretics (even though they admitted the need for grace for every action) because they claimed that grace left the human will with power to obey or disobey.

5. It is a renewal of Semi-Pelagian heresy to say that Christ died for all men without exception.

Two questions arise: are these propositions heretical? Are they in the book as expressing the teaching of the book? The first question falls within the undoubted right of the hierarchy of the Church to declare a doctrine sound or otherwise; it therefore became known as the *Question de Droit*. The latter question is clearly on a matter of factual evidence. An opinion that such and such a doctrine occurs, or does not occur, in a book is not itself a doctrinal opinion. Granting that the hierarchy has full authority to pronounce on a matter of *doctrine*, would it be temerarious to question a ruling of the hierarchy on a matter of factual *evidence*? This is the *Question de Fait*.

The petition to Rome had been the delayed result of an agitation worked up by the Jesuits under Habert, Bishop of Vabres, and supported by a number of French bishops. Many bishops kept aloof on Gallican grounds and at least twelve refrained through Jansenist sympathies and wrote saying so. Sainte-Beuve gives a lively account of the negotiations in Rome, especially of the relations between the charming and diplomatic old Pope and the delegation of defenders of the *Augustinus*, to whom he extended a warm but non-committal friendship. Any Jansenist who approached him with a leading question was rewarded with a brilliant smile and the Papal blessing. At the last, when the Bull had been decreed, he gave the Jansenists a special reception. They asked him whether they could honourably sign their acceptance without ceasing to be Augustinians (that is, champions of the *Augustinus*). He replied, 'O, questo è certo!' 'My dear friends, *of course!*' So far as he was concerned he had merely pronounced certain doctrines as unsound. The body of the Bull contained no reference to the book, though the Preamble referred to it as the occasion of the inquiry and a Postscript contained the implication that the views condemned had been defended by Jansen.

Sainte-Beuve deplores as a quibble the raising of the *Question de Fait*. 'Une fois dans cette voie double, le Jansénisme est perdu, et j'ajouterai, il le mérite. Saint-Cyran, où est-tu?' But this seems unjust. Arnauld's fault was not in raising the question of *Fait* but in mishandling it. A man accused of false teaching has a plain right to challenge his accusers to quote; and the briefer his challenge the better. But Arnaud had a fatal incapacity for brevity and gave his enemies a large and ever-expanding target.

We may perhaps pause to consider the disproportion of this strange debate at this juncture. On the one hand, the five Cardinals with their band of consulting theologians; the urgent, ubiquitous, powerful Society of Jesus; the numerous French bishops; the anti-Jansenist majority in the Sorbonne; somewhat later, the thundering oratory of the young Bossuet (though he fired broadsides both to port and starboard); and on the other hand—what? The devout laity touched by Port Royal were ill-equipped for polemics. Jansen and Saint-Cyran were dead. The nuns in the convent of Port Royal, one convent among many, were attending to their prayers; their directors, Singlin and de Saci, gave themselves to direction with hardly a passing glance at controversy (de Saci's maladroit excursion into controversy, *Les Enlumineures*, rather proves this than otherwise). Saint-Cyran's successor Barcos, and the solitaries headed by le Maître, lived away from the world. We are reduced to the fitfully-appearing figure of Antoine Arnauld, with his as yet somewhat dim lieutenant Nicole. About two years later, Blaise Pascal will make a third.

Nothing would have seemed less likely at the moment when we see him entering and studying the society of his time. Recent writers on Pascal have discarded the former view that this was a mere lapse of five or six years during which Pascal turned his back upon religion and science for social relaxation. For one thing, the crucial period is much reduced, almost to the eighteen months from May 1653 to November 1654, and, far from being months of mere relaxation, they were a period of intense though sporadic thinking. The writings he will leave at his death will be largely the fruit of these months. Moreover, the new social code which he studied while it was in process of formation was not something which he subsequently dropped. He enjoyed and approved it. The fashionable friends whom he acquired were retained until he died, along with his admiration of their aims and of the atmosphere of their society.

The social ideal of *l'honnêteté* was an aristocratic standard for people of breeding and culture; it had little of the democratic spirit, but within its limits it was admirable. The basis of it was consideration for others, present or absent. No one must be bored or humiliated or crowded out of the conversation or unkindly slighted. *L'honnête homme* is the man who can play his social part without overplaying it, who has learnt enough about human feelings never to wound them gratuitously. He is the perfect host or the perfect guest; he brings out the best in his fellows without obtruding himself.

The immediate cause of this movement towards good manners based on good feeling seems to have been a healthy disgust for the coarseness and violence of the Fronde and the pushfulness of the leading Frondeurs. Its more remote source was Montaigne, who in some of his Essays (notably ii, 8, 25, 27) draws an ideal portrait of the *gentilhomme*, the man who repays an education marked chiefly by kindness and understanding, with a gentle, unassertive, undogmatic but independent and well-stored mind.

It is certain that Pascal spent much of 1653–4 immersed in Montaigne's Essays, with the intricate and in some ways paradoxical results which inspired Sainte-Beuve to some of his most brilliant pages.*

It is likely that Pascal had read Montaigne early in life. His father had educated him on the model of Montaigne's father, and in any case the Essays were favourite reading in that class. Here is one of the great Montaigne paradoxes. The sedate, honourable, respectable men of position read Montaigne for edification; and at the same time Montaigne was the 'Breviary of the Libertines', the charter of free thought and very free behaviour. If we would follow Pascal's line of thought we must seek some light on this riddle.

Montaigne is edifying because he is honest and hates cruelty, because his references to religion are almost invariably respectful and his interest in human nature is vivid and variegated, and because in an evil time he practised and preached a stoical tranquillity and strength of soul, overcoming his own considerable dread of pain and horror of death by recognizing that 'ces choses ne sont ni doloreuses ni difficiles d'elles-même, mais nôtre faiblesse et lacheté les fait cettes'. Such were the qualities which won the approbation of the upright, and which no doubt appealed to Pascal along with the vast expanse of human observation which Montaigne offers and the supple strength and vivacity of his style.

But Montaigne is insidious. The reader has fallen completely under his spell long before he begins to discover that he is accepting and on the verge of approving a number of dubious propositions. Religion, it appears, is venerable because it is celestial, beyond this mundane sphere of ours, beyond our reach and not in any really practical way touching human affairs at all. Human nature, described in these essays with enchanting amplitude, with

* *Port-Royal*, Pléiade ed., tome I, see esp. pp. 826, 859, 860.

urbane sympathy and apparently kindly humour, gradually comes
into view as utterly contemptible, the prey of passions and foolish
imaginations and delusions. In Montaigne, says Sainte-Beuve, 'il
n'y a de riant que l'apparence'; what looks like a smile is something
more like a snarl. Of course this needs to be qualified, and of
course Sainte-Beuve qualifies it. Montaigne is too big to be boxed
into an epigram. His humanity is rich and benevolent and genuine;
he had kindness for another's troubles, courage in his own. The
real point about Montaigne, the thing that made him important
for Shakespeare and for Pascal, is his demonstration that humanism is not enough. His inexhaustible interest in his own kind, his
unparalleled abundance of instances from ancient and contemporary history, his frank and shrewd reflections, led him in-
exorably out on to the waste land. Having made his noble onslaught on all forms of pedantry and intellectual tyranny, having
proclaimed the gospel of naturalism, he emerges at last unable to
find any dividing line between the natural and the bestial or the
trivial.

Like Thomas Hobbes in the *Leviathan*, he considered the condition of men who 'live without other security than what their
own strength and their own invention shall furnish them withal';
and his conclusion, if less bluntly expressed, is not far different
from Hobbes', that 'the life of man is solitary, poor, nasty, brutish
and short'. Perhaps in nothing else does Pascal show his greatness
as much as in his self-identification with what was true and fine in
Montaigne's portrait of man, coupled with his refusal to accept
Montaigne's final verdict.

Pascal went more than once to the Court, frequented the salons
of great ladies, became almost (perhaps quite) one of the Roannez
household, went sometimes, with no great enjoyment, to the
theatre, joined in the sports and games, possibly even the gaming,
which were in fashion; above all he revelled in the practice of the
art of conversation which was society's chief interest.

There was no reason, no apparent reason, why he should not
accept with both hands these new interests and pleasures. He was

released from family responsibilities; his livelihood depended upon the creation of influential connections, which also stimulated the genius of which he had already given proof. To himself and to his friends he must have appeared well over the threshold of a dazzling career.

But he was profoundly unsettled. This is not a guess; his own later admission dates his worst and longest period of spiritual uneasiness and dryness from this time. Behind his business-like attention to business, his growing ease of manner in society, the delight of new friends, the quiet pleasure of reading Epictetus, the thrill of reading Montaigne, lay an unappeasable distaste for it all and a great weariness.

CHAPTER 6

THE VOID

'*We possess nothing in the world—a mere chance can strip us of everything—
except the power to say "I". That is what we have to give to God—in other
words, to destroy. There is absolutely no other free act which it is given us to
accomplish—only the destruction of the "I".*'

SIMONE WEIL, Gravity and Grace

It may not have escaped the reader, though it quite possibly
escaped Pascal, that he had lately been in a sense (a perfectly
sincere sense) making the best of both worlds. His two sisters
were both practising religion, one in the world, the other in community, largely under the encouragement of his spiritual counsel.
He had, with immense fervour and moral authority, mapped out
a path which they were following but he was not.

For the course of the present chapter we accept M. Mesnard's
chronology which he convincingly bases upon certain docu-
mentary clues. In September of 1653 Pascal travelled to Poitou
with the Duc de Roannez, returning with him to Paris in January
1654. These four months and the seven months that followed are
a period described by Strowski as 'la plus féconde et la plus
dramatique de la vie de Pascal'.

The journey to Poitou is almost certainly described, in distinctly condescending terms, in a later writing of the Chevalier
de Méré who was one of the party:

'I once made an expedition with the Duc de Roannez, who
talks both wisely and well and is excellent company. With us
came M. Miton, whom you know and whom everybody at
Court finds so entertaining. As it was simply a party of
pleasure, we thought of nothing but our amusement and left

few subjects untouched. The Duc is interested in mathematics and had brought with him a man *entre deux ages* who was little known at the time but has since made a great stir in the world. He was a great mathematician but nothing else. The man had *ni goût ni sentiment*. This did not deter him from joining in everything we said and did. He admired the mind and eloquence of M. du Vair and told us the jokes of the Criminal-Judge d'O. . . . after a while he noticed that he was striking a wrong note, and became a listener, asking occasional questions and now and again pulling out tablets to record his reflections. By the time we reached Poitou he was conversationally on level terms with his companions, and was himself astonished and pleased at the change. . . . After that journey he thought no more of the mathematics which had always occupied him.'

We can accept this as referring to Pascal. No one else satisfies all the requirements—a noted mathematician who knew Roannez and Méré and Miton, and is known to have visited Poitou with the Duc. We certainly need not accept Méré's picture of an awkward savant with a single-track mind, though it is not difficult to suppose that Pascal at this time might monopolize the conversation. There is clear evidence that he had already acquired social ease in the big houses and at Court. Méré's statement that he gave up mathematics from this time conflicts with the fact that his chief mathematical discoveries were soon to be made, and to some extent in collaboration with Méré himself. But it seems true that just at this juncture he did give up the practice, resolutely and for several months, while in the grip of a larger and more vital interest:

'I spent many years in the study of the abstract sciences, and the small amount of human contact which they afforded filled me with disgust. When I began the study of man I found that the abstract sciences were not suited to humanity, and that I was drifting further from my proper condition by my knowledge than other men were by their ignorance. . . . I did at least expect to find many companions in the study of man . . . but there I was mistaken. Even fewer study human nature than those who study geometry. . . . They may be right. May it not be better for a man's happiness that he should not know himself?' (144).

The study of man was Pascal's object for the rest of his life, but intensively so in the months opening with this journey to Poitou.

He must have been a miraculously quick reader, with an intellectual metabolism which converted all that he could use of what he read into the formation of his own mind, whence it issued, adopted, adapted, clarified, deepened, redirected. Thus at this time he must have devoured Epictetus and Montaigne, but his first studies and his permanent object lessons were the men about him, Roannez, Miton, des Barreaux, and always Méré, to whom he owed much and gave more.

Miton seems to have held some especial appeal for Pascal. He had held a high position in the State and remained in high favour for his social gifts. Madame de Sablé declared that she found the rare gift of natural eloquence only in him and Montaigne and Voiture. A man of powerful but rudderless mind, possessing no faith, little hope and abundant charity, gambler and wit, keeping his house filled with boisterous guests whose antics (and his own) he observed with disillusioned tolerance, somehow he makes us think of Charles James Fox. Miton frequently came to Pascal's thoughts as he penned them later: 'The self is hateful. You, Miton, hide it up; but you do not succeed in getting rid of it. You are, then, always hateful? No; for in acting to oblige everybody we give no more occasion for hatred of us' (455). 'Miton sees well that men are corrupt; what he does not see is why they cannot fly higher' (448). 'Reproach Miton for not being troubled, since God will reproach him' (192). So far as Pascal had any one individual in mind as the typical free-thinker to whom he wished to cast the life-line of Christianity in forming his Apology for religion, it was probably Miton.

Another member of that circle, des Barreaux, might have similarly interested Pascal if they had met earlier, when the former was a brilliant intellectual rebel. He was now that unpleasing spectacle, the voluptuary run to seed. The stock joke about him was that his periods of religious devotion coincided exactly with his illnesses. Someone reported to the Abbé Bourzéis some daring atheistical sallies of des Barreaux. 'Dites-lui de ma part,' replied the Abbé, 'que je veux bien discuter avec lui, mais à la première maladie qu'il aura.' Pascal's one written reference to him is contemptuous.

Antoine Gombaud le Chevalier de Méré was a far more considerable and interesting character. He was the Lord Chesterfield of his day, with a great deal of Max Beerbohm's 'Duke of Dorset' (in *Zuleika Dobson*). A member of the great house of Condé, he had fought bravely, been wounded and decorated; had travelled in England, Germany, Spain and even America; had mastered many living languages and found time to become an accomplished classical scholar with a particular liking for Demosthenes, Homer and Plato. From his estates around the Château de Boussaq in Poitou he became the self-appointed mentor of society and devoted his life to the cultivation of *l'honnêteté*, that ideal of good manners described in our last chapter. He wrote voluminously, but as it was one of his canons of good form not to rush into print, the earliest of his published works is dated 1671. His book-titles indicate his *genre*: *Les Conversations* (1671), *Les Agréments* (1676), *De l'Esprit* (1677), *De la Conversation* (1677), *Maximes* (1687). They reveal him as a man of very wide but detached interests, like Montaigne in his breadth but completely unlike him in that Méré has no wish *de se peindre*, having more taste than talent for metaphysics, in religion a sceptic, in conduct a cultivated libertine. He applied himself to the vocation of teaching good manners as an artist, a doctor or a priest might dedicate his life to a high duty. The world owes much to Méré for Pascal's incomparable literary style, for although Pascal had shown himself able to write with directness, and with his own verbal music, before this, his writing might not have attained such complete freedom from affectation and verbiage but for Méré's teaching.

While expanding in this high and congenial company Pascal read passionately, chiefly in Epictetus and Montaigne.*

Pascal's interest in Epictetus was a transient but vital stage in his development. M. Strowski has given reasons for concluding that Pascal, characteristically, by-passed the popular Christianized versions of this Stoic teaching, du Vair and Charron, to read Epictetus himself in the excellent translation of Dom Jean Goulu, formerly Provincial of the religious house of the Feuillants. We ourselves think that he certainly had read and admired du Vair, and his acquaintance with Charron's *La Sagesse* is proved by *Pensée* 65: 'Parler de ceux qui ont traités de soi-même; des divisions de Charron, qui attristent et ennuient.' Charron had done for Epictetus and Montaigne precisely what Jansen did for Saint Augustine, laying their teachings out upon the dissecting table and accurately ticketing the lifeless remains.

Epictetus seemed to offer what Pascal was looking for: a clue to life's meaning and a rule for life's conduct. A crippled slave of the time of Domitian, he had humbly practised his moral philosophy many years before he began to teach it. It was based upon a resolute and contented submission to the will of God, Whose Spirit is the soul of the universe. All that happens comes within a drama of which God is the author, and man must learn to play his part whatever part may be assigned to him. He must learn to acquiesce. 'Never say, I have lost such a thing; say rather, I have given it back: my son is dead; I have given him back. . . He who deprives you of your property is guilty, you say? But why disturb yourself about the mere instrument? He who lent you these things is claiming them again.'

Pascal, with his poor health and his uncertain financial prospects, was fortified by such precepts; and even more he felt the appeal of a doctrine which offered him interior peace. 'Les

* 'M. Pascal dit que ses deux livres les plus ordinaires avaient été Epictète et Montaigne, et il lui fit de grands éloges de ces deux esprits.' *Entretien avec M. de Saci.*

Stoiques disent, *Rentrez au dedans de vous-même; c'est là où vous trouverez votre repos.'*

But before long he was compelled by experience both exterior and interior to add the four or five words which complete this *Pensée*: . . . 'et cela n'est pas vrai' (465).

For as we have seen Pascal was inveterately a realist, concerned always with facts before theories, and with theories only as they were divulged by the facts. His complaint of Descartes was that in physics he sought a short cut to truth by scorning the labour of observation and experiment. Similarly he perceived that the Stoic doctrine of man was a false simplification. Epictetus, *ce grand esprit* who knew so well what man ought to do, quite failed to recognize the limits of what in fact man could do.

Pascal was keenly observing, with growing consternation, what man could do and was doing around him. It was all so gracious and pleasant and cultured, the conversations and the expeditions, the hunting parties and the games in the evening and the elevated, easy, unaffected exchange of classical allusions; but how artificial, how superficial and brittle! Those who spent their lives in such diversions only seemed to be making a full and generous use of life's opportunities, while in fact they were living with blinds drawn to shut out the contemplation of life's more unwelcome realities.

From this point we can quote the *Pensées* with increasing confidence, for even if Pascal did not actually write down until his last years his thoughts on human nature (we believe that many of them were written in this period of 1653–4), it was now that he formed them.

'Men are responsible from infancy for their honour, their welfare, their friends, and even for the honour and welfare of their friends. They are thronged with business affairs, the study of languages, physical exercise. They are made to assume that happiness is impossible unless their health, honour and fortune are in good order; and that one thing wrong will make them unhappy; so they are given cares and affairs to keep them bustling about from daybreak. An odd way, you will protest, to make men happy! What more could one do to ensure their misery? Very well, what more *could* one do? This; we could relieve them from such cares. Then they would be face to face with themselves, would reflect on what they are, whence they came, whither they go; indeed, we can hardly give them too much to divert and distract them. . . . How hollow, how stuffed with rubbish, is the heart of man!' (143. The final exclamation is scribbled in the margin.)

He turned to Montaigne with a well-founded impression that Montaigne had a more realistic idea of his fellows than Epictetus or the contemporary exponents of Epictetus.

So he read again the Essays and was captivated. The amplitude and variety, comparable with Shakespeare's, of the picture of man; the reckless candour of the portrait; the championship of intellectual freedom and scorn of barren dogmatism; the unquenchable vitality of the style; all these qualities entranced him. Pascal was a humanist from the very heart, and Montaigne's claim that the rules of virtue should be attuned to man's nature, should be simple and natural and practicable, won his assent as it had earned the admiration of S. Francis de Sales and S. Vincent de Paul. 'The strength of a man's virtue must not be measured by his efforts' (i.e. his periods of exceptional piety) 'but by his ordinary life' (352). 'To leave the mean is to abandon humanity. The greatness of the human soul consists in knowing how to preserve the mean. So far from greatness consisting in leaving it, it consists in not leaving it' (378). This is Pascal echoing but amplifying Montaigne. Such thoughts as these were alien from the whole teaching and spirit of Jansenism, yet for Pascal they were of primary importance up to his death, and were integral to his plan for a defence of the Christian religion. The natural man of Montaigne, says Sainte-Beuve, is precisely that which Port Royal most hated in him.* It was precisely what Pascal most loved in him.

Montaigne avoided the Stoic error of crediting human nature with a strength it did not possess. You never found Montaigne saying loftily, 'Quant à moi, je n'ai jamais empêché de faire ce que j'ai voulu, ni forcé de faire malgré moi ce que je n'ai pas voulu.' To read Montaigne's wealth of anecdotes about men of ancient times and of his own time, and about himself was, for Pascal, an exercise in his favourite occupation, the observation of real things, a feast of facts.

For all these reasons Montaigne became, in Sainte-Beuve's phrase, anchored in the soul of Pascal. Of this relationship Sainte-Beuve uses two other really splendid metaphors. Pascal, he says, was like the Lacedaemonian youth, and Montaigne the concealed wolf who tore at his entrails; and later, when Sainte-Beuve is describing Pascal's use of Montaigne, he refers to 'les nombreuses pensées sur la vanité, la faiblesse et la contradiction de l'homme, que Pascal reproduit, et dont il s'empare *en les couronnant, comme des minarets, de la Croix*, ce qui eut doit frapper plus que la ressemblance . . . c'est la différence du ton et le sérieux du dessein opposé au jeu de l'escrime'.†

Pascal constantly refused, on the one hand, to follow where Montaigne beckoned or, on the other hand, to jettison Montaigne and all he stood for, all his disciples of Pascal's generation, as being outside the sphere of redemption. 'Pascal,' writes François Mauriac, 'released a torrent of infinite love over the men of Montaigne. . . . It is Pascal who throws Montaigne into the current of redemption.'‡ To take one course or the other would have been easy. The Jansenists recognized (but not as clearly as Pascal) the dangerous attraction of Montaigne's spiritual nonchalance, his fundamental scepticism; accordingly they shunned and condemned him. The libertines responded (only less eagerly than

* *Port-Royal*, Pléiade ed., tome I, p. 827.
† *Op. cit.*, tome I, p. 860.
‡ *The Living Thoughts of Pascal*, Cassell & Co, 1941.

Pascal) to the gay and generous tolerance of Montaigne; it emancipated them from the stark austerity of the religion of the Cross. Only Pascal, of that generation, gave himself the pain and the glory of sifting the grain from the chaff.

As yet, there was only pain. Pascal's own faith was dimmed and he could only fight what he felt to be wrong in Montaigne with a dumb, obstinate conviction that man was better than the Essays painted him. 'Despite all our miseries which press upon us and grip us by the throat, we have an instinct which we cannot repress, and which raises us up' (411).

The chief arena for this conflict was Montaigne's longest essay, the twelfth of the second volume, called *An Apologie of Raymond Sebond*, which also powerfully affected Shakespeare (echoes of it appear in *Hamlet*, *The Tempest* and perhaps in *Macbeth*). As the title suggests, it sets out to defend a book, the *Theologia Naturalis* of Raymond Sebond, from certain criticisms. This book deals with the testimony made by the natural world to the natural reason of man concerning the things of God. It would have satisfied the conditions of the Bampton Lectureship. Probably Pascal read it before embarking on his own very different Apology. Montaigne had felt a special interest in it, as he was its translator into French from the original Latinized Spanish; so he sets out to defend it from detraction. The essay has many astonishing features, and among them this: that if among the criticisms of the *Theologia Naturalis* there was any so complete, so savage, so devastatingly destructive of Sebond's whole line of argument as Montaigne's 'defence' of his pet book, then Sebond was a much ill-used author.

This was clearly not Montaigne's original intention. He starts by speaking up well for what was, in fact, a fine treatment of natural theology. 'His drift is bold and his scope adventurous; for he undertaketh by humane and natural reasons to establish and verifie all the articles of Christian religion against Atheists. Wherein I find him so resolute and so happy, as I deeme it a thing impossible to doe better in that argument.' '. . . we should accompany our faith with all the reason we possesse.' It is only gradually that the note changes. What happens is that (as is almost usual with Montaigne) he quickly forgets what he started to write about and settles down to something which interests him more, in this case the folly of human pretensions.

Natural theology rests upon certain assumptions: that the universe is rationally controlled; that universal laws may be inferred from natural laws; that the processes of human reasoning lead to reliable conclusions; that the human senses yield trustworthy information of nature. Upon all these assumptions, except possibly the first, Montaigne opens the floodgates of doubt. How do we know that natural laws apply outside our little world? 'Tu ne vois que l'ordre et la police de ce petit caveau où tu es logé, au moins si tu la vois. Cette pièce n'est rien au prix du tout ... c'est une *loi municipale* que tu allègues, tu ne sais pas quelle est l'universelle.' We may be mistaking a set of parochial bye-laws for Statutes of the Realm.

Montaigne begins his invective against vanity with a long section in which he assigns to man his place 'in the ample bosom of nature', and shows it to be an extremely humble place. His ostensible target is the presumption of the atheist: 'The means I use ... is to crush and trample this humane pride and fiercenesse underfoot, to make them feele the emptinesse, vacuitie, and no worth of man; and violently to pull out of their hands the silly weapons of their wisdom; and to make them stoope and bite and snarle at the ground, under the authority and reverence of God's Majesty.' 'Is it possible to imagine any thing so ridiculous as this miserable and wreched creature, which is not so much as master of himselfe, exposed and subject to offences of all things, and yet dareth to call himselfe Master and Emperour of this Universe?' We are shrivelled by the mere contemplation of the stars. But even on this globe we have no great title to eminence: 'When I am playing with my Cat, who knowes whether she have more sport in dallying with me than I have in gaming with her? We entertain each other in mutual monkey tricks.' He proceeds to compare, at leisure and in detail, man with his fellow animals, not at all to the advantage of man. Many animals excel us not only in strength but in sureness of instinct, in constancy of friendship.

We are the prey of trivial chances: 'A gust of contrarie winds, the croking of a flight of Ravens, the false pase of a Horse, the casual flight of an Eagle, a dreame, a sodaine voyce, a false signe, a mornings mist, an evening fogge, are enough to overthrow, sufficient to overwhelme and pull him to the ground.' Among the animals 'such as most resemble man are the vilest and filthiest of all the rout'.

So Montaigne puts us in our place. Nevertheless, even in this humble condition, we feel able to study the truth of things. What (asks Montaigne) have we to encourage this confidence? 'We have for our part inconstancy, irresolution, incertitude, sorrow, superstition, the fear of things to come, ambition, avarice, jealousy, disordered appetites, war, lies, disloyalty, distraction and vain curiosity.' But at least we have religion? Yes, says Montaigne, we have the religion which chance flung in our way. 'Man cannot make a worm, but he makes Gods by the dozen'; 'We are Christians by the same title as we are Perigordians or Germans'. All is reduced to a fundamental relativity. And what had Christianity in fact done for man and made of man? (It is to be noted here that the year in which Montaigne retired to his castle, to spend his days in study, coincided with the massacre of S. Bartholomew.) 'Notre religion est faite pour extirper les vices; elle les couvre, les nourrit, les incite.'

But what of the wise men of the past, the philosophers? As though Montaigne had not yet properly let himself go, he now covers page after page with acid analysis and angry ridicule of the diverse and contradictory theories of the philosophers. 'Trust to your Philosophie, boast to have hit the naile on the head, to have found the beane of this Cake, to see this coile and hurly-burly of so many Philosophical wits.' We look to them to tell us what is the Sovereign Good, the purpose of living; they supply us with at least two hundred and eighty different replies.

Man then is reduced to the evidence of his own senses and the sober employment of his own commonsense. This consideration leads Montaigne to his climax. What worth is there in man's senses or his sense? Our judgment is enfeebled and distorted in a thousand ways, by maladies, passions, sentiments, prejudices, sensory illusions, extravagant imaginations. 'In few, there is no constant existence, neither of our being, nor of the objects. And we, and our judgement, and all mortall things else do uncessantly rowle, turne, and passe away; . . . we have no communication with being; for every humane nature is ever in the middle between being borne and dying; giving nothing of itself but an obscure appearance and shadow.'

At this final moment Montaigne remembers that he is defending religion, and indeed defending the rational defence of religion, and modulates into the original key. 'Oh what a vile and abject thing is man *unless he raise himselfe above humanity!* . . . He may elevate himselfe by forsaking and renouncing his owne meanes and suffering himselfe to be elevated and raised by meere heavenly means. It is for our Christian faith, not for his Stoicke vertue, to pretend or aspire to this divine Metamorphosis or miraculous transmutation.'

We have summarized the *Apologie* at this length because no other piece of writing outside the Bible entered so far or reverberated so constantly as this within the soul of Pascal. He loved it and he loathed it. He hated the hard note of contempt which Montaigne, at least here, allowed himself in dismissing as worthless man's trust in reason, man's attempts at virtue, man's sense of some dignity attaching to his own species. He welcomed and dwelt upon and incorporated into his own writings this exposure of all falsely idealistic or complacently optimistic accounts of man's condition. Moreover, this essay was more than an element in the progress of Pascal's thought; its closing words were to be an illuminating comment upon the course of his life. Pascal would never kick down the ladder of reason by which he had ascended. 'All the dignity of man consists in thought. Thought is a wonderful and incomparable thing .... How great it is in its nature, though how vile in its defects!' (365). But he knew that it was not by thinking or by his own striving that he could attain that 'Divine Metamorphosis' for which, unconsciously, he had begun to crave.

At this moment Pascal had, in Hegelian terms, his Thesis and his Antithesis, but no hint or clue of the necessary Synthesis. Epictetus had very nobly shown that man must consider God as the supreme object of his regard, and of all philosophers he had given the best account of man's duties; but he had shown himself unaware of man's real weakness. The elevation of the Stoic argument was magnificent, but the foundations were faulty. Montaigne gave an unsparingly candid view of man's limitations, and since these were drawn from accurate observation they were undeniable and must form the basis of any system of faith or ethics; but Montaigne did not show how man could ascend from his pitiable condition; and did not even seem greatly concerned that he should.

It was this unconcern about primary and eternal issues which horrified and puzzled Pascal, not so much as he found it within the covers of a book as in the men of his daily converse. That men should fill their days with useless, tedious and vacuous occupations seemed to him not merely deplorable; it was monstrous, not sane. 'A man in a dungeon, not knowing whether or not his sentence is pronounced, having just one hour in which to secure its repeal if it is pronounced—to spend that hour in playing piquet, it is unnatural' (200). 'We run heedlessly to the precipice, having put something between to block out our sight of it' (183). 'C'est une chose monstrueuse de voir dans un même cœur et en même temps cette sensibilité pour les moindres choses et cette étrange insensibilité pour les plus grandes' (197).

It was not that Pascal himself abjured at this time the futilities which wearied him. Outwardly he did whatever his friends did. Émile Boutroux* quotes some courtly lines inscribed in Pascal's writing on the back of two pictures at the Château de Fontenay-le-Comte not far from Poitou:

* *Pascal*, p. 57.

De ces lieux, jeune et charmante hôtesse,
Votre crayon m'a tracé le dessin;
J'aurais voulu suivre de votre main
La gràce et la délicatesse.

Mais pourquoi n'ai-je pu, peignant ces dieux dans l'air,
Pour rendre plus brillante une aimable déesse,
Lui donner vos traits et votre air?

The party returned to Paris in January 1654. Pascal took up again his lodgings in the Rue Beaubourg but often visited, and perhaps stayed at, the Hôtel de Roannez. He was fully occupied with settling his estate, buying property, renewing his efforts to sell the arithmetical machine. And before long his scientific interests 'awoke from a long sleep'.* They seem to have been touched off by Méré who asked him to solve two problems of practical use to gamblers.† The first was: When playing with two dice, what is the minimum number of throws on which one can advantageously bet that this number will contain a double-six? This was an easy one for Pascal; twenty-four throws would be a bad bet, twenty-five a good one. The other question was much more knotty.

Two players have agreed that the stakes will go to the one who first wins three games. They are interrupted and have to end the playing before this happens. In what proportions ought they to divide the stake? Pascal found a typically ingenious and simple method of solution. Given that the stake was sixteen pistoles, that A had won two games and B one game; A should receive twelve pistoles and B four pistoles. For, assume that one more game could be played. If A won it, he won all the sixteen pistoles; if B won it, at that point he could claim half the stakes. So that when only three games had been played, A can say to B, 'Win or lose the next game, I have at least eight pistoles due to me. That leaves the other eight for the next game, in which the chances are

* V. Giraud, *Pascal*, Vol. I, p. 82.
† Jacques Chevalier, *Pascal*, p. 101.

equal, so if we cannot play the next game we divide equally, and I get four.' By similar reasoning he worked out the proportions for interruption after two games and after one. He sent the problem to Fermat at Toulouse, who solved it by strictly algebraic methods and arrived at the same results, to Pascal's great pleasure: 'Je vois bien,' he wrote, 'que la vérité est la même à Toulouse et à Paris.' Thus independently but simultaneously these two great minds founded the mathematical Theory of Chances.

As we should by now expect, Pascal at once flung himself into an intensive study of the generalized theory of numbers and chances. Loyal always to arithmetic (rather than algebra), he devised his Arithmetical Triangle, consisting of columns of figures so constituted and so arranged that they handed to Newton the Binomial Theorem almost ready-made, and to Leibniz the Integral Calculus. The whole Calculus of Probabilities 'which' says Professor Chevalier,* from whose book we derive these details, 'tends to become the general form of all sciences' is completely contained or prefigured in the Arithmetical Triangle.

Clearly Pascal had refound his true *métier* and had struck a particularly rich vein of his genius. The clarity of his methods, the fecundity of his results, forbid us to write off this sudden intellectual activity as *only* a desperate diversion; yet our knowledge of his spiritual state at this very time, his 'contempt of the world and disgust with everyone in it', warn us that something of this sort is present. It is to be noted that Pascal has gone back to pure mathematics, away from his more characteristic interest which was in physics. Even geometry would have been nearer the actual world than these integers. Was he, then, unconsciously turning from the pain of the actual world?

'A pure idea,' wrote Malebranche, 'has not the strength to pick a straw off the ground.' It is possible that Pascal did not wish to pick straws off the ground. There is, indeed, something unmistakably feverish about his sudden enthusiasm for the abstract. At least it indicates a recoil from the study of human nature, and we

* *Pascal*, p. 105.

have only to glance at the programme of work which at this time he laid before the 'tres célèbre Académie parisienne des sciences', work which he undertook to complete *within the next few weeks,* to be aware that he was over-driving himself. He proposed to complete the Theory of Numbers, to complete his long-delayed Treatise on the Equilibrium of Liquids and write a new Treatise on the Arithmetical Triangle, to write a paper on magic square problems, and another on the properties of a circle tangential to three other contiguous circles, to pursue his earlier work on conic sections, to study the rules of perspective, and 'to reduce to an exact art, with the rigour of mathematical demonstration, the incertitude of chance, thus creating a new science which could justly claim the stupefying title: the geometry of hazard'.

It was grand, but it was fantastic and desperate. No two philosophies can be less alike than those of Pascal and Omar Khayyam, but Pascal was using abstract problems as Omar used draughts of wine:

> What! Without asking, *hither* hurried *whence?*
> And, without asking, *whither* hurried *hence?*
> Another and another cup to drown
> The memory of this impertinence!

He was in great need. He knew now why men took to diversions, why he himself had learnt polite conversation, hunted, played games, danced perhaps, versified, and now was attempting all this. The alternative was an intolerable vacancy. Surely it was at this time that he penned the *Pensée* No. 131 which we shall print here in the strange strophic form in which it appears in Pascal's handwriting:

ENNUI

> *Rien est si insupportable*
> *À l'homme que d'être*
> *dans un plein repos,*
> *Sans passion, sans affaire,*
> *Sans divertissement, sans application.*

Il sent alors
Son néant, son abandon,
Son insuffisance, sa dépendance,
Son impuissance, son vide,
Incontinent, il sortira du fond
De son âme, l'ennui,
La noirceur, la tristesse, le chagrin, le dépit,
Le désespoir.

Even God was absent. That was the void within the void. Externally Pascal was a made man and a celebrity. Those hostesses were fortunate who could now include him among their guests. One of these was Madame de Sablé, who soon would be found encouraging La Rochefoucauld to coin *Maximes*. Pascal revisited the Court. Roannez became more and more dependent on his counsel and companionship. Men like Fermat watched him with admiration and great expectations. Inwardly he was beaten to his knees, looking every way for help but not greatly hoping for any, for who could give him what was not there to be given? And even if it were there, who of those he knew could bring it? Rebours? Singlin? Méré? He needed contact with a mind cognate with his own, but wiser, more experienced, calmer; and he thought of Jacqueline.

CHAPTER 7

THE CONVERT

. . . εἰ μή τις δύναιτο ἀσφαλέστερον καὶ ἀκινδυνότερον ἐπὶ
βεβαιοτέρου ὀχήματος λόγου θείου τινός, διαπορευθῆναι.

PLATO, Phaedo

On December 8 of that year, 1654, Soeur Sainte-Euphémie
(whom we shall continue to call Jacqueline) wrote to Gilberte: 'Although for over a year past he had felt a great scorn of
the world and an almost unbearable disgust for all the people in it,
feelings which might have excited one of his fiery nature to great
excesses, in fact he displayed a moderation which filled me with
hope.'

Seven weeks later, on January 25, 1655, she wrote again, telling
the glad story in fuller detail but still not knowing the inner
kernel of it as we can:

'Towards the end of last September he came to see me and
opened his heart in a way which wrung mine, saying that in the
midst of all his great occupations, and among all those things
which might have combined to attach him to the world (things
which we naturally thought he was thoroughly enjoying) he
had been so longing to get away from all that, having so great
an aversion for the follies and amusements of the world and
being incessantly stung by his conscience, that he had now
broken away from everything as never before; he had known
nothing approaching it. And yet, for all that, he felt completely abandoned from God and with no attraction whatever
of that sort. But he believed that he was merely making an
intellectual struggle to find God; it was not a genuine movement of himself towards God. In his present detachment he

121

felt that if only he could recover his former sentiments towards God he could overcome the horrible temptations which assailed him, to resist God's grace.'

Sedate, lucid and penetrating, in the Pascal manner, Jacqueline is here recording her own personal joy and one of the more notable conversions of Christian history; in which she was the chief human instrument.

For Blaise's sudden decision in September to go and see Jacqueline had been followed up by other visits. In her second letter to Gilberte she remarks with compassionate humour that Blaise came so often and stayed so long that she might have had nothing else to do. But she was profoundly happy and thankful; he was like a child and she was his mother in God. Even so she did not know, nor anyone else until after Pascal's death when the Memorial was found upon him, of the 'Divine Metamorphosis and miraculous transmutation' which came to him two months after these visits began.

From the first visit onwards, Pascal naturally engaged himself in sacred reading and prayer. He had acquired a pleasant small house in the Faubourg Saint-Michel, installing a modest domestic staff. On the night of November 23 he was studying the seventeenth chapter of S. John's Gospel where Jesus Christ prepares Himself for the final sacrifice. Among its other claims to his attention this passage may have had a special appeal to Pascal because his physical illness had returned and his thoughts were attuned to that wonderful prayer (whether he wrote it now or later) for the right use of sickness, in which occur the words: 'Ouvrez mon cœur, Seigneur . . . l'idée du monde y est tellement gravée que la votre n'est plus connaissable. . . . Que je vous trouve au dedans de moi-même, puisque je ne puis vous chercher au dehors à cause de ma faiblesse. . . . Entrez dans mon cœur et dans mon âme. . . .' It was in the spirit of that prayer that he directed his attention upon Jesus Christ, Himself advancing to the endurance and the use of pain.

While he so thought and prayed there was given him that time-
less eternal moment (he meticulously timed it afterwards; it lasted
two hours) which some are allowed. During that space or on that
level (our language is not competent for this matter) common experience loses its opacity. It is still there and still real, indeed still
visible as is the window through which a man looks; but he is no
longer looking upon it. No secular event, no earthly thing, can
give or take away that which is seen and which is equally and
eternally there whether it is seen or not; and the man who has
seen is now permanently aware that pain, injustice, the defilements of guilt, the corrosion of time, failure, the brevity of life,
all the *lachrymae rerum*, are indeed still present; sorrow can still
move him, temptation can still assail; but they can never again
assume their appearance of finality or their power to crush the
spirit.

On emerging from the vision Pascal seized a paper and wrote
at headlong speed an account, copying it afterwards on to a piece
of parchment. Both were found after his death, sewn into his
doublet. The parchment has been lost; the paper original survives
among the Pascal MSS together with a careful copy made by
Blaise's nephew, the Abbé Louis Périer.

The year of grace, 1654.
Monday, 23rd. November, Feast of S. Clement, Pope and Martyr,
and of others in the Martyrology
Vigil of S. Chrysogonus, Martyr, and others,
From about half-past ten in the evening until about half-
past twelve
FIRE
God of Abraham, God of Isaac, God of Jacob, not of the
philosophers and savants
Certitude. Certitude. Feeling. Joy. Peace.
God of Jesus Christ.
My God and Thy God
'Thy God shall be my God'

123

Forgetfulness of the world and of everything except God
He is to be found only in the ways taught in the Gospel
Grandeur of the human soul
Righteous Father, the world hath not known Thee, but I have
known Thee
Joy, joy, joy, tears of joy
I have fallen from Him
'They have forsaken Me, the Fountain of living waters'
My God, wilt Thou forsake me?
May I not fall from Him for ever
This is life eternal, that they might know Thee, the only
true God, and Jesus Christ Whom Thou has sent
Jesus Christ
Jesus Christ
I have fallen away: I have fled from Him, denied Him crucified
Him
May I not fall from Him for ever
We hold Him only by the ways taught in the Gospel
Renunciation total and sweet
Total submission to Jesus Christ and to my director
Eternally in joy for a day's exercise on earth
I will not forget Thy word. Amen.

Men have discussed and will continue to discuss the psychological clues afforded by this document. Aldous Huxley has re-
marked on the curious alternation of devotional and philosophical
statements (in Pascalian terms, the alternation of *l'esprit* and *le
cœur*). Others have hesitated over the orthodoxy of the phrase
'God of Jesus Christ', or over Pascal's reasons for dismissing the
'philosophers and savants'. Strowski (who gives a beautiful
analysis of the whole Memorial), noting the accuracy and fullness
of the Biblical quotations, observes, 'Pascal has not lost his sang-
froid'. Men have picked out and dwelt upon the characteristic and
significant words: Feu, certitude, joye, grandeur de l'âme humaine.
They have asked whether the Fire is a metaphor or an actual

perception, and if a perception whether present to the senses or only to the mind. They have pondered over the meaning, for Pascal, of 'renonciation totale et douce'.

All this is well and just and necessary. It is the duty of a biographer to scan and analyse the documents which throw light on his human subject, and the Memorial is an incomparable human document. Nothing else that he wrote reveals him to us as this single page does. But its main interest does not lie there.

How shall we pose this main point? If Pascal was in fact alone in that room that night, then the interest and importance of his particular thoughts and personal reactions dwindle considerably, since they were based on some sort of illusion. If in fact Pascal was not alone there that night, then again the interest of his personal reactions dwindles to vanishing point, in the presence of a more compelling interest.

Men put pen to paper for many reasons and with many effects. Among the writings of men there are some which convey a sort of claim, or conviction, or impression, that the writer as well as the pen has been used as an instrument. It is a tenable suggestion that such writings are, on the whole, those which should command our attention above all others, for they may be evidential.

Outside Holy Writ is there, in any language of any age, any extant writing which conveys this impression with more immediacy than Pascal's Memorial?

Professor Chevalier says that the best comment upon the Memorial is Pascal's life from then onwards. While agreeing, we would point out that the commentary afforded by Pascal's post-conversion life is not simple. Certainly from now onwards prayer and sacred study are his main concern; if he had entertained any prospects of marriage he gave them up; except in private correspondence he seems never again to have attached his name to any of his writings, an evident discipline against vanity; to some real extent, but not completely or on principle, he frequented less the society of his more fashionable friends. He definitely, and for a considerable while, ceased to occupy himself with science, though again not on principle, not as one renouncing an evil or dubious habit. Mylon wrote to Huyghens early in 1657: 'It seems difficult to get hold of M. Pascal as he is immersed in devotions; but all the same he has not lost sight of mathematics. When M. de Carcavi met him and put to him some question he did not refuse to reply, he gave the solution of it, and principally on the subject of games of chance, which he was the very first to deal with scientifically.'* The biggest mistake that can be made as to the effects of Pascal's conversion is to imagine him putting on the trappings of woe. Rather, he put them off. 'Joye, joye, joye, pleurs de joye', he had written that night; and his new-found happiness could not be bottled up. Jacqueline was slightly shocked, or at least disconcerted, by an effervescence which Port Royal did not encourage in its penitents. Who would have guessed, from Pascal's history so far, that his next considerable work would be chiefly distinguished by a daring hilarity which would startle opponents and friends alike? But he had cause for joy; the prisoner leaps to lose his chains.

We have attributed the change in Pascal, on the human side, to his approach to Jacqueline and his study of S. John's Gospel. It must be again remembered that no one (except possibly his confessor) knew about the experience on the night of November 23. Two other stories became current, as accounting for his conversion. Either of them is possible, as an event which may have happened and may have contributed; but each comes in questionable form.

There is Marguerite Périer's statement that on December 8, 1654, Pascal listened to a sermon from M. Singlin and was converted by it. This is the exact date on which Jacqueline wrote her first letter on the matter to Gilberte. We already know that he 'found God' a fortnight before this, but it is also known that Singlin was ill in bed throughout December. But nothing is more

* Stewart, *Holiness of Pascal*, p. 101.

likely than that Pascal at this time should have been greatly moved by some sermon.

And there is the story of the accident on the Neuilly Bridge, of which Voltaire made capital at the expense of Pascal's sanity. He had it from some unnamed person who claimed to have had it from d'Arnauld de Saint-Victor as having been reported by the Prior de Barillon as from Mme Périer. It relates that 'a few years before his death' Pascal was driving in a carriage drawn by four or six horses, and at the Neuilly Bridge, when halfway across the Seine, the leading horses plunged over the parapet and the carriage was only saved from following by the snapping of the traces. Pascal (like de Quincey on a later occasion not unlike this) had a 'vision of sudden death'. From that moment he gave up his fine carriage and other possessions and lived in complete solitude. That is the legend. History relates that he did not give up his carriage until 1660. There is nothing impossible, or unlikely, in his having had an accident of the sort about then.

Reverting to the question of a sermon preached on December 8, it does seem likely that Pascal about then heard some spiritual counsel which overcame his strong reluctance to place himself under a director. Jacqueline had been urging this, and had discussed it with Singlin. Singlin had, for his part, been not only ill, but frankly scared by the prospect of directing someone of Pascal's eminence, and the matter had hung fire. At last Pascal resolved to go into retreat, and the obvious place for this was Port Royal des Champs. Singlin was relieved; this solved the problem, and put Pascal under the direction of M. de Saci who looked after the souls of the solitaries.

Pascal announced his intentions to the Duc de Roannez who had just returned from another visit to Poitou, and to whom Pascal was bound by some mutual undertaking as a member of the Duc's entourage. 'He gave his consent, not without tears.' Early in January Pascal entered retreat, first at the Duc de Luynes' château of Vaumurier and then completing the fortnight in the solitaries' hostel at Les Granges.

De Saci was the incarnation of all that was best in Port Royal, living almost hourly in the realized presence of God, reserved, quiet, gentle, studious and shrewd. Philippe de Champagne's portrait of him perfectly illustrates the impression he has left, but we have also a word-portrait, equally masterly, in the famous *Entretien de M. Pascal avec M. de Saci sur Epictète et Montaigne*, by de Saci's secretary, Fontaine, who was present at the first interview between the gentle director and the formidable penitent. His account is a minor classic of French literature and an indispensable source of information on Pascal at this crisis of his life.

Fontaine begins, 'I do not pause here to give an account of a man who was the admiration not only of France but of all Europe', and then pauses to do just that. Then de Saci is respectfully but naïvely introduced: 'The sacred interest which he felt in the study of the Scriptures and the Fathers led him to hope that he would not be too greatly dazzled by all the brilliant qualities of M. Pascal. . . . He found in the result that he could approve of all his sentiments.' He discovered, according to Fontaine, that although Pascal had never yet studied S. Augustine his views were completely Augustinian and therefore acceptable. 'M. de Saci's habit in conversation was to adapt his topics to the several tastes and pursuits of the person he addressed', so he conversed with Pascal on philosophy (unaware of the writing sewn up in Pascal's doublet). So opens the wonderful dialogue on Epictetus and Montaigne which gives us both the history of Pascal's inner struggle arising from his study and his contrasting of these two opposite poles of thought, and also, even at second hand, our first taste of the richness and strength of Pascal's matured style.

First, Pascal describes and pays tribute to the finer elements in the Stoic teaching: 'Voilà, Monsieur, les lumières de ce grand esprit qui a si bien connu le devoir de l'homme. J'ose dire qu'il méritait d'être adoré, s'il avait bien connu son impuissance.' But Epictetus imagined that men can by will-power compel their minds to exclude what is false, and their passions to avoid what is

PASCAL'S MEMORIAL

wrong. 'Ces principes d'une superbe diabolique le conduisent à d'autres erreurs. . . .'

He turns to Montaigne, with greater enthusiasm and therefore at greater length. He is unsparing on Montaigne's faults and begins with the worst of them, his fundamental scepticism: 'C'est dans ce doute qui doute de soi, et dans cette ignorance qui s'ignore . . . qu'est l'essence de son opinion . . . ne voulant pas dire: "Je ne sais," il dit: "Que sais-je?" . . . Sur ce principe roulent tous les Essais.' But this mocking at all certainties and tearing apart of all received opinions serves a purpose. It confounds all self-assured systems of truth. It humbles the human mind 'ne lui donnant pouvoir d'agir cependent que pour remarquer sa faiblesse avec une humilité sincère'.

De Saci was impressed, but he was there to direct and he did not shirk his duty. Admitting that he had not read Montaigne, 'who might well, indeed, wish to be known only through such accounts as you give of his writings,' he questioned whether any profit was to be gained from a writer of such destructive scepticism and such misdirected wit. Pascal gives his tremendous answer: 'I confess, Sir, that I cannot but be pleased to see in this writer the pride of reason so thoroughly crushed by its own weapons . . . *et j'aurais aimé de tout mon cœur le ministre d'une si grande vengeance*' if only Montaigne had been able to build up as well as pull down; and Pascal proceeds to show in detail what a negative, hopeless, heathen thing is Montaigne's humanistic ethic. 'Ignorance and incuriousness are (to use his own words) the softest pillows for a well-regulated mind.'

So there are the Thesis and Antithesis which have been torturing Pascal's mind for the past year. 'Epictetus and Montaigne appear to me, beyond question, the most powerful champions of the two most important sects among the infidel world. The first says, there is a God, who has made man able to raise himself, by his own understanding, to God. The second says, man cannot elevate himself to God, he seeks his happiness in things of sense.' There is error on both sides, and it is impossible to exclude it by any forcible effort to combine what is good in each system; they refuse to mix. 'One sect, knowing only the impotence of man, and not his duties, fall into laxity; and the other, knowing his duties but not his impotence, wrap themselves in pride . . . they cannot subsist alone, on account of their deficiencies, nor unite, because of their contrariety; they can only wound and destroy each other.'

But on the night of November 23 Pascal had discovered his Synthesis. In this quarrel between the assignment of moral power and of moral weakness, 'faith teaches us to assign these two in-clinations to different things: infirmity to human nature, but power to grace. This is that new and astonishing combination, which it was the right of God alone to reveal, and only His power could achieve.' Pascal was no longer torn between presumption and despair; for the recognition of his fallen nature preserved him from the one, and the experience of the redeeming love of God preserved him from the other.

Thus were determined the two focal doctrines which domin-ated Pascal's religious thought and his conception of the Catholic religion. They occur and recur continually in the *Pensées*: 'Elle enseigne . . . aux hommes ces deux vérités: et qu'il y a un Dieu dont les hommes sont capables, et qu'il y a une corruption dans la nature, qui les en rend indignes' (556).

These two pivotal Catholic doctrines became pivotal for Pascal, it must be noticed, in the *Sturm und Drang* of his own per-sonal adventure, and particularly in that part of his adventure where he was furthest removed from theological influences of any school or tendency. They happen to be the doctrines which at Port Royal were stressed and, in the opinion of some, over-stressed; but it was not at Port-Royalist bidding that he adopted them, and it was never quite in the Port-Royalist sense that he held them. This conversation with M. de Saci revealed a rift, which would never be bridged, between his attitude and that of the late M. Saint-Cyran which continued to dominate Port Royal. He rejoiced in the proper humbling of the human reason; he would never agree to its annihilation or its expulsion from the spiritual life.

Port Royal taught that the will of fallen man is completely enslaved by concupiscence. Pascal not only agreed but crossed the t's and dotted the i's of this; no man has insisted more strongly on the theme that we are tied and bound with the chain of our sins. But he believed in, and worked out, a function for the human will which was contrary to Jansenist teaching, in his conception (learnt from Montaigne and integral to Pascal's defence of religion) that 'custom', the repetition of acts of faith and of devotional practices, even almost mechanically, can put a man on the road to realizing the truths and the dispositions indicated by those habits. 'La coutume est notre nature. Qui s'accoutume à la foi, la croit, et ne peut plus ne pas craindre l'enfer' (89). 'Il faut que l'extérieur soit joint à l'intérieur pour obtenir de Dieu; s'est à dire que l'on se mette à genoux, prie des lèvres, etc.' (250). Finally and most daring, from the end of his great passage on the Wager: 'There are people who know the way. . . . Follow the way by which they began; by acting as though they believed, taking the holy water, having Masses said, etc.'

One perhaps need not be a Jansenist to be startled by this deliberate advice to practise a religion one does not yet hold; but how practical, and how modern, is the psychology of it!

He returned to his house in the Faubourg Saint-Michel, keeping in occasional touch with Port Royal. At some time in 1655 he invented a new method of teaching reading for the pupils at the Petites Écoles at one of which his nephew Étienne was being taught. In the latter part of the year Antoine Arnauld made some of his rare reappearances at Port Royal des Champs, and Pascal met him there.

CHAPTER 8

THE PAMPHLETEER

'Courage, my soul, now learn to wield
The weight of thine immortal shield,
Close on thy head thy helmet bright,
Balance thy sword against the fight;
See where an army, strong as fair,
With silken banners spread the air!
Now, if thou bee'st that thing divine,
In this day's combat let it shine,
And show that Nature wants an art
To conquer one resolved heart!'

ANDREW MARVELL

The Bull *Cum Occasione* in which Innocent X had condemned the five propositions and (implicitly though not explicitly) the *Augustinus* had been received quietly in France. Arnauld and Port Royal felt no difficulty in assenting to it since it did not, they maintained, force them to admit that Jansen had distorted S. Augustine's teaching. Arnauld offered to keep silence on the whole matter if his antagonists would do the like; but Annat, now Provincial of the Jesuits in Paris, returned from Rome too jubilant for silence. The Society had tasted blood and had marked Arnauld down. His *Fréquente Communion* had seemed as deliberate an attack upon them as the *Augustinus*. The Jesuits celebrated the Bull with an Almanach, January 1654, having a frontispiece showing the Pope under the heavenly Dove, flanked by Religion bearing a cross and The Church, helmeted and armed, casting down Jansenius who hurtled, clasping his book and endowed with mitre and bat's wings, towards Calvin who philandered in a lower corner with a spectacled Jansenist nun.

It is perhaps fair to say that the frontispiece of the *Augustinus* showed S. Augustine trampling on Pelagius and two other heretics who have all the appearance of Jesuits. Throughout the year 1655 Arnauld was using his over-worked pen to fight for his cause and (a minor consideration) for his position.

In the same month that Pascal made his retreat, January 1655, the Duc de Liancourt, whose granddaughter was being educated at Port Royal, had made his customary confession at S. Sulpice. His usual confessor, M. Picoté, referred the matter to M. Olier his Abbé, who refused absolution on account of Liancourt's Jansenist affiliations. This high-handed action drew from Arnauld a *Lettre à une Personne de Condition* which began with the ingenuous and remarkable phrase, 'The desire which God has given me to avoid every kind of controversy and dispute. . . .' It drew a swarm of replies. Inevitably he wrote again, a *Second Letter to a Duke and Peer*, much longer and more incautious. It elaborated the theory of the distinction between *Droit* and *Fait*, claimed that the *Augustinus* was completely orthodox and did not contain the five propositions, and even seemed to maintain the orthodoxy of the first proposition by quoting S. Peter's defection. The Pope said kind things about this letter but it was two hundred pages of ammunition for Arnauld's enemies.

It was published in July; by November a Commission was examining it with a view to Arnauld's degradation from office in the Sorbonne. On December 1, the Commission reported to the Faculty condemning (1) as temerarious, the asserted orthodoxy of Jansen, (2) as heretical, the assertion that grace had been withheld from S. Peter. The Sorbonne discussed their action during the next six weeks, with an almost avowed intention of expelling Arnauld.

His theological distinction, and the heat engendered by the dispute, made it a *cause célèbre*. By Royal direction the Chancellor Séguier attended regularly from December 20. His procession through the streets with an escort of bowmen made a daily pageant which aroused popular interest, though few outside academic circles had any idea what it was all about. A brief summary of what it was about may best introduce Pascal's intervention.

Views on the subject of Divine grace were distributed among three groups of theologians.

The 'central party' were those (largely represented among the Dominicans) who stood by the teachings of S. Thomas Aquinas. They desired to preserve the whole teaching of S. Augustine, that man was fallen and helpless, needing grace; that in every stage of spiritual recovery God's action was sovereign. They sought to mitigate the rigour of S. Augustine by saying that God's grace not only operated upon man but co-operated with him; a man's willpower, enlightened and invigorated by grace, could play some real part in his recovery. (The 'official' doctrine since the Council of Trent had allowed even more scope for the human will, saying plainly that man had it within his choice and power to resist grace when given).

These Thomist teachers were flanked on one side by the Jesuits, on the other by the Jansenists.

The Jesuits followed the theory of Luis Molina, a Jesuit of the late sixteenth century, that man, aided by or resisting God's grace, determines his own fate. Every man is granted sufficient grace for the good life and it rests with him to use it.

The Jansenists affirmed with the *Augustinus* that man's fall had destroyed his will for effective purposes. In his fallen condition he necessarily followed the stronger of two pulls, the downward pull of concupiscence or the upward pull of grace. Grace is given at God's pleasure and only to some. When given it could not be resisted; but it might be withdrawn. Grace, when present, was invariably effective.

In trying to avoid technical terms we have used in their natural sense the adjectives *sufficient* and *effective* (or efficient). The water standing in a watering-can may be sufficient for a rose-bed; a sudden shower of rain is efficient. The two words became technical. For Jansenists, grace when given was efficient; it worked. For Jesuits, grace for all men was sufficient; its working depended upon the human response.

The Thomists in their mid-way position might have gravitated towards the Jansenist position since they were loyal to S. Augustine and their battle against the too-human doctrine of Molina was still a recent memory; but they dreaded Calvinism. Calvin had reinforced all the concrete in S. Augustine's system, and now the Jansenists, for all their determined loyalty to sacraments and hierarchy, were doing much the same. Consequently in this new struggle the old foes, Thomists and Jesuits made an uncomfortable but formidable alliance.

So through the latter half of 1655 Arnauld, almost single-handed, had faced a coalition bent on his professional ruin. The rules of procedure in the Sorbonne were designed for the one end. The jury was packed by the introduction of forty friar doctors (instead of the statutory eight) whose vote was safe. Speeches were limited to thirty minutes and Arnauld was allowed only to state his case and forbidden to argue. The meetings were dominated by the presence of the Chancellor whose bias was not disguised. Arnauld had the dignity to refuse to speak under these conditions, and instead wrote his defence and circulated it among members of the Sorbonne. His powers of dialectic, probably unsurpassed among his professional peers, had effect and a substantial minority were for him.

What he lacked, and what was needed, was the gift of making his case intelligible and vivid to society and the man in the street. Paris was excited without knowing why. Arnauld's friends urged him to write a popular pamphlet and he did his best, and read the result at Port Royal in January 1656. It was received in respectful silence. He said, 'I see you think that this is no good; and I agree with you.' Pascal was present at this gathering and Arnauld turned to him: 'You are a young man. Couldn't you do something?' Pascal demurred. He was no theologian and he had not followed the intricacies of the matter. It was put to him that all that was needed was an exposure of the unfairness of the attack. He undertook to do something.

He returned very shortly with an article headed 'Letter Written to a Provincial by one of his Friends'. It was read with awed delight, rushed through the Port Royal press over the assumed name of Louis de Montalte, and on sale in Paris on January 23. It was quickly sold out.

In the Sorbonne it created consternation and anger. Séguier (whose contacts with the Pascal family were not uniformly fortunate; see p. 41) was in danger of a fit and had to be bled seven times. Otherwise, the pamphlet was received with joyful surprise and mounting laughter. Readers were startled to find French handled as a living language. Not Arnauld nor anyone else would be likely to open a serious disquisition with the words, 'Monsieur, we *were* off the target. I had really been thinking that this fuss was about something . . .'. For us now it may be difficult to realize the full impact of the familiar direct style when it was new. Rabelais was ancient; Montaigne was colloquial but discursive, he lacked Pascal's deadly concentration on the point; Corneille was formal to the point of stiffness; Molière was hardly beginning, and his matured style, at least in *Tartufe*, surely owes something to the Provincial Letters.

To grasp the portent of the *Provincial Letters* we have to remember several things. First, perhaps, that Pascal was highly inflammable with a low flash-point. We have seen him flare up over conic sections, Petit's experiments, Forton's philosophy, Jacqueline's vocation, Noël's theories, Montaigne's Essays. Now he saw a good man outnumbered and out-manoeuvred and he erupted. Add to this that he was one of the leading brains of his century, whose thinking became most logical when his feelings were most engaged; and that lately, under the influence of Montaigne and Méré, he had been reflecting much on the problems of style and the art of persuasion.

Add above all that he was free; his conversion had been a liberation. He was free to do a plainly good turn, and to be as creative in doing it as he knew how.

The first 'Provincials' were distinguished almost more for the gifts of a playwright than those of a controversialist. He creates a character, Louis de Montalte, and endows that myth with flesh and blood. He establishes immediate contact with his audience. He discovers and exploits a talent for dialogue. Montalte is precisely the same sort of person as those he addresses, an educated cultivated man of some position, with an open mind but little acquaintance with theology. He goes to the trouble of inquiring into 'les Disputes présentes de la Sorbonne', and tells his friend in the Provinces the progress of his inquiries.

He has been astonished to find how slight were the apparent grounds of the Sorbonne discussions. The mountain was in labour and brought forth two mice—a mouse of *Fait* and a mouse of *Droit*. As to the *Fait*, Arnauld had been censured for rashness in saying that the five propositions were not in the *Augustinus*, but no one seemed anxious to explore the *Augustinus* to find out. 'If I had any curiosity on this point I should not consult the Sorbonne; I should consult the book. It is neither so scarce nor so large that I could not settle the question that way.' In this first Letter (though not afterwards) Pascal is rather slap-dash. He has evidently not set eyes on the *Augustinus*, which is the size of a family Bible and has nearly twelve hundred pages of closely printed Latin in double columns. Then what of the question of *Droit?* Arnauld seems about to be condemned for heresy, having supported Jansen in saying that grace was lacking to a righteous man when S. Peter lapsed. This is thin ice and Pascal skims off it towards his real objective, to expose an injustice. We follow Montalte on his inquiries.

He calls upon a Thomist doctor of the Navarre College (Bossuet's Alma Mater), and asks whether it is right to say that 'grace is given to all men', for if so the Jansenists are wrong in denying it. He is snubbed by the information that this is not the point. Many Thomists agreed with the Jansenists here. Well then, asks Montalte, were the Jansenists heretical in saying that God's grace determined the human will? 'Certainly not! That is perfectly orthodox.' Then on what point *was* Jansen wrong? 'In saying that just people have not the power to obey God's commands.'

Montalte hastens with this information to a Jansenist friend and tells him that the Thomists are claiming that a just man *can* obey God's commands. 'But of course he can!' says the Jansenist. 'What could be more Catholic and true than that?' Montalte is bewildered to find that Jansenists and Thomists apparently agree on every point; but also he is artlessly delighted. He, a nobody, an amateur theologian, can now settle the whole great dispute. He trots back to the Thomist. 'Look! I've found that the Jansenists say that the just can keep the commandments! We will get them to sign that and peace will be restored.' 'Wait a bit,' says the Thomist, 'I'm afraid you will not find them agreeing that this power is *immediate* power.' Montalte is brought up all standing. He has never heard of immediate power. The rest of the Letter relates his slow discovery that Immediate Power was a term favoured by the Jesuits and *for that reason* readopted (though in a different sense) by the Thomists. Its use was part of the price of an unholy alliance.

In his second Letter, dated only six days after the first, Pascal directed his spotlight on to a similar misuse of the term 'sufficient grace'. 'There are two things about this term. There is the sound of it, which is mere air; and there is the meaning of it, which is real. You Thomists agree with the Jesuits in using the word *sufficient* and disagree with them as to its meaning. You visibly quarrel over the substance and fraternize over the sound. Is that honest?'

Pascal is getting into his stride. The raillery is more vigorous; the thrusts are delivered with more assurance. Between this letter and the third he slipped in a mischievous intermezzo in the form of an 'Answer of the Provincial to the First Two Letters from his Friend. 2nd February, 1656', forty-five lines of enthusiastic acknowledgment, in which the friend quotes from two letters of praise which have come his way. It has all the irrelevance which is one hall-mark of humour. A member of the Académie Française writes eleven lines of encomium in the course of which he works himself into a passion of fury over a private grievance. A lady of exalted position drops a few affected words of approbation. The portraits of the Academician and the *précieuse* are etched in less than a page and a half.

Pascal had come on the scene too late to save Arnauld. The censure was voted on January 31 and Arnauld was degraded fifteen days later. The Third Letter, dated February 9, is a masterpiece of cold irony. Montalte has awaited eagerly the publication of the Sorbonne's grounds for condemning Arnauld. He is *extrêmement surpris* to find them reduced to one utterance of Arnauld's which was a direct quotation from S. Augustine and S. Chrysostom. If the Fathers were orthodox what made Arnauld a heretic? The answer was, votes; 'monks being in better supply than arguments'. His concluding words convey an icy contempt:

'My eyes are open now. I see that this is a new sort of heresy. M. Arnauld is heretical not in his opinions, only in his person. He is a heretic not for what he says or for what he writes but for being M. Arnauld. It is the one fault they can find in him. He can never become a good Catholic by doing anything, only by ceasing to be. S. Augustine's doctrine of grace can never be true while M. Arnauld defends it: its one chance is for him to attack it. That would work; and the only way to destroy Molinism is to induce him to embrace it. So there we must leave them. These are disputes of theologians; not of theology.'

This letter was signed 'Vostre trés-humble et trés-obéissant serviteur, E.A.A.B.P.A.F.D.E.P.', initials which doubtless stand for *Et Ancient Ami Blaise Pascal Auvergnat Fils D'Étienne Pascal.* Anonymity was the price of freedom for the writer of these letters. If identified he would certainly have been sent to the Bastille, but Pascal could not resist this cryptogram.

A side-light at this moment reminds us that Arnauld was quite simply a good man. Sainte-Beuve discovered somewhere the following letter to the Prioress of Port Royal: '31st January, 1656: You will smile at my reason for writing this. There is a small boy about twelve years old to whom I wish to teach reading by

M. Pascal's method; so please complete your work on this method and send it to me. Has the Mother Superior approved your reading of the Letter of a Provincial? I should much like to hear what she said about it.' So should we; and perhaps we hardly remember for the moment that the opinion sought so timidly and indirectly by the great theologian is that of his sister. But the significant point of the letter is the date. It may have been written not only on the very day but at the very hour when his academic prospects were extinguished.

Pascal's task was not over but beginning, for the Jesuits wanted much more than Arnauld's condemnation. They were intent to destroy the religious house where Pascal's sister lived with God, and on dispersing the cluster of solitaries who were now Pascal's friends. Elated with victory, they almost at once secured the expulsion of the solitaries and the disbanding of the Petites Écoles, and started lobbying at Rome for a new Bull which would force Port Royal to deny its deepest convictions. The sword of Damocles was about to fall, and Pascal hardly paused.

On February 25 he moved from defence to frontal attack and, almost as swiftly, from theology to ethics. In the next thirteen Letters he directed upon the Society of Jesus such a damaging fusillade of pamphlets as perhaps no other religious society has sustained. Voltaire, who despised equally Pascal's religion and his person, wrote, 'The finest comedies of Molière have no more wit than the earlier Provincial Letters, and Bossuet uttered nothing grander than the later ones.'

Several small printing presses besides that at Port Royal des Champs were available to Arnauld, and by switching from one to another the Port Royalists kept the Government agents guessing. Indeed these humble printers ran great risks, and at least one of them, Savreux, was imprisoned with his wife. Pascal's own secret was well kept though he ran deliberate risks. He changed his address several times but settled down, as M. Mons, mainly at the King David Inn, which attracted him as being situated opposite to the main entrance of the Jesuit College. On one occasion

Florin Périer was about to visit him there when a Jesuit friend accosted him at the door to warn him that the Fathers had some idea that Pascal (wherever he might be) was the author of the Letters. Pascal himself, within ear-shot in his room on the first floor, had the sheets of the eighth Provincial drying on his bed. He delighted in being, as Sainte-Beuve says, 'invincible and invisible', and in that independence which enabled him to be utterly for Port Royal without being of it.

The change of direction in the Provincials after the third Letter is as dramatic as Nelson's tactics at Aboukir. Until the final two Letters we hear practically nothing more about Arnauld or the Sorbonne or Jansen. The target is the Society of Jesus in its organization, its policy, its use of spiritual direction in the confessional. For this there were two reasons.

The obvious reason was that the strategy of open assault was as correct as it was bold. Trench warfare would never overcome the Jesuit animosity. Port Royal was fighting for its life and its chance of survival lay in the crushing of the fighting resources of its enemy. Pascal accepted the task. Whether he ought to have formed that purpose, how far it was consonant with his spiritual status as a convert, whether he fought fairly, we may discuss later. The alternative was to let Port Royal die.

The less obvious, more substantial reason, was that Pascal, always more of a moralist than a theologian, now felt himself to be speaking not so much for Arnauld or Port Royal as for Jesus Christ. He had been reading the books of moral theology authorized and used by Jesuit confessors, and they revolted him. Again a question arises, whether his moral indignation was as justified as it was authentic, whether he made due allowance for the conditions which must govern the direction of consciences in a mixed society; but no question should be raised about the sincerity of his anger. Not only did he catch fire but fire was caught from him. Before he had finished, the clergy of Rouen, of Paris, of most of France with the majority of French bishops and many elsewhere, were raising their voices in condemnation of the moral precepts of the Jesuits as exposed in the Provincials. Whatever in Pascal's campaign was merely polemical, this was not. He fought 'relaxed morals' to his last breath.

The thirteen anti-Jesuit Provincials appeared at intervals from February 1656 to the end of the year, followed in the first weeks of 1657 by two final letters on the Five Propositions.

Pascal's new move like his first seemed to have come too late. Sentence on Port Royal was not only pronounced but in process of execution. The solitaries were expelled from Port Royal des Champs, the boys' school (with Jean Racine among its pupils) was disbanded, and the convent awaited dissolution. Only a miracle could even delay the final blow, and only a miracle did.

On March 24, immediately after publication of the fifth Letter, 'la terrible cinquième' Victor Giraud calls it, an event happened which stirred the Church at large, permanently impressed Pascal and was of capital importance (for good or ill) in the subsequent history of Jansenism.

A spine from the Crown of Thorns had been presented to the chapel of the Convent. Its reception was the occasion for a ceremony at which the pupils of the Port Royal girls' school filed past the sacred relic and made their acts of veneration. Among them was Pascal's little niece and god-daughter, Marguerite Périer, who was in a pitiable state, suffering from a lachrymal tumour. As she made her reverence the Sister in attendance said, 'Pray to God for your eye, child,' and placed the reliquary against the affected spot. Marguerite obediently prayed and, as she no doubt expected, the pain departed; within a few hours the inflammation had disappeared, and in less than a week her condition was normal. No possibility of a natural explanation occurred to anyone at the time (though one is possible; external pressure from the metal reliquary might have dispersed the ulcer), and the surgeons who were called in affirmed that her rapid and complete recovery was inexplicable in terms of their science.

The machinery of persecution was put into sudden reverse. The solitaries were allowed to return and Port Royal enjoyed peace until 1660 and, less fortunately, acquired a heightened sense of being a chosen vessel for the Lord. A crown of thorns may still be seen on the western door of the chapel in Paris where the former convent is now used as a maternity home. Pascal devised for his signet a similar crown encircling an eye, with the motto *Scio Cui credidi*. For him it was a direct sign from God, a renewal of the certitude granted in November 1654, and it accounts for the large amount of attention his far from credulous mind gave to miracles from this time.

It belongs to the regular pattern of this story that Pascal in his campaign against the moral practice of the Jesuits was using a ball which others used, only placing it better. The Jesuits could rarely return his service and when they did his volley settled the point, but his data were supplied to him almost from one hour to the next. M. Strowski tells us* that anyone who went to the trouble to compare the Provincials with Arnauld's earlier books, the *Apologie pour les Saints Pères* and the *Théologie Morale des Jésuites*, books which reposed upon forgotten shelves, would be stupefied to find the extent of Pascal's depredations, 'mais la marche de la discussion, la forme vivante, c'est du Pascal et du plus admirable. Le génie sauve tout!'

The Jesuits were vulnerable on their use of casuistry, and especially on their recourse to the doctrine of 'probability'. Each of these terms is much older than the Society of Jesus and each stands for a valuable if not essential element in the practice of directing souls.

Casuistry is the judgment of particular problems of conscience with the aid of authoritative conclusions which have been recorded. It is for a working priest what case-law is for a barrister or clinical anatomy for a surgeon, and is as necessary. Competence implies knowledge of actual cases and established conclusions. In seventeenth-century France religious conformity was the rule in spite of a loose general moral standard and much 'free

* *Pascal et Son Temps*, III, p. 80, note.

thinking'; actual severance from the Church was exceptional. Conformity involved at least one Communion in the year, which meant that confession had been made and absolution obtained. Therefore every working priest had to be versed in the matter of giving or withholding or delaying absolution.

The Jesuits therefore were not the only casuists; but as confessors they were in great demand. The King's appointment of Annat as his confessor set a royal example which was widely followed. Many besides Jansenists had a misgiving that the Jesuits relaxed the terms of absolution.

In this connection 'Probability' simply means provability. To import the more usual sense of probable, as meaning 'more likely than not', invites verbal confusion, in which Pascal himself became somewhat entangled. An opinion on a moral case, which has been published by some teacher accepted as an authority, is held to be 'proved' and becomes 'probable'. Clearly, two authorities may reach two different conclusions on one problem. Both conclusions are then probable, and either may be adopted by a confessor; indeed either may be pleaded by a penitent, who is safeguarded against arbitrary severity if he can show that some action he has confessed is dispensed or leniently regarded by some accepted authority.

The dangerous side of the doctrine is sufficiently illustrated in the practices exposed by Pascal. Pascal is sometimes criticized for having carefully picked out the worst examples of Jesuit casuistry, displaying rare and accidental blemishes as though they were typical; and he is sometimes defended on the ground that a controversialist is only effective if he hammers at the weak points. Both the criticism and the defence miss the real point. The spots exposed by Pascal were precisely those to which a morally lax confessor would direct a penitent who wished to be let down lightly. The sound doctrine of Probability is open to such exploitation. An accommodating confessor need only ransack his books until he finds one authority which allows a certain action, and, even if all the other books condemn it, it is Probable and is not a barrier to absolution. They were selected for exposure because they could be selected for use.

The button was off Pascal's foil, which he used with deadly effect. His chief source of data for attack was 'Escobar', that is the compendious manual used by the Jesuit confessors, the *Liber Theologiae Moralis XXIV Societatis Jesu Doctoribus Reseratus* by Antonia de Escobar y Mendoza. It had gone through thirty-seven editions in Spanish as the *Examen de Confessores y Practica de Penitentes* before translation into Latin. It was substantially a good and learned book and its author was a good man. His own comments upon the more dubious conclusions in the compilation are on the side of a high ethical standard; but even editorial disapproval did not rob a printed opinion of its Probability. If it was there it could be applied, and the license of French society suggested that some were receiving the Sacraments on easy terms.

Pascal's most lethal weapon was the sword of truth. Insistence on truth was as salient in his character as the nose on his face. Professionally he was a mathematician and physicist, knowing that a minute inaccuracy can ruin hours of labour. In controversy, a scrupulous accuracy of statement and quotation was the first condition of his task. The documents he held up for obloquy were available to the public and one misrepresentation would have discredited his case and himself. The Jesuits of course cried 'menteur'; they had to cry something. It was more a conditioned reflex than a reply. Yet they cried it so persistently that an impression was created which still hangs in the air. Even some of Pascal's admirers, still more of course his critics, write as though he were somehow vulnerable on this point.

Sainte-Beuve, with manifest regret but impelled by the duty of candour, adduces one example where, he says, the discrepancy 'leaps to the eye', and the Jesuit teacher 'ne dit pas, en un mot, ce qu'on lui fait dire'. Examination of this instance shows that Pascal's version was an exact rendering of Escobar's, and that the only thing that leaps to the eye is that Pascal has let down his Jesuit lightly. Such objective scholars as, for instance, M. Strowski,

Dr Stewart and M. Mesnard regard Pascal's veracity as un-assailable. It is reasonable to expect that anyone who would assail it should quote. Pascal's own challenge on this subject occurs in his eleventh letter:

> 'I can say, Father, as in the sight of God, that I detest nothing so much as offending against truth, even in the smallest degree; and I have always taken particular care not only not to falsify (which would indeed be horrible) but not in the least to alter or distort the sense of one passage.'

The Jesuits could not produce parallel passages to refute that, but anyone who can is still free to do so. The sources are extant.

It is not on such grounds that the Provincials may leave, on the whole, an unhappy impression. Indeed it is not easy to define one's reasons for such an impression. Dr Stewart traces it to Pascal's intemperate accusation that the Jesuits deliberately adapted their moral practice to the end of acquiring world-power. This extravagance is a blemish but it occupies a minor part in Pascal's indictment and did no more harm than the ordinary mis-hit.

M. Strowski charges the Jansenists with a persecution complex, 'a veritable hatred born of the wrongs and calumnies which they endured, and which blinded them. It is one of those collective passions which can cloud the clearest minds. Pascal was infected by it, and the Provincials give it terrible expression.' We accept this with considerable reserve. The Port Royalists do not strike us as 'good haters'. Pascal was a headstrong champion and was moved by whatever moved his friends. Partisan feeling no doubt started his engine, but we believe that the fuel tank was stocked with his moral sense. When he found, or believed he found, in-genious explanations from a society claiming the most holy name, that lying, fornication and homicide might be innocent occupa-tions, his reaction calls for no conspiracy mania to account for it.

It has to be allowed that, as his critics complain, he was merci-less. He selected his instances with the cold discrimination of David choosing pebbles for his sling. He ascended to the kill as implacably as Jack climbing the beanstalk. We see that Goliath and Blunderbore are doomed, and our hearts almost go out to them. The reader of the Provincials feels that he has been caught up into a cavalry charge, and that such *élan* must carry all before it. It is not easy to remain aware of the real situation. On our right, the Society of Jesus, international, ubiquitous, closely marshalled, powerfully influential at Rome, unpopular indeed in France but enjoying the favour and protection of the King, the Court, the law courts, a large section of the Sorbonne; on our left, an apprentice pamphleteer with a price on his liberty. Where sympathy is due it must not be withheld but we are puzzled when Pascal seems to be reproved for not hitting someone of his own size.

The real trouble, the deep fault of the Provincials, we submit, is this. There was a good thing in Pascal which was also present in Escobar but not, to anything like the same extent, in Arnauld.

This was a profound concern for human souls at large, a longing for the *many* that they might awake to their possession of souls. It was a readiness to go out in search of them rather than wait for them to come in, even a willingness to take ethical risks or make ethical allowances, to *accommodate* the Gospel in a high and innocent sense, to be all things to all men (as when he elaborated the argument of the Wager for use in his Defence of Religion). All this was as native to Pascal as it was impossible for Port Royal; and, corruptions apart, it was the very *raison d'être* of the Society of Jesus. He saw the bad side of Jesuitry and exposed it. It deserved exposure. He turned a blind eye to its good side which yet happened to be the best thing in himself.

The eighteen Letters appeared in pamphlet form, each being a folder of eight or twelve quarto pages. Twelve thousand copies of the first Letter were printed, Port Royal placing one-half of the number on immediate sale. The supply rose steeply with the demand. After the seventeenth Letter Arnauld assembled the pamphlets into one volume, published 'at Cologne' in 1657, to which was added two years later a collection of anti-Jesuit factums from the Rouen and Paris clergy and others. (A factum is a formal written complaint or remonstrance to be set before authority. Pascal himself wrote a number of these, and declared the fifth factum of the Paris clergy to be the best thing he had written.) In all early collected editions of the Provincials the words of Pascal are discreetly modified, though this did not save them from the Index and from a public burning by Royal order. In 1658, Nicole's Latin translation (by 'Willielmus Wendrockius') extended the fame of the Letters through Europe and ran to four editions within a year. Countless reprints followed, always with the Port Royal glosses, until Ernest Havet in 1889 and Auguste Molinier in 1891 released the full Pascal text.

Voltaire wrote in his *Siècle de Louis XIV*: 'Le premier livre de génie qu'on vit en prose fut le recueil des Lettres Provinciales. Tous les sortes d'éloquence y sont renfermées. Il faut rapporter à cet ouvrage l'époque de la fixation du langage.' It is in the *Pensées* that Pascal fulfils himself as an artist in words but the Provincials display all his gifts in a polemical frame.

The late Miss Dorothy Sayers, in her book *The Mind of the Maker*, argues that the Trinity of Christian belief furnishes the pattern for all creative work. An author must hold in unity a triad of qualities or activities; the 'Father-idea', the thing he has to say; the 'Son-idea', the author's acceptance and use of the means available for incarnating his thought (words, ink, time, terms of publication, etc.); and the 'Spirit-idea', the author's understanding of his readers and his ability to release his idea into their minds.

In the light of this we may read what Gilberte Périer wrote about her brother:

'He had a natural eloquence which gave him a marvellous facility for saying *what he wanted to say*, but to this he added certain rules which he had worked out for himself, which served him so well that he was *master of his own style*, with the result that not only could he say what he meant to say, but he would say it in the very manner of his choice, and so that his discourse *produced just the effect he intended.*'

We have italicized the three basic qualities by which Pascal controlled his purpose, his medium and his audience.

Such control gave him flexibility. The Provincial Letters called for a wide variety of moods and tones; delicate satire, dignified refutation of calumny, humorous relief, stern denunciation; they are all there in their place and none is misplaced.

We have given one example of his irony. His sense of fun is chiefly exercised in his picture of the Jesuit Father, filled with ingenuous admiration of the 'twenty-four Elders' whose opinions are in Escobar; and here Pascal is indeed unique. Having to draw an imaginary representative of the system he condemns, he delineates him as an honest and likeable man.

The most famous instance of his rhetoric occurs in the sixteenth letter, where he is moved to wrath by the persistent calumnies which the Jesuits invented against Port Royal. To feel its force one needs to have seen this wave approaching long before it breaks:

'Cruel and mean persecutors, is no cloister safe from your gibes? Day and night these dedicated maidens adore Jesus in the holy Sacrament; day and night without ceasing you declare that they do not believe Him to be in the Eucharist or at the right hand of the Father. You would openly sever them from the Church even while they pray for the Church and for you. You slander those who have no ears to hear you, no mouths to answer you. But Jesus, in Whom their life is hid one day to appear with Him, He hears you; He replies for them! Even today one hears it, that Voice, holy and terrible, which astounds nature and consoles the Church. And I greatly fear, my Fathers, that those who steel their hearts and stubbornly close their ears when He speaks as God must listen with terror when He speaks as Judge.'

Pascal's is an ascetic style; he rides his Pegasus upon the curb. Such freedom as he allows himself in the quotation above and other forms of luxuriance such as a haunting music in the setting of some phrase ('car la vie est un songe un peu moins inconstant'), or the solemn eloquence which wells up from thoughts of infinity and eternity, or the rush of attributes and adjectives released when he contemplates something which stirs his antipathy or his admiration, gain effect from their seeming to come almost against his will. They are the rewards of pruning. His constant ideal is plain statement.

'La conduite de Dieu, qui dispose toutes choses avec douceur, est de mettre la religion dans l'esprit par les raisons et dans le cœur par la grâce.'

Translation of such a passage is mere transcription of the words as they come: the conduct of God, Who orders all things with gentleness, is to put religion into the mind by reasons and into the heart by grace; but all his idea of religion is distilled here.

The Provincial Letters became more serious though not less lively as they proceeded. The 'Montalte' element faded out and Pascal, still anonymous, assumed the first person. From the eleventh Letter onwards (August 18) the 'friend' disappeared and the Jesuit fathers were addressed directly. The seventeenth and eighteenth Letters were written 'to the Reverend Father Annat, Jesuit'; they met the persistent cry of heresy which was almost the only coherent reply which the Jesuits even attempted. Pascal shows in the seventeenth Letter that Port Royalists, along with other faithful Catholics, accepted the Papal condemnation of the Five Propositions. The eighteenth Letter is a reasoned defence of the doctrine of *Fait*, that no irreverence to the Pope is involved in questioning whether he is infallible on matters of detail.

Indeed Pascal's tone towards the Papacy here, as always except once, is deeply respectful; but he piles up instances of Papal decrees which have had to be revised in the light of later know-ledge, and his veneration for the Holy See is something other than a respect of persons:

'It was in vain' (he wrote to Annat in the eighteenth Pro-vincial), 'that you people obtained a Decretal from Rome against Galileo condemning his opinion that the earth moved. The earth will not halt for a Decretal; and if there are constant observations which show that it turns, not all the men in the world can stop it from spinning or themselves from spinning with it.'

Pascal's triumph was almost too easy; one may wish that the other side of the picture might have been more worthily pre-sented, but the Jesuits had been caught on the wrong foot and never recovered their balance. Replies to the Provincials were numerous and acrid, but feeble. The Society of Jesus had pro-duced, and would yet produce, great minds and great souls, but it was in the trough of the wave. Nouet was no Cornelius à Lapide nor was Annat a Bellarmine, and Pascal could attack with only an occasional deft parry by way of defence.

Thus, in the thirteenth Letter he gravely discusses the learned opinion of Lessius that a box on the ear might be sufficient excuse for homicide. He refers to a recent State banquet at Compiègne where the King's chef had had his ears boxed by a Jesuit. 'It was perhaps fortunate, Reverend Fathers, that the chef had not ac-quired his moral principles in your schools.' Nouet's reply to this, incredibly, was that Pascal could not be sure that the chef had been struck with the palm of the hand; a blow from the back of the hand might not be a box. Pascal in his next Letter seems to ignore this, until at the very end he grants it a careless sentence or two: 'About that affair at Compiègne, that is a very nice point. I cannot be sure whose province it may be to decide it; but it seems to me that it was a Probable box on the ear, and that salves my conscience.'

In 1657 the Assembly of Clergy ordered the reprinting of

S. Charles Borromeo's Instructions to Confessors and severely discouraged the idea of translating Escobar into French; the first tangible effects of the Provincials and the *factums*. The Jesuits decided on a formal exposure of the Provincials and employed their most learned canonist, Père Georges Pirot, to write a definitive refutation.

His *Apologie pour les Casuistes* appeared with the imprint of the Clermont College towards the end of 1657 and was the Society's worst blunder. Pirot played to an empty gallery. His lofty, man-of-the-world approach, alternately ingratiating and menacing, set all teeth on edge. He addressed the writer of the Letters as some misguided though clever young man who had been roped in by a 'negligible cabal'. Casuists were right and Jansenists were wrong and it was tiresome to have to argue such a trivial matter, but after all life had to go on, and moral precepts had to be adapted to its conditions. Half the population would be put out of business if there were over-much insistence on the avoidance of occasions of sin. Did not Jesus Christ encourage an occasion of sin when He entrusted Judas with the money-bag? Did He not resort to an equivocation in saying, of the last day, that 'of that day knoweth no man, but the Father only'?

The book played straight into Pascal's hands. Having finished with the Provincials he was still busy with the *factums*, and in the sixth *factum* of the Paris clergy he made play with the attempt of the Society to be neutral about a book which they could not repudiate since they had commissioned it. They were trying to achieve the golden mean between right and wrong! The *Apologie* was condemned by the Bishops and the Sorbonne and ultimately by Rome.

The Provincials had to wait till long after Pascal's death for anything like a weighty reply. In 1694 Père Gabriel Daniel's book *Les Entretiens de Cléandre et d'Eudoxe* offered a readable and reasonable criticism, but it was thirty years too late, and even so its appearance only set people reading the Provincials again.

Pascal had ended them as abruptly as he had begun them. The

nineteenth Letter (not published as a pamphlet) ends in the middle of a sentence. Why did he drop his pen?

Everywhere in France the law was moving into operation against Jansenist publications and particularly against the sale of the Provincial Letters. The Pope had declared that all who denied that the Five Propositions were in the *Augustinus* were children of iniquity; the King was infuriated with Port Royal which he held responsible for a spirit of continual unrest. Pascal had a threefold choice. He could carry the matter to open defiance of the highest spiritual and secular authority, but he was an ardent Papalist and monarchist; or he could trim and tone down his arguments with more discretion, but a Pascal does not do that; or he could stop. He stopped.

Was he also weary of controversy? The biographer of Pascal must at many points resist the temptation to simplify what is not simple, and at this point the temptation is strong. One desires to say that Pascal ceased to write Provincials as one saying suddenly and decisively, this is not my *métier*. For it was not his *métier*, and already he knew it. God made him to build rather than to cast down, and the miracle of the Holy Thorn had put into his mind the great constructive purpose of drawing a picture of Christianity which would impel the attention of the man in the street and in the salon and the gaming-room. Along with it was a growing personal need and hunger to order his own spiritual life, to grow towards God. These great matters beckoned him and he felt the time was short. He did not know how short it would be. Was he to spend the precious years scoring debating points against fellow-Christians? Such thoughts were in him and they were to dominate his remaining days. In the Provincials *l'esprit* is far more evident than *le cœur*. They belonged to an order which Pascal was transcending.

Yet among the last-written fragments found at his death was this: 'If my letters are condemned at Rome, that which I condemn in them is condemned in Heaven. *Ad tuum, Domine Jesu, tribunal apello.*'

The tone of the Provincials caused some distress among Pascal's devout friends. In 1680 Arnauld wrote:

'The moment he began to deal with the moral teaching of the Jesuits in his grand manner, we began to hear murmurs and complaints from the devout. Some of our best souls thought that this way of writing was not Christian; that it lacked charity; that raillery might not be used in treating holy things, and that the better sort of people were scandalized.'

We shall presently see 'Montalte' acquiring, through the grace of God, the humility and submissiveness of a child. May we not round off this chapter of his life by seeing him coming to share the misgivings and regrets of the pious souls whom he championed? Indeed the temptation is strong.

But it must be resisted. Some facts support it but others negate it. Battle may not have been Pascal's true *métier* but he never ceased to see it as having been his duty. In his eyes the Provincials were a work of highest charity towards the souls endangered by corrupt teaching, and even towards the souls who spread that teaching.

He had one answer for any suggestion that he ought to mitigate and moderate his onslaught. You would never find the Saints holding their tongues. '*Jamais les Saints ne se sont tus*' (920).

CHAPTER 9

THE ORDER OF CHARITY

'Just as I am, though tossed about
With many a conflict, many a doubt,
Fightings and fears within, without,
O Lamb of God, I come.'

CHARLOTTE ELLIOT

———

'M. Pascal,' said the gardener at Port Royal, 'always looks as though he were just about to swear.' It is fair to remember that he only saw Pascal at Port Royal where sobriety of demeanour was *de rigueur* and where Pascal had much on his shoulders including the security of that gardener's job. Pascal's known visits to Port Royal add up to a small aggregate. He probably went there fairly often for material for the Provincials, and Vaumurier would have been a good centre for discussions. On the other hand, he had reasons for restricting such visits.

'I am not of Port Royal,' he wrote flatly; and he was not. When not at his home by the Luxembourg gardens he was at the Auberge Roi David or at the Hôtel de Roannez. He seems to have moved around considerably, but at no time did he dream of taking the step which Singlin must have expected and Jacqueline may have prayed for, becoming one of the solitaries. His theological affinities with Port Royal may seem so close as to appear identical at some points, but the main difference was a deep one. It was the difference between attention to formulae and concern for people. It was more than a tactical prudence, it was a personal need which kept Pascal detached from the party which commanded his affection and his remarkable services.

The miracle of the Holy Thorn crystallized a purpose long

present in his mind, which now became his dominant passion; to set other feet on the rock where his were planted. He would write a book to commend Christianity to the sceptic. He knew himself equipped for it. He could exhibit the lines of an argument without digressions, ambiguities or equivocations. He had contact with his intended audience and the Provincials showed that what he wrote would be read.

He did not hurry. So great a matter must wait its moment. He must ponder long over the method of approach and fill up gaps in his knowledge of the Bible and the Fathers. Étienne Périer wrote in later years of his uncle, 'He often said that he would need ten years of strength for such a task.' In fact he had before him four or five interrupted years of acute controversy and broken health.

In the thick of the Jesuit battle he was allowed to guide a soul. Charlotte de Roannez, the younger sister of the duke, was moved by the miracle of the Thorn to test her vocation to religion, and during the last three months of 1656 Pascal wrote her a series of letters which she preserved. They must have been strong diet for a young girl; S. Francis de Sales would have better known how to make the yoke of Christ seem easy and His burden light; yet Pascal himself quotes this text, and the encouragements and joys of spiritual commitment are the main theme of this counsel. But the rigours of the way and the dangers of lapse are given as he himself saw them. 'Those who repent of their repentance become, as Tertullian wrote, penitents of the Devil.' Such words might have haunted Charlotte de Roannez in later years, for after making voluntary vows she was persuaded by her family to renounce them under dispensation, entered a loveless marriage and never knew happiness again.

These letters reflect Pascal's interests at the time. The day after the Assembly of Clergy had approved the Formulary he wrote, 'I tremble to see persecution approaching, not only against persons (that matters little) but against the truth.' A little later when the problem of his relation with Rome is much on his mind he writes, 'I welcome with all my heart that zeal you show for union with the Pope. The body is no more alive without the head than the head without the body. The Church does not contain any more attached to this unity than those we care for [i.e. Port Royal]. . . . I shall never separate myself from communion with the Pope. At least I pray God to give me this grace, without which I should be lost for ever.'

The dilemma which had faced Port Royal three years before with Innocent X's Bull *Cum Occasione* reappeared more acutely in October 1656, with Alexander VI's new Bull *Ad Sanctam Sedem*, in which the condemnation of the Five Propositions was specifically extended to the *Augustinus*, now named a forbidden book. To every Port Royalist, and no doubt to Pascal at this time, the *Augustinus* was a true reading of the Church's inspired teacher on grace. To surrender Jansen would be to desert the vocation to recall the Church to purity of doctrine. That was unthinkable. Yet to every Port Royalist and to Pascal, the Pope was the head of the body of Christ. A breach with him was equally unthinkable. But two Popes in succession had condemned Jansen.

The only loophole was the old one. The Pope must not be questioned when he spoke on doctrine; he might be misinformed on a statement of fact. Pascal patiently argued this in his last two Provincial Letters. Before writing them he had secured a delay. The new Bull, pronounced in October 1656, needed the consent of King, clergy and Parlement to become operative. The King readily accepted it and the clergy not only assented but attached to it a Formulary to be signed by all 'religious persons' (clergy and those under vows) attesting their individual assent. The last line of defence was the Parlement, to whom Pascal wrote an open 'Letter from an Advocate' appealing against registration of the Bull on Gallican grounds, as threatening the liberties of the Church in France. It succeeded. The Parlement refused to register the Bull, which became a dead letter for several years. Once more Port Royal had been saved at the eleventh hour.

So during 1657 Pascal could give his mind to the shaping of his

Apology for Religion. He thought long about the communication of belief from one mind to another. His *Esprit de Géométrie*, a writing in two sections, may have been written this year. (E. Havet assigns it to 1655. Strowski offers a fascinating conjecture that it was written in 1654 in reply to Méré's letters of that time. Either may be right; we only feel that the writing is too calm to place just before the conversion, and too philosophically detached to place just after.) It seems Pascal's equivalent for Descartes' *Discours sur la Méthode*.

The first part is concerned with the function and limitations of mathematical reasoning. Truths can be ideally and infallibly demonstrated by defining every term and proving every proposition. A sovereign safeguard against equivocation is to form the habit of mentally substituting the definition of a thing every time that thing is mentioned. But this ideal of defining all terms and proving all propositions cannot be realized. One soon comes upon terms too simple for definition and propositions too obvious for proof. Pascal concludes that 'man has a natural incapacity for treating any science whatever in a complete order'. Therefore geometry (a word which the seventeenth century used for mathematics in general) must make assumptions before it can begin to reveal truth.

In the second part, which he called the Art of Persuasion (they are both uncompleted though considerable fragments), Pascal compares two avenues through which belief may be communicated, the understanding and the will of the hearer. The understanding is the more natural road to belief, the will is the more usual, though few admit this. Pascal is here concerned with truths in the natural world of which (as yet) he insists that strictly rational processes offer the only safe road. It is otherwise with supernatural truths, because God has willed to humble man's proud reason by decreeing that these enter the mind through the heart. Natural things have to be known before they can be loved; supernatural things come to be known only by those who love them. The higher truths are apprehended by the faculty of charity.

The Art of Persuasion, then, requires either rigorous intellectual demonstration or an *agrément* which involves an intimate knowledge of the man to whom the argument is addressed. This latter method is 'incomparably more difficult, more subtle, more admirable. I am incapable of it, and indeed it looks to me impossible.' He seems unaware that he will use this method and formulate some memorable rules of persuasion which are anything but geometrical. He proceeds to elaborate the rules of axioms and proofs sketched in the first fragment, but with many wistful glances towards the more human method. 'The same thought can have a different effect upon someone other than its originator; *infertile in its natural field it flourishes when transplanted.*' 'The best sort of book is one which makes the reader feel that he could have written it.' It seems a modest test, but it is also true of the finest batting or billiard-playing and the chess of the masters.

In 1658 (probably) he gave a lecture to his Port Royal friends expounding his forthcoming Apology. They were spellbound by the natural eloquence to which Gilberte testifies; they never forgot the occasion, and two accounts remain of what Pascal said, an abridged summary by his nephew Étienne Périer and a much longer version by a Poitevin member of the de Roannez group, Filleau de la Chaise. Notes for this speech occur in the *Pensées* (72, 416, 417, 436 and doubtless others).

Périer's account forms the preface to the Port Royal edition of the *Pensées*, instead of the account by Filleau de la Chaise which the Périers rejected as being too long and unsatisfactory in other, unspecified, ways. Of course Filleau de la Chaise if reliable is an authority of the first importance towards the understanding and right arranging of the *Pensées*; he is so accepted and used by the late Dr Stewart, and Professor Chevalier almost bases upon him his treatment of Pascal's theory of knowledge.* But Filleau de la Chaise makes at least one glaring blunder. He reports Pascal as

* *La Méthode de Connaître d'après Pascal*, 'Études sur Pascal', *Revue de Métaphysique et de Morale*, pp. 73–7.

having illustrated his theory of the communication of belief by a reference to the Great Fire of London, which happened four years after Pascal's death.

Périer's account, though perhaps not first-hand, is clearly authentic, and Filleau de la Chaise's has the same general outline. We learn that Pascal proposed to perform an old task in a new way.

The line of Apologists from before Tertullian to the successors of Paley is a long one, and some notable Defences of Christianity were current in Pascal's day. He seems to have studied them all, with particular attention to Raymond Sebond's *Theologia Naturalis* in Montaigne's translation, Charron's *Les Trois Vérités*, which he found tedious but of which there are certainly echoes in the *Pensées*, the *Traité de la Vérité de la Religion Chrétienne* of Hugo Grotius, and a very remarkable book which was already four hundred years old, Raymond Martini's *Pugio Fidei Christianae*. In 1264 the royal Saint Louis, wishing to stop the infiltration of Averrhoist ideas through Talmudic writings, but not destroy writings which might be found to bear important testimony to the Catholic faith, commissioned five scholars to study these books. Martini, a Dominican monk, was one of the five. He had access to a unique collection of sources for knowledge of Jewish and Arabic philosophy, and of Greek philosophy through Semitic eyes; also, he knew what to do with his material. His book had a temporary success and then was forgotten for nearly four centuries, till the manuscript was discovered at Toulouse in Pascal's time and published with heavy annotations by Joseph de Voisin. Pascal's impression of the value of this book may be measured by the fact that he learned Hebrew to follow it better. Chiefly, it gave him his necessary background of knowledge of the Old Covenant as a preparation for the New.

Pascal gave long thought to the form of his argument. He considered, weighed and rejected the metaphysical approach, the attempt to produce conviction by beginning with abstract principles (as did S. Thomas and Descartes) and deducing sure inferences from them, testing the logic at every step. Conclusions so reached, he felt, would be sterile. Freethinkers would not be interested enough to try to refute them. Hypotheses (as Professor William James pointed out in his *The Will to Believe*) are not merely true or false, they are also (whether true or false) alive or dead. To the average libertine of Pascal's time the hypothesis of God's existence was very likely a dead one. Pascal's first task was to make it live.

Pascal's 'target-reader' would be someone like Miton, affable, courteous, keenly intelligent, lazy, a little more than dubious about Pascal's extravagant interest in religion, hugely amused by the Provincials (which made no demands upon him) but likely to close the Apology the moment it looked like a sermon directed at himself; and he would detect the homiletic accent by the appearance of allusions from the vocabulary of evangelism; Grace, Repentance, Salvation. When such terms appeared he would shrug his shoulders, close the book and look around for something interesting.

He would be impervious to the 'hot Gospel' approach; and the exclusively rational approach would only, at best, engage his intellectual assent. Was there any alternative? Pascal found one, and we have found something like a parallel to it:

> 'Marshall opened the defence. For the first twenty minutes he did not touch the facts of the case, but used all his eloquence and dramatic power to instil into the jury a sense of their tremendous responsibility. J. B. Melville, K.C. . . . then a very "white-wigged" spectator, describes this prelude as a masterpiece of advocacy, the most effective jury-speech he ever heard. "After twenty minutes of this passionate and pulverizing rhetoric," he said to me, "the jury were in a state of pulp." '*

For the first large section of his book Pascal would hardly mention God or the Bible or grace. He would draw a picture of

---

* *The Life of Sir Edward Marshall Hall, K.C.*, by Edward Marjoribanks (Gollancz; pp. 246–7).

the dark and draughty spaces stretching infinitely in all directions from just outside the pasteboard setting of the genteel but brief and trivial comedy of Miton's existence. He would show Miton that he lived a lie because the truth scared him. The reader would have the choice between going on reading or admitting to himself that he dare not. Evidence for Christianity could wait until the reader was actively demanding it. It would be the Montalte strategy of carrying the war into the adversary's camp. The reader would be convicted of regarding truth as something to conceal and time as something to kill, and challenged to say whether that was the philosophy of a sane man.

Having painted the feebleness and fragility and folly of man's condition and existence he would, by a swift transition, write of his greatness, his capacity for noble conduct, his intimations of immortality. The resultant picture would be thoroughly bewildering. Man's nature seems an insoluble riddle.

Pascal would take his reader through some of the answers that had been attempted, and show their inadequacy; the philosophies, the non-Christian religions.

Finally, in true Pascalian manner, he would draw attention to a queer fact. One human race was different from others. It was not a question of better or worse, but the Jews are visibly different. If we inquire why, we find that they have an explanation, contained in their book. So the great argument is opened which would lead (from a flagrant fact) through history, prophecy, miracle, to the life of Christ and the work of the Church.

In the early summer of 1658 Pascal's thoughts suddenly reverted to mathematics, and he solved a problem which Galileo had declared almost insoluble and which had in turn baffled Descartes and Roberval: the mathematics of the cycloid.

The line traced by a point on the perimeter of a wheel moving in a straight line on a plane surface has been called the commonest line of all next to the straight line and the circle; but the calculation of its properties (such as the area bounded by it) proved quite intractable to the cluster of brilliant scientists of that time. Pascal's own account is among the collection of his latest writings:

> 'On one unexpected occasion, turning my attention to geometry which I had long abandoned, I formed certain methods of ascertaining the dimensions and centres of gravity of solids and surfaces and curves, which seemed to me applicable to almost all such things; and in order to attack the most difficult thing of all I set myself to find out all that remained unknown about the nature of this particular line, the roulette or trochoid.'*

Gilberte Périer's account is more picturesque: 'One night when my brother had a violent toothache, which made sleep quite impossible, there came uninvited into his mind some thought on the problem of the roulette. It was followed by another, and that by another, a whole crowd of thoughts leading on and showing him, as though in spite of himself, the proof of all these things even to his own surprise.' The good devout lady does her best to show that there was nothing really deliberate in this sad lapse (of which nevertheless she was proud). We can accept the reference to the toothache, for it was characteristic of Pascal to cope with pain by bending his attention upon something else. His health began finally to break up in this year, 1658, but he does not mention it himself; and that perhaps is a point not sufficiently noticed.

There have been some notable literary invalids: Donne, Nietzsche, Stevenson, Kafka, Francis Thompson, Barbellion. None of them excels Pascal in banishing from his writings the atmosphere of the sick room. His beautiful Prayer for the Right Use of Sickness offers a complete contrast to the famous 'Devotions upon Emergent Occasions' in which John Donne follows with fascinated interest the stages of his illness. Pascal fought illness all his life, with pain in the entrails and head. He accepted it robustly, and dismissed it. No doubt it left its mark upon his spirit but his writings show no trace of hypochondria or self-pity.

* *Oeuvres Complètes*, ed. Lahure, III, p. 339.

He did not broadcast his solutions of the cycloid problems but told them to his friends. They at once urged that he must publish them. Roannez in particular advanced the specious argument that they would add to the effect of his defence of religion. Pascal yielded against his inclinations. He might have felt little scruple in publishing the work simply as a contribution to knowledge, but the idea of stage-managing it held spiritual risks.

The *libido excellendi* was his Achilles heel. He had gone far to overcome his taste for glory, but let him once get intoxicated with success and he might start strutting and crowing as of old. However, he agreed; just this once perhaps he might further the cause of true religion by blazoning his fame. It was indeed plausible but— who sups with the Devil should use a longer spoon than that!

The plan was to publish the problems without Pascal's solutions, in the form of a competition for scientists at home and abroad, with a prize for the correct solutions and a date by which they must be submitted. Such challenges were not unknown. When Huyghens discovered rings around Saturn he made a brief statement of it in Latin, jumbled the letters up and sent the cipher to all the astronomers known to him. To us this way of celebrating a discovery must seem precarious. If any solutions identical with Pascal's had been received who would have got the credit? It was assumed that no satisfactory solutions would be sent, and none were, but the assumption might have strained the impartiality of the judges.

The challenge went out in June 1658, over the name of 'Amos Dettonville' (an anagram of Louis de Montalte; another will be found in *Pensée* 18). 'If within the three months no one has solved these problems we shall give our own solutions, and indicate others from which may be drawn greater discoveries, and posterity will assuredly acclaim us.' The long-discarded trumpet has not lost its vibrancy.

The two prizes of forty and twenty pistoles were held by Carcavi, one of the panel of judges. Entries came from Huyghens (not for competition) and a considerable number including the

Dutchman de Sluse, the Italian de Ricci, and 'M. le Chevalier Wrenne' under which title (Strowski's) we may identify the creator of S. Paul's, at that time a young Fellow of All Souls. Pascal greatly admired his entry. The best replies came from John Wallis, Savilian Professor at Oxford, and a Jesuit of Toulouse, Père Lalouvère. Both of these protested vigorously against the verdict that their work did not earn a prize. Wallis's was admittedly incomplete; his grievance was the shortness of the time allowed. In Lalouvère's work there was a mixture of brilliance and confusion. He came uncomfortably close to the central principle of Pascal's discovered method but his calculations were far too muddled to justify his conclusions.

'Amos Dettonville' dealt with these claims by correspondence, rather more than firmly. In mid-October, Pascal published his *History of the Roulette* and, at the beginning of 1659, he published a letter with three short treatises giving full solutions to the problems.

They were an intellectual feat of the first order, and opened a chapter in knowledge. Leibniz's own copy of Pascal's book has marginal annotations which constitute his first draft for expounding the Integral Calculus, which he inferred from these pages.

But, alas! the *History of the Roulette* had covered twenty years of scientific rivalry. In earlier days Roberval, vain and violent, had claimed priority over Torricelli in suggesting a way to calculate its area and had even imputed plagiarism. Torricelli had withdrawn from the field for the sake of peace. In his *résumé*, Pascal (on his friend's behalf and under his influence) revived the unfair imputation, which Torricelli could not answer from the grave. It was not like Pascal, but it happened.

The labour and excitement of this affair told heavily on Pascal's health. He bade a final farewell to the glories and quarrels of science, and this may be the moment at which he began to wear next his skin an iron belt with small spikes which he pressed at any temptation to pride, a concealed substitute for a crown of thorns. It aroused the doubts of Condorcet and the mirth of

Voltaire, for whom the conception of intellectual pride as something to be fought might have seemed as whimsical as the means taken to fight it.

The key to Pascal's remaining days is his written meditation on Gethsemane, called the *Mystère de Jésus* (see below, p. 225). Humility, charity and patience are now his ambitions, and he was learning patience in a particularly hard school, for his illness robbed him of the faculty he chiefly needed for the writing of his book, his marvellous memory.

Beethoven composed his deepest music after becoming totally deaf; Pascal wrote his most searching sentences in brief intervals of release from prostration and of the return of energy and clarity. The *Pensées* are in a sense his *Rasoumouvsky Quartettes*.

In the matter of charity he advanced to the stage which is easily misunderstood except by the saints who know it well, and by clergy who (saintly or not) know that it is a condition of their work, where love for others imposes detachment from them.

'It is wrong', he wrote, 'that men should bind themselves to me, even if they do so with pleasure and of their own free will. I should deceive those in whom I had created this desire, for I am not the last end of anyone and have not the means to satisfy them' (471).

With this we may compare some sentences by Simone Weil who in some respects was the most Pascalian person of our own time: 'I must withdraw so that God can make contact with the beings whom chance places in my path and whom He loves. It is tactless for me to be there. It is as though I were placed between two lovers or two friends,'* and 'In a perfect friendship the two friends have fully consented to be two and not one. . . . Man has the right to desire direct union with God alone. Friendship is a miracle by which a person consents to view from a certain distance, and without coming any nearer, the very being who is as necessary to him as bread.'†

Gilberte Périer misunderstood this and was much troubled by

* *Gravity and Grace*, Routledge & Kegan Paul, p. 36.
† *Waiting for God*, Routledge & Kegan Paul, p. 135.

Blaise's apparent coldness. Jacqueline understood, and was able to reassure her sister. It is quite likely that Blaise sometimes over-did the control of his natural feelings; none of the Pascals did things by halves.

He became a familiar figure in several of the Paris churches where he particularly loved to attend the Little Hours of prayer for the joy of hearing his favourite 118th Psalm (our 119th). He was not a hermit; the drawing-rooms still sometimes welcomed him, and about this time he gave some instructions to a boy of high rank in the duties of the station he would occupy.

This boy was almost certainly that du Plessis, son of the Duc de Luynes, who later became the Duc de Chevreux and supported Fénelon in the reform of the Court. Nicole's record of Pascal's instructions, like Fontaine's *Entretien*, testifies to the enduring impression Pascal's words made on those who heard him speak. Pascal's task in these *Trois Discours sur la Condition des Grands* was to teach the boy his social duties (someone else no doubt was directing his soul) and he sticks to the point. He treats the social order as a fact, not one of the highest importance since social dis-tinctions occur by accident and are accepted by custom, but there they are, and they create duties. Natural excellence of body or mind had greater worth than social position. Pascal hopes that his pupil will display such qualities also, but his concern is with rank. *Noblesse oblige.* The man of high position must be *honnête*; he must be just and considerate in his dealings with those of lower degree. He must realize that the respects paid to him are *grandeurs d'établissement* merely. The code proper to them is a fine one so far as it goes, but that is not really very far. 'If you content your-self with *honnêteté* you will lose your soul, but at least you will lose it as a gentleman.'

Up to now Pascal still lived with some elegance, maintaining his carriage and horses, while tapestries and well-stocked book-shelves graced his rooms. If the accident on the Neuilly Bridge happened at all it happened about this time, let us say early in 1660, for then he made a spiritual retreat which left him with two simple resolves, to write his book and to find God. He shed all his possessions except bare necessities. The carriage and horses were discarded, and the tapestries, and even his books except the Bible and one or two of the Fathers and (surely) Montaigne.

Increasingly, his more perceptive friends must have felt like those who watch a solitary climber making a difficult ascent. The easiest part of his climb was the mastery over the body. The pain he had always been able to accept he now welcomed and offered. His food was limited to the minimum which the doctors would sanction and he practised indifference to its taste. It was only possible for him to take liquids slowly, almost drop by drop, and he never showed awareness of any difference between comforting drinks and nauseating medicines.

To his friends, and still more to his critics, he showed a kindliness which moved them not because he had ever been wanting in it, but because there was a new depth of courtesy. Even now he could sometimes be brusque but he would quickly apologize and make amends; there was perhaps something new in that.

It is sometimes thought of Pascal that science was a labour which he forsook; more correctly it was an intense pleasure which he sacrificed. He probably thought of it as his largest offering of all, but if so he was mistaken, for an even more costly oblation was required when the moment came (we do not know when) of realization that he would not complete his book.

His feeling for the poor moved towards the standard Christian pattern, that of S. Francis and S. Vincent, in which the aim is more than benevolent action, is identification; helping the poor, not from outside or still less from above, but from amongst or below. It is the pattern of the Maundy feet-washing and it is more than that, a method not only of the imitation of Christ but of mystical union with Him.

One aspect of this phase calls for delicate judgment and especially for freedom from theological bias. How far, if at all, did he seek to extricate himself not only from science and worldly contacts and social obligations but from his Jansenist ties?

If this question arose it must have been delicate for himself. His relations had no qualms about Jansenism and cannot have supposed him to have any. Their Church was the Catholic Church, their creed was the Catholic faith, and Jansenism was a word used by their enemies to describe the type of devotional life at which they were aiming; and was not Blaise their outstanding champion in all this?

Here is no question of recantation, or of abandonment of a cause. It is rather a question of spiritual reorientation, and the evidence that some such process happened to Pascal at this time is of that various, accidental, convergent sort from which (according to Pascal's own theory of belief) the greatest certainties arise. We have some sentences written by Nicole as late as 1680; some passages in the memoirs (not discovered until the present century) of the Abbé Beurrier who attended Pascal in his last illness; the last two Provincial Letters read in the light of this evidence; the note struck by a number of the *Pensées*.

What Nicole wrote in 1680 was that twenty-five years previously he had begun to think that Jansen's interpretation of S. Augustine was too harsh, that the Dominicans and Thomists were nearer the truth, and that 'the late M. Pascal, with whom I had the fortune of being closely united at that time, helped me not a little in encouraging that inclination'.* With that in hand we compare the first two Provincials with the last two and recognize that Pascal in the interval has acquired a definitely more respectful attitude towards the Thomist theory of grace and its teachers. The Abbé Beurrier wrote in his notes: 'He told me that in the last two years he had retired prudently from these disputes in view of the great difficulty of these questions about grace and predestination, following the example of S. Paul himself when he cried, *O Altitudo!*'

Pascal had made some attempt to straighten out for himself the intricacies of the theology of grace in three short tracts written about 1660 and assembled as his *Écrits sur la Grâce*. Their purpose

* Jovy, *Pascal Inédit*, tome II, p. 362.

is to find a rational formula for a mystery, the conjunction of God's sovereignty with man's freedom of will. Jansenism regarded man as a puppet and that is one epithet, some might say *the* one epithet, which Pascal would never accept for himself or apply to his fellows; but after this essay in theology he ceased to inquire and redirected his attention to worship.

The authentic note of Pascal's last phase, hidden but unmistakable, is joy. Gilberte's account of his closing years gives an impression of sunset and evening star and one clear call, but not (since this is Blaise Pascal) of any process that moving seems asleep.

Illness made a visit to the country imperative, and he was taken by leisurely stages, mainly by canal, to Clermont. Fermat heard he was that much nearer Toulouse and wrote suggesting a meeting at some midway place since they were both too weak for the whole journey: '. . . though if you do not agree you run a risk of my coming all the way and you will have two invalids in your house.' There is so much self-potraiture in Pascal's reply that it deserves giving in full:

'Sir,—You are the most delightful person in the world and I am one of those who can appreciate your qualities and admire them unboundedly when I find them allied to talents such as yours. All this compels me to acknowledge with my own hand the offer you make, in spite of the difficulty I have in writing or reading. I tell you, Sir, that if my health allowed it I should fly to Toulouse, and I would not have allowed a man like you to take one step for a man like me. This must be added, although I consider you the leading geometer of Europe it is not for that reason that I should come, but because I should enjoy the fun and *honnêteté* of your conversation.

'Speaking frankly, I find geometry the noblest exercise of the mind, yet I know it to be so useless that I see no difference between a geometer and a clever artisan. I call it the loveliest occupation in the world, but only an occupation. I have often said that it is good as a hobby but not as a vocation. I would not take two paces for geometry and I feel perfectly sure that that is your own view. But also, I am now engaged upon studies so remote from these that I should find it difficult to remember what they were all about. A singular chance about a year or two ago did set me at mathematics, but having settled that matter I am not likely ever to touch the subject again, apart from the fact that I am not yet well enough.

'I am too weak to walk without a stick and cannot stay on a horse, or drive more than two or three leagues in a carriage. It took twenty-two days for me to come here from Paris. The doctor orders me to take the waters at Bourbon in September, and I am pledged since two months ago to spend Christmas at Saumur with the Duc de Roannez, who has much too high an opinion of me. But my route to Saumur by river would take me through Orleans and if my health forbids further travel I should return to Paris from there.

'There you have my present condition. I had to tell you, only to make clear the impossibility of my enjoying the honour you offer, and to say how greatly I wish to meet you, either in your person or in your sons to whom I am devoted, having a particular veneration for those who bear the name of the world's greatest man.

I am, etc.,

Pascal.'

He wrote from Bienassis, the Périers' country home outside Clermont. He returned to Paris in November, to find that Jacqueline had 'wished' on to him the care of his two younger nephews Louis and Blaise Périer, who were at Paris waiting for school vacancies. He was already housing their older brother Étienne. Jacqueline's letter seems to have broken a long silence:

'November 10th 1660. My dear Brother: Good morning to you and a happy New Year; and please believe that I wished you this in January though I only write it now! This year which I have from my heart offered to God, has made no difference to the feelings which (in Him) I ought to have for you. It has sped past and has given little pain from a separation which seemed to defy nature; it all makes me long for eternity. I will not pursue this subject; it could take us too far. I had no intention of starting it. I only write to felicitate you on being the father of a whole family, in the sense that God is the Father of all of us; and to ask your pardon for the trouble it gives you. It is my doing entirely; it will not last long, and I believe you will enjoy it.'

As Lord St Cyres observes* this was planting rather a load on a very sick man whose income was engaged to the hilt in doctors' bills and charities; but Blaise loved his nephews and probably did enjoy having them.

He did want more money. A recent famine had especially hit the poor of Blois and he wished to send relief there. The Paris Infirmary needed funds. He never walked the streets without finding someone to help from his purse. Already he had in mind a happy idea whereby to make money for the poor of Blois by doing a good turn to the poor of Paris, giving them cheap transport by lines of public vehicles. He discussed with Roannez and others the launching of this enterprise.

In December 1660, Louis XIV, wearied by always having Annat at one ear and 'ces Messieurs de Port Royal' at the other, ordered the Assembly of Clergy to end the matter. The Bull *Ad Sanctam* was to be enforced and the Formulary must be signed. By the early summer of 1661 the crisis faced the clergy and nuns of Port Royal. Signature was compulsory, but could they attach some reservation to save their allegiance to Jansen?

Here yet once again, in all probability, it was Pascal who stepped in to the rescue. The Vicars-General of the absent

* *Pascal*, p. 355.

Archbishop, not ill-disposed to Port Royal, added a *Mandement*, or Pastoral Letter, to the Formulary probably in consultation with Pascal. Its wording was clever:

> 'To avoid every pretext for dispute . . . we ordain and enjoin that in regard to the facts decided by the said Bulls and contained in the said formulary, all shall show the complete and sincere respect which is due to the said Bulls, without preaching, writing or disputing anything to the contrary, and that the signature made by everyone on the said formulary shall be a public and inviolable witness, promise and engagement binding them as to their belief to this decision on the Faith.'

It looks cast-iron; but examination shows that Port Royal could sign without giving away anything. Those who signed would be bound to accept the doctrines in the Bulls; as to the facts mentioned in the Bulls, signatories promised respect for the Pope's views and silence on their own! Arnauld, Nicole and Singlin welcomed this *Mandement* with profound relief and directed the nuns to sign. Most of them were ready to do so but one voice, speaking for a few, rang out like a clarion. Sister Sainte-Euphémie (for in this we must give Jacqueline her name in religion) was in an agony of choice between two evils. Refusal to sign would be disobedience, a breach of one of the sacred vows of her espousal with Christ. To sign would be (as she saw it) to put her name to a lie, implying that a book which she had not read held passages which she condemned. Either way, she would incur an intolerable load of guilt.

She sent a firm courageous letter to Arnauld; and to Soeur Angélique de Saint-Jean she wrote almost in letters of flame. It is one of the searching ironies of this story that perhaps the most Pascalian thing in it was a writing having all the molten logic of the Provincials written by Blaise's sister and at least by implication (if he composed the *Mandement*) with him as target.

'I know well that it is not for girls to defend the Faith, but when Bishops are showing the courage of girls it is time for girls to show the courage of Bishops. . . . If we cannot defend the truth we can die for it, and suffer anything rather than abandon it. . . . Sign? I ask you, my very dear Sister, in the Name of God what difference do you find between these contrivances and the giving of incense to an idol under pretext of a crucifix hidden in the sleeve?'

Arnauld reasoned with her and prevailed on her to sign, but she felt stained by the act. 'I speak', she wrote afterwards, 'under such a weight of sorrow that I should die of it if I had not the consolation of seeing some who hold out and conserve the truth by their person.' The consolation was not enough. Thirteen weeks after signing Jacqueline died, broken with grief. When they told Blaise he said, 'God give us all grace to die so well.'

His iron control covered a profound impression. M. Brunschvicg says, 'This death enlightened Pascal.' Sainte-Beuve wrote of Jacqueline, 'She explains Pascal, completes him, in some respects surpasses him, and now for the last time she converts him.' If these judgments convey that Pascal's sudden change of front was wholly caused by his sister's passion they seem excessive. Before Jacqueline died the situation had radically altered. The nobility of her protest is not affected if we think that Port Royal might have honourably accepted the olive-branch of the *Mandement*, but it was withdrawn.

The Pastoral Letter was forbidden by the King, disapproved by a Papal Brief and in November replaced by another which left no loopholes for reservations.

The Port Royalists discussed their situation. They had to save the convent from dispersal somehow, and keep flying the flag of S. Augustine. Could they even now frame some Postscript such as authority would pass and the Sisters would adopt? The sorely harassed men failed to see that the campaign, though far from over, had reached a decision.

They had been out-generalled. The Jesuits had not only chosen

their battleground, the *Augustinus*, but had contrived to shift
the burden of proof to Arnauld and Nicole. The latter could at
any time have fairly stated their case thus:

> 'We are loyal servants of the Church who happen to have a
> particular veneration for one of the Fathers who is specially
> honoured by the Church. If we are thought to misrepresent
> his teaching, let the offending passages in our teaching be
> pointed out.'

That being said, there might have been little need to say more.
But how much more had been said! Every Latin disquisition on
the subject from Arnauld's pen had served to strengthen the suspicion, diligently fostered by the Society, that the Jansenists regarded as their Bible a book which, if all were known and if one
had time to read it, probably contained a lot of dangerous matter.

The theological clamour was getting on people's nerves, and
the Bull *Ad Sanctam* was much less a definition of a heresy than
an admonition on the lines of 'Stop this talking!' Anne of Austria's exclamation, 'Fi! fi! fi! de la grâce!' may have echoed what
many thought, though they had not her regal freedom to say it.
Three years later, Bossuet, as emissary for the Archbishop of
Paris, said to the Port Royal nuns, 'We have no prejudice whatever against Jansen, whom we esteem very highly'; it was just a
matter of accepting the Pope's ruling.* If at this juncture the gift
of wisdom had enabled Arnauld to say, or Pascal to advise: 'We
stand fast by S. Augustine. As for the *Augustinus*, we submit to
higher authority' (in other words, to sign the Formulary), the
Jesuits would have won the skirmish but lost the campaign.

But Arnauld and Nicole still put their faith in expedients and
in Pascal who had been so prolific in them. They received a dis-
abling rebuff.

Pascal, tired and ill and grieving for Jacqueline, realistic as
always, saw that the day of expedients had passed. The distinction
between *Fait* and *Droit* had been hunted to death and no longer

* Bossuet, *Oeuvres*, Vol.. **XXVI**, p. 221.

meant anything. They must choose between S. Augustine and the Pope. Echoes of Jacqueline's letter recur in the trenchant sentences he wrote to Arnauld.

'If you sign you exclude, formally and necessarily, the teaching of Jansen. . . . To imagine now that there is any Fact distinguishable from the Pope's Right is pure illusion. . . . Whence I conclude, (1) that those who sign the Formulary simply, without reservation, condemn Jansen and S. Augustine and efficient Grace; (2) that those who explicitly make exception of Jansen's doctrine save him and save the doctrine of Grace; (3) that those who sign, meaning that they agree on the doctrinal side but not making it clear that they disagree on the condemnation of Jansen, take a middle line; and that is abominable to God, contemptible to men, and perfectly useless.'

Arnauld, Nicole and Singlin were thrown into great perplexity by this challenge. Their champion was calling them to commit open schism. Arnauld wrote him a long, affectionate and pathetically jocular letter of expostulation. Nicole wrote saying that Pascal's attitude would be magnificent against the enemies of the Church, but this was against its anointed rulers.

A meeting was arranged at Pascal's rooms as he was too ill to attend elsewhere. The situation was reviewed and Pascal rose to speak. After a few powerful sentences he faltered, lost the thread and fell senseless. The room was cleared and he was brought back to consciousness. He explained to Gilberte, 'I saw these men, trustees of the truth, caving in; and it finished me.'

For this brief fantastic interlude Pascal was almost alone (his lawyer friend Jean Domat was with him) in contending for Jansen at any cost. How may this be reconciled with the belief implicit throughout this present book, that Pascal had a deeply un-Jansenist side to his nature? We think he was at the end of his patience with hair-splitting. He was contending for truth in action, not for truth in a volume; at least not for truth in the volume of the *Augustinus*, of which he has left no evidence that he ever read it. He looked before and after, on years of intrigue at Rome, on Annat always at the King's elbow, on Arnauld's continual word-spinning, on all the interminable lobbying, to which indeed he himself had made notable contributions. A line had to be drawn and he suddenly felt it must be drawn here.

He did not forfeit the love and respect of 'les Messieurs', nor they his, but there was a rift. He wrote a few more protests to Arnauld (which were destroyed eventually, as they were only to be published if the nuns signed), and then returned to his 'O Altitudo', a dying man composing his being for eternity.

Almost at once he was immersed in the details of the formation of his Société for placing public vehicles on the streets of Paris. Letters Patent were obtained from the King in January 1662. The company was inaugurated on March 18 and the first line ran from the Porte Saint-Antoine to the Luxembourg.

A long letter from Gilberte to M. de Pomponne (son of Arnauld d'Andilly and Minister of State for Foreign Affairs) gives a lively picture of the *éclat marveilleux* with which the venture had roused all Paris. Every omnibus had been overfilled and had made its way through excited crowds. A second line was added in April and a third in May. A topical comedy, *L'Intrigue des Carosses à Cinq Sols* enjoyed a run. Unlike the Calculating Machine, this industry made money. Pascal sent his proceeds to the relief fund at Blois and bequeathed half his interest in the company to the hospitals of Paris and Clermont.

His daily life now was a waiting upon God, meditating when he could, filling a page of *Pensées* when he could, otherwise taking his medicine and giving as little trouble to others as he might. Gilberte relates as characteristic his interest on behalf of a young girl who begged from him outside S. Sulpice as he came away from Mass. Learning that she was from the country and that her father was dead and her mother in hospital, he took her to the hostel managed by the S. Sulpice clergy and left money for her board. On the morrow he sought out a woman who would know what clothes to buy her and enable her to find a situation.

In his house by the Luxembourg he had installed a poor family with few obligations since he attended to his own simple needs. The man's son fell ill, and rather than send the family away Pascal left the house to them and went to live with the Périers 'between the gates of S. Marcel and S. Victoire' in the parish of S. Étienne-du-Mont.

There in June his last illness befell him. His friends and his doctors agreed that he was less ill than he felt, and for that reason they steadily discouraged his requests for the last Sacraments. His only approach to fretting arose from their reluctance that he should make a general confession and receive Communion.

He pleaded to be transferred to the hospital for the incurable poor, where he would find the real presence of Christ as authentically as in the Eucharist. That not being granted, he asked that some pauper invalid might share his room, so that Pascal could perform the humblest offices for him and thus 'communicate with the Head through His members'. It is at last perhaps briefly possible to refer to 'the anguish of Pascal' as a fact, and not as a romantic misreading of his nature, when we see him, with death almost upon him, separated by the solicitude of his friends from his last remaining need.

On August 17 his headache became insupportable. There was a consultation and the doctors pronounced him to be suffering from acute migraine but not in danger. Gilberte, however, took alarm and arranged for the curé to spend the night with them. It seemed too late, for Blaise was manifestly dying, with continuous convulsions. Near midnight an attack left him apparently dead, but after a while he opened his eyes. Gilberte called the priest. Blaise answered quietly to a few questions on his faith and dispositions and received his Viaticum with deep emotion. After being blessed with the ciborium he spoke a phrase from his own Memorial, 'Que Dieu ne m'abandonne jamais.' Some hours of convulsions followed but he did not speak again.

Earlier in this story we described Pascal as being by conviction and convention a loyal member of the Catholic Church. We have seen a heavy strain cast upon his loyalty to the Papacy, but it took the strain. His will, dated August 3, 1662, opens with the words: 'Premièrement, comme bon chrétien, catholique, apostolique, romain. . . .'

Two and a half years after Pascal's death the new Archbishop of Paris, Hardouin de Péréfixe, a Pharaoh who knew not Joseph and a harsh persecutor of Port Royal, took the Abbé Beurrier to task for having given the last Sacraments to a Jansenist, adding some threats about exhuming the body and dismantling the monument. Under obedience Beurrier put into writing Pascal's final words about his religious attitude. Beurrier had understood (or more correctly, misunderstood) Pascal as having broken with Port Royal because 'they went too far in the matter of grace and did not seem submissive to the Pope'. Péréfixe published it, to the joy of the Jesuits and the dismay of Port Royal. Gilberte Périer challenged Beurrier's account, and he frankly acknowledged that he must have misunderstood Pascal, who meant that the Port Royalists 'went too far' in concessions to authority.

It seemed now that the natural conclusion was that Pascal died in the last ditch of Jansenism, defying the Pope almost with his last breath. This became the traditional picture, as for instance Sainte-Beuve gives it, but it was at least as misleading as the other. Light was at last thrown on the subject in 1908 when the manuscript of Beurrier's memoirs was discovered and published by M. Ernest Jovy. These make it clear that after his final flare-up Pascal had resolutely closed his mind to all the controversial points of the theology of grace, 'et ainsy qu'il se tenoit au sentiment de l'Église touchant ces grandes questions, et qu'il vouloit auoir une parfaite soumission au vicaire de Jésus-Christ qui est le Souverain Pontife . . .'

Room for some misunderstanding remains. At the Tercentenary celebrations in 1923 the panegyric delivered by the Abbé Bremond, generous in substance, was somewhat tempered and hesitant in detail. 'In the person of the Abbé Beurrier it is the whole Church which absolves the dying Pascal and recognizes him as hers.' We get the impression of a death-bed recantation, the turning home of a prodigal from the husks of a far country. Does it accord with the facts?

Perhaps Pascal would never have been a comfortably docile son of Rome, but only at one brief moment of impatience and clouded judgment was he anything but a loyal son; and Port Royal (even if he had belonged to it) was not a sect. All of the characters in this story, except a few libertines and sceptics, were men and women who accepted, and wished to accept, only the doctrines, discipline, ministry and sacraments of the Church of their baptism. In later years the Jansenist movement aroused passions, acquired forms, hardened into attitudes and terms which are irrelevant to Pascal's career because they were subsequent; but they can colour our judgment. We look back through the refracting atmosphere of the intervening years. If we could quite rid ourselves of that or make due allowance and correction for it, we might find ourselves reflecting how nearly France possessed an earlier Lourdes. Is it too great a flight of fancy to suppose that the Calendar might have acquired a second S. Blaise?

Such speculations are outside the theme of this book, which is written not to contend for Pascal's orthodoxy or his sanctity, but as one of the many (and how various!) honest attempts to see and describe him.

Writers have presented him as a humanist, and as an anti-humanist; as a great defender of the faith, an anguished sceptic, a devoted Catholic, a repressed Protestant, a scientist *manqué*, a foe to metaphysics, an outstanding philosopher; the list could be extended to four times this length and there is no indication that it is closed. Ever since Pascal's strong voice was stilled and his mobile features were composed in the noble dignity of his death-mask, men have probed and assessed and conjectured about the mind of this indomitable man. Through it all, he slept and sleeps.

PART II

CHAPTER 10

THE BOOK OF THE PENSÉES

'If from the whole of French literature I could only save one book I should certainly feel death in the soul at the mere thought of sacrificing such a wealth of masterpieces. I should be inconsolable at not being able to read again Ronsard or Rabelais, Montaigne, Corneille or Racine, Molière, Bossuet, Chateaubriand or Lamartine, or how many others. Yet I should not hesitate; and I should consider that the world would still contain a high and pure example of the French genius if we rescued from this appalling hecatomb the one volume of the *Pensées*.'

This judgment of an acknowledged critic (it is translated from M. Victor Giraud's Introduction to Messrs. Dent's edition of the *Pensées* in the Collection Gallia) is representative, not of course in the sense that all Frenchmen would make the same choice; but because few French critics would regard it as a surprising or extravagant choice. In the general estimation of his own countrymen Pascal occupies not only a high place but the top place. 'He is to France', writes Professor Chevalier, 'what Plato is to Greece, Dante to Italy, Cervantes and S. Theresa to Spain, Shakespeare to England.' The Bibliothèque Nationale guards none of its treasures more jealously than the Pascal manuscripts.

We on 'the other side of the water' may be allowed our surprise if we feel it. A nation rich in exquisite poetry, great drama, hilarious satire, torrential eloquence, subtle and precise philosophy, places in our hands what may seem a curiously random collection of aphorisms, quotations and exclamations, and says, 'This is our very best.'

Admirers of Pascal have never been lacking in England,

but the general English attitude has given Pascal an almost secondary place among notable French writers. English opinion has one peculiarity; we may not place him high but we do not seem able to do without him. Examining the name-index in almost any considerable English book on religion or philosophy we might conclude that no French author is quoted in so many books or with so few quotations (usually one to a book) as Pascal. The reference will be slight and may even be slighting, but it will be there. The ranking given to Pascal by his own countrymen is a challenge to our understanding.

When Pascal died, some finished treatises were found in his room awaiting publication and were published without much delay. They included his essays on the Weight of Air and on the Equilibrium of Liquids, written long before, about the time of the Puy de Dôme experiment. With these were found nearly a thousand fragmentary writings flung down in Pascal's rapid script (except such as he had dictated) upon a very great number of separate sheets of paper of various shapes and sizes. These had been sorted into rather over twenty bundles by means of one sewn thread for each bundle.

At the beginning of the eighteenth century, Pascal's nephew, Canon Louis Périer, deposited these for safe keeping in the library of St Germain-des-Prés, after binding them in an album measuring forty-three centimetres by twenty-eight, the fragments being mounted on four hundred and ninety-two pages. Until recent years scholars concluded that the fragments were assembled completely haphazard, and the work was attributed to some illiterate bookbinder, but M. Lafuma has disposed of this legend and shown that although there has been some disarrangement, the album contains strong and numerous traces of the intention to keep together the contents of each of the bundles found in Pascal's room.

The album eventually found its present home in the Biblio-thèque Nationale, and is of course the source of all editions of the

Pensées; but the fragments already had a history before scholars got to work upon them, which was not until 1842.

At Pascal's death an informal Committee was set up, consisting partly of the Périer family and their Clermont friends, such as Jean Domat; partly of the Duc de Roannez and his circle; partly of the Port Royalists. The Provincial Letters had created a public hungry for writings from Pascal's pen and it was widely known that he had spent several years preparing a book; but the task which faced the 'committee' was both immense and delicate. The fragments were hard to decipher, and Port Royal was in deep trouble. Some of Pascal's more outspoken views would have aggravated the situation. They resolved to defer publication to a more convenient season. In 1670, when the situation had eased, they were still discreet and published an innocuous selection (in face of strong protests from Gilberte Périer) in which the fragments were not only abridged but considerably modified. Attached to it was a preface written by Étienne Périer, consisting mainly of an account of the lecture which Pascal had given to outline his plan (*supra*, p. 159). Filleau de la Chaise had first been asked to supply this preface but his *Discours* was found too long and perhaps too imaginative.

This imperfect 'Port Royal' edition, in which a distinctly muted Pascal gave the world a collection of edifying spiritual reflections, had a great and continued success. For nearly two hundred years Pascal's actual words and full text lay unexamined except by Condorcet and the Abbé Bossut, who had access to them. Successive publications of the Port Royal edition were augmented from time to time by opuscules. Thus in the 1687 edition Gilberte's *Vie de Blaise Pascal* was added. A reprint in 1727 by Père Desmolets of the Library of the Oratory enriched the volume by adding the *Entretien avec M. de Saci*, and Pascal's *L'Art de Persuader*. Condorcet's version, about 1770, incorporated *L'Esprit de Géométrie* but mutilated the fragments by cutting out all references to the supernatural, as one might improve the *Origin of Species* by liberating it from all disfiguring references to

Natural Selection. Shortly afterwards, Voltaire published his similarly expurgated version with notes contemptuous of Pascal's philosophy. In 1779 the Abbé Bossut restored, in his own arrangement, the religious element, using the manuscript as a means to supplement the Port Royal edition, but all this while, and for much longer yet, the manuscript awaited full and scholarly study.

Criticism of the Périers is stilled in the face of what we owe them. They anxiously preserved Pascal's manuscripts; they went to the great labour of making two complete and accurate copies of the whole work, and they arranged one of these copies in chapters which almost certainly correspond to the sewn bundles, thus preserving Pascal's filing system, whatever it meant.

In 1842 Victor Cousin delivered a lecture to the Académie Française drawing attention to the great discrepancies between all previous editions of the *Pensées* and what their author had written. He called for a new and authentic edition. The task was taken up by M. Prosper Faugère, who studied the manuscript, decided on his own order in which to present the fragments (following the plan indicated in Périer's preface) and scoured the country for more material.

At Clermont he found an aged judge, M. Bellaigue de Rabaneau, whom he calls 'the last of the Jansenists' as he found him still scrupulously observing the Port Royal Calendar. He possessed some precious manuscripts which he had refused to show to anyone, but he yielded them up to Faugère.*

E. Havet's edition in 1851 had the fullest and most valuable commentary yet published. A very sumptuous and exact edition was produced in 1877 by A. Molinier. Of subsequent editions the best known and most used is in M. Léon Brunschvicg's production of all Pascal's works.† His enumeration is adopted throughout the present book.

* *Pensées, Fragments et Lettres de Blaise Pascal, publiés pour la premier fois conformément aux manuscrits originaux en grande partie inédites*. Paris, 1844.

† *Les Grands Écrivains de France*, Brunschvicg–Boutroux–Gazier. Hachette, 4 vols., 1904–14.

Other notable editions have been compiled by M. Strowski, 1923; Professor M. J. Chevalier, 1925; the Abbé Dedieu, 1937; M. Z. Tourneur, 1938; Dr H. F. Stewart, 1942; and M. Louis Lafuma, 1948.

The first task of any editor is to decide on some principle for the order in which he will print the *Pensées*, which, as we have seen, bear few (though important) traces of the order which Pascal intended to impose on them.

About one-quarter of them may be separated out (though M. Brunschvicg does not do this) as having no connection with the Apology for Religion. These include meditations on the Passion of Christ, notes for letters to Charlotte de Roannez, for the discourses on the Condition of the Great, numerous notes for the Provincial Letters, rules for literary style, etc. When these are strained off the remainder forms a rich miscellany of material for maintaining the truth of Christianity.

Now, the sort of book which an editor makes of the *Pensées* depends on the sort of question he asks himself. If it is, 'How can I arrange these fragments so that Pascal's main ideas on various subjects are made plain and readily available to the reader?' then M. Brunschvicg's method is indicated. He took all the fragments together, ignoring any indications as to Pascal's literary intentions, except such as he himself might have left (and Brunschvicg overlooked the existing clues), sorted them into sections under subject headings, and then arranged these sections into the most logical order he could devise. The book becomes coherent, with a coherence frankly imposed by the editor.

An alternative question is, 'How did Pascal himself intend to arrange these?' A correct answer, if available, would give us the perfect edition. Within limits, some sort of an answer is made possible by three sources of information; the reports of the lecture he gave on his plan, the chapter-headings of the Port Royal copy, and the occasional groupings of several different thoughts on to one sheet by Pascal himself.

Dr Stewart's *Pascal's Apology for Religion* uses Filleau de la

Chaise as the basis for the order in which he prints the Thoughts with suitable section-headings. The result is certainly more dynamic than M. Brunschvicg's; the reader is more aware of the unfolding of a powerful argument, which he knows to have been the very argument in Pascal's mind. Yet the very attempt to assemble the fragments into a single-line piece of reasoning emphasizes that they do not fit into that mould, and reminds us that Pascal's book would not have been quite like that. For making the argument intelligible by means of the *Pensées* we do not expect to see a better arrangement than Dr Stewart's, but we doubt whether it brings us much nearer than M. Brunschvicg's to the book which Pascal did not write. Rather than leave bare the bones of his logic, he would have deliberately *mingled* his material so as to convey conviction by convergent testimonies.

Such mingling is actually to be witnessed on some of the manuscript sheets, and is further indicated in the chapter groupings of the copy. MM. Z. Tourneur, L. Lafuma and J. Mesnard have worked upon such indications and they seem to offer the most fruitful line for research.

We ourselves venture the view that the book of the *Pensées* with all its great evangelistic and apologetic force can never re-create the book of the Apology.* The Apology was not even something which Pascal carried to his grave. A book not written is not a book; and only the writing of it would have brought it into Pascal's beloved world of actual things. The *Pensées* are at once something much less and something much more than that unwritten masterpiece.

They are less in the same way as a painter's palette can never deputize (if this opinion may still be hazarded) for his picture. When an artist's idea is known, and when the materials he has gathered to express it are also known, it is still impossible to know what he will do with them. A work comes into being only in the

---

* This does not put in question the great value of the textual researches initiated by Tourneur and Lafuma. Every new light on Pascal's methods must illuminate his meaning.

actual labour of creation. The Apology never received that immediate fusion of purpose with material which might have given us a very great Christian classic; and the *Pensées* cannot yield it.

They fail there, but in their own right and in their peculiar quality they give us a Christian classic of another sort; for what are the *Pensées*?

They are of course a miscellany. There are some long passages so thoroughly worked over that (notwithstanding anything written above) they might have gone straight into their appointed place in the Apology (e.g. 72, 82, 194, 233). At the other end of the scale there are a number of fragments so fragmentary that much knowledge of context may be needed even to guess their meaning: 'Sceptic for obstinate' (51); 'He lives on the other side of the water' (292). Every writer makes brief jottings which would seem cryptic to anyone else, perhaps to himself next day. The remarkable thing about them here is their fewness. The outstanding quality of the *Pensées* is their lucidity. Whether we accept his meaning or not, his meaning is plain in both senses. It is clear, and it is unadorned. Pascal's sentences have no beauty except their own. A few examples:

> 'Every religion is false which as to its faith does not worship one only God as the origin of all things, and as to its morality does not worship one only God as the goal of all things' (478).

> '*Miracle*: It is an effect exceeding the natural force of the means employed to produce it' (803).

Having once shaped this definition Pascal will never use the word miracle without meaning precisely that.

> 'Le nez de Cléopatre: s'il eût été plus court, toute la face de la terre aurait changé.'

We have seen this translated as though it only meant that Cleopatra's nose affected the future fortunes of the world, but it is the *face* of the Universe which he sees as depending on the face of the Seleucid minx.

'It is not from space that I must seek my dignity, but from the control of my thinking. I shall possess no more if I possess worlds. By space the world engulfs me and dwarfs me to an atom; by thought I comprehend the world.'

Whatever the length of the sentence or the paragraph, there is always the alert shaping of the thought and nothing else; no digression, no ornament. But Pascal is not a thinking machine. His athletic mind is at the service of an intensely ardent and sensitive heart. While he is musing the fire kindles and still he finds the words; we get the great unforgettable phrases:

'L'homme ne sait à quel rang se mettre. Il est visiblement égaré et tombé de son vrai lieu sans le pouvoir retrouver. Il le cherche partout avec inquiétude et sans succès dans des ténèbres impénétrables' (427).

'Le dernier acte est sanglant, quelque belle que soit la comédie en tout le reste. On jette enfin la terre sur la tête, et en voilà pour jamais' (210).

Chateaubriand exclaimed at this 'brief and glacial' history of man with its curt transitions; the comedy, the handful of earth, eternity.

'Toutes ces misères là mêmes prouvent sa grandeur. Ce sont misères de grand seigneur, misères d'un roi dépossédé' (398).

'Le silence éternel de ces espaces infinis m'effraie' (206).

'Que l'homme contemple donc la nature entière dans sa haute et pleine majesté, qu'il éloigne sa vue des objets bas qui l'environnent. Qu'il regarde cette éclatante lumière, mise comme une lampe eternelle pour éclairer l'univers, que la terre lui paraisse comme un point au prix du vaste tour que cet astre décrit . . .' (72).

In his character as Louis de Montalte he had discovered and exploited powers which reappear in the *Pensées*. Even the epistolary form was considered as perhaps the best form for his Apology. 'Lettre pour porter rechercher Dieu' (240). 'After the letter *That we ought to seek God*, to write the letter *on removing obstacles*; which is the discourse on the machine . . .' (246). '*Order* . . . a letter of exhortation to a friend to induce him to seek. And he will reply, "But what is the use of seeking? Nothing is seen." Then to reply to him, "Do not despair!" And he will answer that he would be glad to find some light . . . but it would be no use to him, and so he prefers not to seek. And to answer to that; *the machine*' (247).

The last-quoted *Pensée* is a brief sketch for what might have become an important early section of the Apology, but we think it may also throw some light on the mystery of the argument known as Pascal's Wager. The Wager (283) is a long and ingenious argument which undertakes to persuade the unbeliever that he has everything to gain and nothing to lose by believing in God. It is perhaps the most difficult of the *Pensées* to place either chronologically or logically. There is no indication when Pascal wrote it, and nearly all his biographers query why he wrote it.

He had a double interest in gambling; it offered a field for studying the mathematical theory of chances, and it was a favourite occupation of the men he wished to convert. His application of it to the spiritual life is frankly mathematical, mercenary and mechanical. Its pragmatism caught the interest of the philosopher William James, who (in his *The Will to Believe*) gave the same argument a less egocentric form.

Those who would date it before Pascal's own conversion or treat it as a lapse from the height of his general argument have to account somehow for its references to the truth of Christianity (it has all the appearance of a stage in his apologetic argument) and for the passion of its closing words: 'If this discourse pleases you and seems forcible to you, know that it comes from one who has gone down on his knees before and after, to pray this infinite and limitless Being, to Whom he submits the whole of himself, to submit himself also on your behalf for your blessing and His glory.'

We suppose the truth to be this; for Pascal the standard to be set before men, of Christian vision and Christian living, could not be pitched too high as an ideal of which all men might become capable by grace. At the same time, within the plain limits of morality, it could hardly be set too low when the aim was to persuade men at least to make a beginning. The man who acts on the advice in Pascal's Wager will have gone no distance spiritually. He has everything to learn; but his attention has been caught, the thought of eternity has lodged in his mind, his feet are on the road. The Wager is the furthest limit of Pascal's concession to worldliness to bring the worldling in; and the whole long passage ends with the advice to the hesitant unbeliever to perform religious actions. Pascal recognized (as did Descartes; it was a much-discussed aspect of human action) that much of our experience is purely automatic. Hence his numerous references to 'the machine'. We suggest that *Pensée* 247 is a first short draft for the Wager. Many would say that religious actions performed unthinkingly have no moral value. Pascal gave them a subordinate but definite value. Our vital processes, breathing, digestion, the beating of the heart proceed without our taking thought. The important thing is to keep them going, or in emergency to start them going. The argument of the Wager is a sort of artificial respiration of the soul.

Also it offers us an excellent example of Pascal's most compelling quality as a writer, his use of a sort of 'interior dialogue'. The long passage begins as a soliloquy but imperceptibly it becomes a debate: 'Do not then reprove them for having made a choice; you do not know what led them to it. "No, but I do blame them, not for making that choice but for making any. Heads or tails, you cannot be certain. The fault is in betting at all." Yes, but you *must* bet; you are not free to do otherwise. You are embarked.'

We come upon it time after time in the *Pensées*. To some extent this resort to dialogue is a consciously adopted device. Pascal says as much himself: '*Order by dialogues*;—What ought I to do? I see only darkness everywhere. Shall I believe that I am nothing? Shall I believe I am God? "All things change and follow each other." You are mistaken. There is . . .' (227). ' "What? Do you not say yourself that the sky and the birds prove God?"—No.—"And does not your religion say that?"—No, for however true in a sense it may be for some souls to whom God has given this light, yet for most people it is false' (244). In the manuscript these two *Pensées* run into each other. We see that Pascal definitely contemplated throwing his whole argument into this conversational form, as well he might after the imagined conversations of the early Provincials.

But in fact Pascal's feeling for dialogue goes back far beyond the Provincials, to his vigorous discussions with Méré, Rebours, Roberval, and further back still (we do not doubt) to the interminable self-questionings of his childhood at Clermont when, as his sister wrote, 'il voulait savoir la raison de toutes choses', and when the for and the against, which had to be given an equal voice for truth to emerge, were so personified in his mind that interior dialogue became the very pattern of his thinking and would give peculiar depth and vitality to his writing.

This native, intimate habituation must have been greatly reinforced when he came to reflect on the art of persuasion. There is a *Pensée* on this which recalls a passage between Hamlet and Polonius:

'One imagines one is playing on ordinary organs in dealing with men. In fact they are organs, but not ordinary ones; strange, changeable, wavering, their pipes are not arranged in proper sequence. Skill on other organs will not help us to produce harmonies with these. *One must learn the placing of the keys*' (111).

Consequently in all his writing Pascal is reaching out to his reader, trying to learn his keys, producing harmony from him, bringing him into the interior debate, making him contribute to it.

This is what makes so many readers of Pascal feel that the roles are almost reversed; he seems to be reading them. He cultivated and mastered that mysterious quality which he had discovered in Montaigne: 'It is not in Montaigne but in myself that I find all that I see in him' (64). 'When a natural discourse paints a passion or an effect, one feels *in oneself* the truth of what one reads; it was there all the time but one did not know it. Hence one is inclined to love him who makes us recognize it; he has opened up to our sight not his own riches but ours' (14). It is almost uncannily true that Pascal's writings do awaken and stir into life the reader's most private intimations of truth.

'Ce qui fait la force éternelle de Pascal,' wrote Miguel de Unamuno in the *Revue de Métaphysique et de Morale* (Avril-Juin 1923) 'c'est qu'il y a autant de Pascal que d'hommes qui en le lisant, le sentent et ne se limitent pas à le comprendre,' and M. Gilbert Chinard, an acute and objective critic of some aspects of Pascal's thought, declares that 'the enchantment which he exercises over his reader-listener comes above all from that . . . veritable communion which he has intended and achieved between himself and those whom he would move, touch and convince.'*

No writer, not Montaigne, not Shakespeare, is more universal than Pascal; and none is more intimately or mysteriously personal. That is the innermost quality of the *Pensées*. They were not written for publication; we are eavesdropping when we read them, and paradoxically that brings us the more closely into his confidence. Whenever illness relaxes its grip and allows him some brief period of mental ease and energy, the thoughts are flung down on paper as they arise in his mind. He takes no thought for the form, except in the case of those fragments which he did deliberately shape and reshape for use. Then indeed we get erasures and alternative versions in great number; but in most cases the thought shapes itself; a habit of right expression has become second nature for Pascal; so it all goes down, intellectually

* *En Lisant Pascal*, p. 15 tr.

precise, emotionally charged with his love for God and for his fellows, alive with the drama of the intricate debate between the self that affirms and the self that questions, and also between himself and his reader who is pictured as not only present but argumentative. If he had prepared it for publication there must have been (as in some cases there are) modifications, bridge-passages making more clear the sequence of the logic, enabling us to distinguish when Pascal is uttering his faith, when he is putting a question merely to externalize it and look at it, when (possibly) he is expressing not his own convictions or his own doubts, but those of his interlocutor.

There is no time, and apparently no need, for these discretions. All comes straight from the heart through the brain to the paper, and all is passionate; even the calmest reasonings, the catenas of Old Testament texts, the cool philosophical observations have behind them the same passion as his occasional and famous exclamations. They come from one living in the Order of charity, intent on our finding Heaven. He wrote as never like to write again, and spoke as dying man to dying men.

CHAPTER II

PASCAL'S THEORY OF KNOWLEDGE

At the beginning of this book we described the one known meeting between Pascal and Descartes. It was hardly more than a social encounter, yet for that short while one room contained the mind which, while originating the scientific era, bequeathed to the twentieth century a philosophical riddle, and the mind which perhaps contained the answer to the riddle.

Professor Bertrand Russell in the Introduction to his *History of Western Philosophy* writes: 'Modern philosophy begins with Descartes, whose fundamental certainty is the existence of himself and his thoughts, from which the external world is to be inferred. This was only the first stage in a development, through Berkeley and Kant, to Fichte, for whom everything is only an emanation of the ego. This was insanity, and, from this extreme, philosophy has been attempting, ever since, to escape into the world of everyday common-sense.'

It is not clear why modern philosophy should be so acutely embarrassed by what is recognized as an insane extreme, and it is reasonable to inquire whether the trouble may not have been already present in the first stage of the process traced by Bertrand Russell; that is, whether Descartes himself did not direct Western thought into an attractive *cul de sac*.

Although the few definite references to Descartes in Pascal's writings are critical or derogatory, these two admired each other and had much in common. Both of them thought little of tradition in matters of natural inquiry. Each of them revered reason as man's chief and unique natural endowment.

Perhaps the most fundamental difference between them was that Descartes was, and Pascal was not, a schematic thinker. Equally with Descartes he perceived the reign of order, but was not tempted into drawing a large-scale map of it. He was quite sure that he could not do so, and that no man could do so. In both directions, that of the infinitely little and that of the infinitely great, the scheme of things entire passes human comprehension, and even that section of reality which falls within man's observation presents him with mysteries and with seeming contradictions which he must accept as observed data without distortion. Truth must never be amputated or compressed to fit into the box of some preconceived system. As Professor Chevalier writes,* for Pascal 'connaître c'est chercher'.

Consequently, to speak of Pascal's theory of knowledge is very far from indicating that he had drawn up any general chart of truth into which he could pencil and locate new data as they presented themselves. With Pascal we can only use the word theory in its original meaning, as referring not to a constructed scheme but to a perception, a thing seen. By his theory of knowledge we mean his understanding of some ways in which certitude of fact enters the mind. We may best consider the features of this theory by first recalling that of Descartes.

The scientific age began on a winter day in Bavaria some three years before Pascal was born, when Descartes was shut up in a cottage room so small and so heated that he calls it an oven. He occupied his enforced idleness considering one problem: of what can we be really sure? To reach firm ground, he resolved to exclude as though it were demonstrably false anything whatever upon which reasonable doubt could be cast. That involved the exclusion of all religions and philosophies, all history, all personal memories and even the immediate evidence of his senses (since they could mislead). He seemed to be left with a complete panorama of uncertainties, discarded as such. *He* was left with all this debris; so at least *he* was there; *Je pense, donc je suis*. He had arrived at an unshakable fact.

The solid ground was very cramped ground. The function of

* *Études sur Pascal*, p. 55.

thought was reduced to the thinker thinking of himself (of himself, that is, in the act of thinking, and thinking of himself . . .) At this point Descartes pulled himself together and did a little honest cheating. He must, if only for the moment, bring God into it, and it is evidence of his great intellectual power that he improvised a version of the ontological argument for God's existence which stands up much better than S. Anselm's argument to logical examination. 'I cannot forgive Descartes,' Pascal would write later. 'In all his philosophy he would willingly have done without God; but he had to bring Him in just to give the world a flick to set it in motion; after that, he had no further use for God' (77). Now that God had come upon the scene, Descartes felt free to reflect that he had certain quite clear notions about the existence of things, their extension in space, their duration in time. Such ideas were too clear to have any origin but God, and being from God they must be true. The external world came into view as a realm of facts. There is an excellent modern series of philosophical works (*Être et Penser*, La Baconnière, Neuchâtel) whose slightly mischievous motto 'Sum ergo Cogito ergo Sum . . .' exposes the circularity of Descartes' argument, but nothing can rob him of his place in history as having inaugurated a new approach to nature, and a new epoch of technical progress.

He had drastically simplified both the field of observation and the methods of observing. As to the field of observation, he admitted three basic facts: God, Descartes, and the world of objects in space and time. The properties of objects were such as arose from 'clear ideas'. In a later day Locke would elaborate the distinction between primary qualities, such as are mensurable, and secondary qualities, such as may be to some extent contributed by, or dependent upon, the observer; but this distinction is already noted by Descartes in his Sixth Meditation. As to the methods of observing, by sweeping aside all appeal to Aristotelian or other authority he was able to reduce research to three or four plain simple rules. He streamlined the whole subject, formulating a basic routine, intelligible to all, of approach to physical nature.

'We note', wrote Professor Whitehead, 'its astounding efficiency as a system of concepts for the organization of scientific research. In this respect it is fully worthy of the genius of the century which produced it. It has held its own as the guiding principle of scientific studies ever since. It is still reigning. Every University in the world organizes itself in accordance with it. . . . It is without a rival.'

'And yet,' he adds, 'it is quite unbelievable. . . . Thereby modern philosophy has been ruined.'*

So we encounter the note of doubt about this marvellous intellectual instrument, a note which (apart from Pascal) was sounded first and unconsciously by Spinoza, who himself had no doubts. His own great and original contribution to metaphysics makes free though discriminating use of the *Méthode*, as is shown by the geometrical setting of his Ethics; but it leads him into difficulties. Readers of the Ethics who persevere to the fifth Book, which is largely on the love we owe to God, can hardly fail to be aware that something has crept into the argument which does not seem to belong.

'The essential incoherence of Spinoza is one of the first warning signs of the false lead given to modern thought by its founder,' wrote the late Archbishop Temple.†

The late Baron von Hügel attacked that feature of Descartes' thought which was probably felt by Pascal as a defect worse than any other, though Pascal was not enough of a metaphysician to define it in von Hügel's terms. If we follow Descartes 'we thus take for granted, as rock-certain truth, that which is demonstrably non-existent: "I think" instead of "I think such and such objects" . . . for all experience is always threefold; it is always simultaneously experience of the subject, and of the object and of the over-bridging thought. Indeed, clear consciousness always concerns first the object, and only much later on the subject.'

A formidable indictment occurs in Professor Jacques Maritain's

* *Science and the Modern World*, Cambridge University Press, pp. 69, 70.
† *Nature, Man and God*, Macmillan & Co Ltd, p. 69.

Trois Réformateurs.* This long essay is based on the thought-provoking thesis that the world-view which Descartes harnessed upon posterity, the sort of attitude which the human mind has been taught to adopt towards the outer world, is such as the Scholastic theology attributes to the angels; such knowledge claims to be intuitive as to its mode, innate as to its origin and independent of things as to its nature. As men are not angels, in each of these particulars the claim to such knowledge distorts and impoverishes our grasp of facts.

'Il (Descartes) a fait de la connaissance un abîme d'inquiétude, parce qu'il a conçu la Penseé humaine sur le type de la Pensée angélique' (p. 78). 'Connaissance inhumaine parce qu'elle s'est voulu surhumaine! C'est là le principe, non seulement du brutal mépris affiché par Descartes à l'égard des humanités . . . c'est le principe et l'origine de la profonde *inhumanité* de notre science moderne' (pp. 92–3). 'Nous voyons de nos jours les réjouissants effets de cette matérialisation de la science, et l'étonnante indigence intellectuelle qu'un progrès, admirable en lui-même, de la spécialisation technique et des procédés opératoires est capable de procurer' (p. 94).

Pascal's own references to Descartes, besides the one quoted above (p. 198), are brief: 'To write against those who have made too profound a study of science: Descartes' (76); 'Descartes useless and uncertain' (78) '(*Descartes*)—We must say summarily: "This is made by figure and motion", for it is true. But to say what these are, and to construct the mechanism, that is ridiculous' (79). These opinions must be taken in due perspective. Pascal was engaged in the task of finding the strongest arguments for the truth of Christianity, and was reflecting upon the degree of support which the philosophy of his time might afford to religion. His conclusion that *for his apologetic purpose* Descartes was 'useless and uncertain' falls a long way short of an opinion on his status as a philosopher. Yet in the last-quoted *Pensée* a general

* Paris, Librairie Plon, 1925; II. Descartes et L'Incarnation de l'Ange.

opinion is implied, which includes Descartes in condemnation along with all other builders of *à priori* systems; they 'construct the mechanism', that is, not content with making true observations they undertake to draw up a complete scheme of the Universe, and that, in view of the contrarieties and mysteries and contingencies with which experience presents us, is in Pascal's eyes a ridiculous presumption.

What Descartes offered was not only a system, but a closed system, a completely mechanical universe so interlocked that any part of it might in theory be inferred from any other part. Experience told Pascal that existence was indeed very largely mechanical, but that one could not possibly say of everything that it was *necessarily* what it was. 'I feel that I myself need not have been, for my ego consists in my thought; and I who think would never have existed at all if my mother had died before I was animated; so I am not a necessary being. Neither am I eternal or infinite; but I see clearly that there is in nature a being necessary, eternal and infinite' (469). Here Pascal is launched on a line of reflection which led Professor Whitehead to postulate God as the Principle of Concretion, the Power deciding which events should be awarded the high and exceptional distinction of happening!

There are two sentences in the *Pensées* which seem to distil the essential difference between Pascal and Descartes. 'Le moi est haïssable' (455), and 'L'homme, par exemple, a rapport à tout ce qu'il connaît' (72).

'Self is hateful.' As it stands this might be no more than a social axiom; it is bad form to push oneself forward. Very possibly Pascal heard Méré enunciate this first rule of *honnêteté* in these very words; but in writing them he had got far beyond matters of deportment. Here is one secret of intellectual and spiritual advance. When Pascal studied any object he was concerned with that object, not with Pascal studying it. The world which he studied was a direct datum, not an inference from his own existence, neither was his own existence (as for Descartes) his 'fundamental certainty'.

'Man, for instance, is related to all that he knows.' Professor Maritain's chief complaint of Descartes is that he claimed (like the angels) to study the natural universe as from a position quite outside it, forgetting or ignoring that he was part of it. 'He scorned the place of the body in the labour of science; refused that animal knowledge which links us from the first to the created world. He set aside this properly human condition of only being able to know anything by the senses and the intellect together. See, now, what happens to this fine science! Is it sure of itself? It will indeed go far; but Kant is waiting at the turn of the road. If the senses (he will say) only report to us pure appearances, and are not the vehicle to our mind of that which is, you will need (presumptuously) a *suprasensible* intuition to give you the actual thing. Angels may have it, but you do not carry such a thing in your luggage. *Ergo* you never will be able to know that which is, and all your *à priori* is nothing more than a traffic in appearances.'*

On the contrary, Pascal insists on the *nexus* with nature which Descartes would rule out. There is an inescapable give and take between man and his world which is both help and hindrance. Because of this alliance we can never see things quite in focus or in their totality. It is not only Heaven but this world also which we necessarily see as in a glass, darkly. But without this alliance we cannot see things at all, except in diagram or skeleton outline, in the abstraction of their formal relationships. We shall have parted with the 'thing in itself'.

Here, then, are two features of Pascal's approach to fact. The sense of *contingency* (the Chestertonian feeling that events are caused not by any dead mechanism but in response to some deliberate, conscious choice) and the sense of *rapport*, these are the first steps in Pascal's ascent to a theory of perception.

He never renounced or modified his dictum that man's first privilege and duty is to think, and to think clearly; but he came to recognize and carefully to distinguish two different ways of thinking, the mathematical and the intuitive.

* *Op. cit.*, p. 102 tr.

'For mathematical thinking the principles are palpable but removed from common use; you have to wrench your mind aside to attend to them, but having done so you see your way ahead; you would need to have a very muddled mind to argue inaccurately from such plain principles. But intuitive thinking deals directly with the things before you; there is no turning aside. You need only use your sight, but it has to be good sight. The principles involved in such thinking are many and subtle. So for intuitive thinking one needs very clear sight, and a habit of accurate thinking' (1).

But already before working upon this distinction, and within a purely mathematical setting, Pascal had noticed the presence in things of a *hierarchy*, an arrangement in ascending orders, which fascinated him by its implications and which grew into perhaps the most characteristic feature of his thought. Of course it was at least as old as Plotinus, but Pascal developed and used it in his own way.

His doctrine of Orders begins modestly enough in a passage from his arithmetical treatise *La Sommation des puissances numériques**:

'If you have a magnitude of a certain order, you cannot increase it by adding any number whatever of magnitudes of a lesser order. Thus, a line cannot be prolonged by adding points to it at either end however many points you add. A plane surface is not increased by laying lines along one edge, neither does a solid get any larger by surrounding it with a number of surfaces.'

Since lines have no breadth and surfaces no depth this was a truism, but it was a fertile truism. It germinated in Pascal's mind, and from that time onwards he tended to dwell on ascending triads of reality: mineral, vegetable, animal; body, mind, soul. It would be interesting to know whether, when he became a

* Tome III, p. 366.

profound student of the Bible, he halted over the great text, 'The earth bringeth forth fruit of itself; first the blade, then the ear, after that the full corn in the ear,' which exactly describes the later habit of his thinking.

Of these triads he noticed two things, of which the first has already been noted. No amount of magnitude in a lower order could amplify a higher order. This would seem to make the various 'orders' completely separate from each other; but the other quality linked them together. He found one law prevailing throughout all experience. 'La nature s'imite; une graine, jetée en bonne terre, produit; un principe, jeté dans un bon esprit, produit; les nombres imitent l'espace, qui sont de nature si différente. Tout est fait et conduit par un même maître; les racines, les branches, les fruits; les principes, les conséquences' (119).

Give Pascal a few years to digest this idea and at last we get his doctrine of the Three Orders. The great *Pensée* 793 (792 in the Everyman Library edition) is best known for its three closing paragraphs, but it calls for quotation in full:

'The infinite distance between bodies and minds is an emblem of the infinitely more infinite, the supernatural, distance between minds and charity.

In all the glory of high rank there is no splendour for those whose researches are of the mind.

The greatness of men of intellect is invisible to kings, to the wealthy, to captains and to all the worldly great.

The greatness of wisdom, which is nothing if not from God, is invisible to the worldly and to men of intellect. These are three orders, different in kind.

Great geniuses have their empire, their glory, their greatness, their victory, their splendour, and have no need of worldly greatnesses with which they have nothing in common. They are seen not by the eyes but by the mind; it suffices.

The saints have their empire, their glory, their victory, their splendour, and have no need of worldly or intellectual distinctions, with which they have nothing in common, and which can neither increase nor diminish them. They are seen by God and the angels, not by bodies or by curious minds; God suffices them.

Archimedes, without renown, would have had the same veneration. He conducted no battles to glut the eyes, but all minds can share his discoveries. Oh! how he has shone for those who think!

Jesus Christ, without wealth and without any external display of knowledge, is in His own order, that of sanctity. He gave the world no invention; He did not reign; but He has been humble, patient, holy, holy towards God, terrible to demons, without any sin. Oh! the pomp, the prodigal magnificence of His appearance to the eyes of the heart, which see Wisdom!

It would have been useless for Archimedes to act the prince in his books of geometry, though he was so entitled.

It would have been useless for our Lord, that He might shine in His kingdom of sanctity, to come as a king; but it well became Him to come in the glory of His own order.

It is very absurd to be shocked at the lowliness of Jesus Christ, as if this lowliness were of the same order as the greatness in which He did appear. Let us only contemplate this greatness in His life, in His Passion, in His obscurity, in His death, in the choice of His disciples, in their desertion, in His hidden resurrection, and in all else, and it is all so grand that we have no ground for offence at a lowliness which does not touch it.

But there are those who can wonder only at worldly distinctions as though there were no intellectual grandeurs; and others there are who admire only intellectual eminence as though Wisdom did not offer something infinitely higher.

All bodies, the firmament, the stars, the earth and its kingdoms, are not equal to the smallest gleam of intelligence: for it knows them and itself, and they know nothing.

All bodies together, and all minds together, and all their products, are not equal to the slightest stirring of charity. That is of an order infinitely more exalted.

From all bodies together we cannot obtain one little thought; that is impossible and of another order. From all bodies together, and from all minds together we cannot derive one movement of· true charity. That is impossible, of another order, supernatural.'

This is a devotional *Pensée*. It is evidently meant as the climax, or a climax, of his presentation of Jesus Christ as the object of the convert's faith. Pascal did not write it as a contribution to epistemology; yet it deserves attention as such.

In his final statement of the three orders, consider the first two terms, the distinction between bodies and minds. It is completely dualistic, as every writing on this subject was bound to be of that time. Matter belongs to one realm and mind to another. Our opinion that Pascal was ahead of his century is not a claim that he foresaw Einstein's Theory of Relativity or Bertrand Russell's technique of Logical Analysis, the latter of which at least would seem almost to obliterate the difference between mind and matter.

Even now we suspect that not many people, and they not all the time, can quite overcome the habit of regarding a material object as being somehow other than a thought. We may acquiesce in the doctrine of neutral monism and agree that (for example) the ink used in writing this sentence is homogeneous with though in important respects distinguishable from, for instance, the meaning expressed, but still we are more impressed by the difference than by the common nature of the two events.

For Pascal the difference is nearly absolute. The only connecting link is 'the admirable liaison' prevailing in the universe; 'La Nature s'imite . . .' For him there are these three orders, layers, storeys, which constitute the totality of being, and of which the material world is the basis and the point of departure for studying the whole, yet is as remote from the realm of thought as linear geometry is from solid geometry. The distance, he says, is infinite. The emergence of intelligent life at some definite period in the past is sometimes referred to in much the same way as though it were some new form of vegetation, and as though no problem were created by the existence of a natural order before that event, and as though 'appearance' or 'emergence' meant anything, or 'meaning' meant anything, except within a centre of intelligence. What Pascal exposes is the absurdity, the strict nonsense, of reducing mind to terms of matter.

The pre-eminence of mind over matter is referred to by Pascal in words which may be commended to the special attention of any who entertain the idea (itself an emotional judgment) that Pascal, like Rousseau and perhaps Bergson, substituted emotion for thought. The empire of the mind, by which he meant the sphere of cold, exact, strenuous logical brain-work—the sort of work which solved the cycloid and which is today applied to the problems of linguistic analysis—was for Pascal an empire indeed; and be it remembered that this *Pensée* was written in his last days and represents his mature conclusions. He has not suffered any emotional relapse.

He has, however, acquired an emotional advance. He has become certain that there is a realm of truths which the reasoning intellect cannot, by itself, comprehend. We do comprehend these truths, but not by analytical reasoning.

The perception of an order of charity, whose distance above the order of mind was 'infinitely more infinite' than that of minds over bodies, implied our possession of a means of grasping the truths that are in this highest order. He calls this faculty *le cœur*, a name with romantic associations but not here used with romantic intention.

Through the discursive reason we receive a very great deal of information about the world and (as the Church would affirm) about God; but *all* information so acquired suffers one general disability which is more visible today than it was in Pascal's time; it can only be statistical.

'What we can know of physical objects . . . is only certain abstract properties of structure. We can know that the sun is round in a sense, though not quite the sense in which we see it is round; but we have no reason to suppose that it is bright or warm, because physics can account for its seeming so without supposing that it is so. Our knowledge of the physical world, therefore, is only abstract and mathematical.'*

Pascal found that purely intellectual inquiries into the being of God yielded a similar result. The discursive mind could at best give only a completely abstract picture. It could not penetrate to that order of charity where the 'brightness' and 'warmth' of God are felt as facts. Yet something in us could reach that realm, for what else was religion?

He called that something *le cœur*. He did not mean that it was cardiac rather than cerebral; probably so far as physiology comes into it *le cœur* uses the brain as much as *l'esprit* does, but uses it differently. It composes instead of separating; it replaces analysis by cognition; and it goes much more immediately to the core and meaning of the object perceived.

'C'est le cœur qui sent Dieu, et non la raison' (278). Thus far Pascal is hardly more than echoing S. Augustine's *Pectus facit Theologium*, but in *Pensée* 282 he somewhat extends the idea. He had always been (like Bertrand Russell) irked by the fact that geometry did not start from scratch; it had to be given a start in the form of initial propositions which could not be proved and had to be accepted. He was inclined at first, as we see in *L'Esprit de Géométrie*, to attribute this to the frailty of human nature, and consequently to despair of all prospect of real knowledge. His later verdict is less despondent:

'We know truth not only by the reason but by *le cœur, and it is in this last way that we know first principles;* and reason, which has no part in it, tries in vain to overcome them. . . . We

* Bertrand Russell, *A History of Western Philosophy*, p. 862.

know that we are not dreaming, and however impossible it is for us to prove it by reason, that impossibility only illustrates the limits of reasoning and not, as sceptics affirm, the uncertainty of our knowledge. For our knowledge of first principles, such as space, time, motion, number, is as sure as any knowledge we have. Reason has to trust these intuitions of *le cœur*, and has to base upon them every rational argument. . . . Principles are intuited, propositions are inferred; there is certainty throughout, but there are different roads to certainty' (282).

We observe that Pascal has imported or extended the operation of *le cœur* from the grasp of heavenly things to the study of the natural world; or it would be truer to say that he finds the order of charity permeating the natural world and, to that extent, employing *le cœur* for its study. He has indeed almost come to the point of saying 'C'est le cœur qui *sent* quoi que ce soit'; that there is nothing at all in the real world which we fully apprehend by the reason only, since the reason can only give us its statistical properties.

We desire to suggest that this conclusion is the one to which his whole argument points, even though he stopped short of drawing the conclusion himself. 'Would that God had enabled us to know everything by instinct and feeling. But nature has given us only a few instances of this sort of knowledge; all the others can only be acquired by reasoning' (282). In Pascal's day the gap between the scientific picture of nature and that painted by common experience was much smaller than it is now. If he had foreseen that rational process could give us no assurance that the sun was bright or warm he would certainly have progressively extended the function of *le cœur* to account for these certainties. If the reason can only give us H_2O then it must be *le cœur* that gives us water. A completely scientific account of an apple today would be a sheaf of symbols and pointer-readings from which the whole of its appleness would have evaporated; yet it is as an apple that we should claim to *know* it. What is the nature of such knowledge, now that it has transpired that it is not rational knowledge?

Pascal gives his answer in the most famous and most misunderstood of all his sentences: 'Le cœur a ses raisons, que la raison ne connait point' (277). He did not write this in the vein of minor poetry or religious emotion. He was observing, with an eye for facts unequalled in his generation, that the scientific picture is an incomplete picture, and that we know things which the discursive reason fails to convey.

Perception of a whole fact involves more than the analysing mind; it involves the personality. We are *en rapport* with our world, in some sense akin to it, and so our knowledge has something of the character of immediate recognition.

CHAPTER 12

THE PORTRAIT OF MAN

This chapter will consist mainly of extracts from the *Pensées* illustrative of Pascal's portrait of man. This portrait is in some features at variance with the main currents of modern thought, and therein perhaps lies its claim to modern attention.

There is of course no one theory of human nature which is universally adopted in the present age; but there is a twentieth-century climate of opinion which fosters the growth of the purely scientific and naturalistic approach to the subject. The process of thought which began with Descartes has issued in a society in which man increasingly regards his own species as he regards any other class of natural objects endowed with life; as with them, it is held that his only attributes and needs are biological and are confined to the spatio-temporal framework within which they can be studied. This view is incompatible with the religious view of man which it seeks to replace. The naturalistic view of any living object is that it can progressively adapt itself to its environment and evolve within that environment. The religious view of man is that the natural world is not man's final environment, and awareness of this creates in human nature a permanent tension which sets up his moral conflicts and his spiritual hungers.

The modern tendency is to discard, with a sense of relief, this spiritual view of man as the product of primitive superstitions and taboos, and to apply all the resources of modern science to the cultivation and development of human life conceived in exclusively naturalistic terms.

We should note about this view that it is new and even recent. 'The fundamental moral struggle within the individual was for many centuries accepted as the essential characteristic of man. This being, suspended between good and evil by a law inherent in his nature, is the man of Dante and Shakespeare, and of Balzac and Tolstoy. He occupies a country of his own with unique rights and needs, quite apart from the biological sequence.'* The belief that man is in some sense an exception in nature not only held the fort throughout all the centuries of pre-scientific history but survived over three centuries of the scientific era. It is within living memory that the idea of limiting man to his natural framework has taken any root. To quote again Mr Edwin Muir, 'For the separate autonomous drama of mankind we have gradually substituted a natural process. The result has been a reduction of the image of man, who has become simpler, more temporal, more realistic, and more insignificant.' We might add—and more insecure.

Pascal's account of the human condition is incidental and introductory to his defence of Christianity. It relies mainly upon personal experience and observation. It opens with the long and well-known *Pensée* on man's place in the universe.

THE TWO INFINITES (72)
Disproportion of Man

'So let man contemplate the whole of nature in her full and splendid majesty and turn his attention from the low things around him. Let him gaze on that brilliant light, set like an eternal lamp to illumine the universe; let the earth dwindle for him to a point compared with the vast ambit described by that great star and realize with wonder that this great circle is itself a minute point beside the revolutions of the stars in the surrounding firmament. Our vision may be arrested there but our imagination can pass beyond, and nature's power to supply material will not be exhausted sooner than our power to conceive of it. The entire visible universe is only a speck in the ample bosom of nature. . . . Nature is an infinite sphere, the

* Edwin Muir, 'The Natural Man and the Political Man', Penguin New Writing, No. 26.

centre of which is everywhere, the circumference nowhere. . . .

Returning to himself, from his remote little corner where he is lost; from the minute cell in which he is lodged (and I mean the visible universe), let him estimate at their real value his kingdoms, cities, himself. What is he, in the Infinite?

But a prodigy equally astonishing awaits him. Let him examine the most delicate things he knows. Let him take up a mite with its tiny body, its parts infinitely tinier, the legs with their joints, veins in the legs, blood in the veins, humours in the blood, drops in the humours, vapours in the drops. Let him further split up these last things to the very limit of his power, and let the last object which he thus arrives at be now the subject of our discourse. Perhaps he will suppose that it is Nature's smallest object. Allow me to show him its infinite greatness. Let me compel him to see within it a new abyss. I would depict for him not only the visible universe but all that he can imagine of nature's immensity within the womb of this fragment of an atom. . . .

For what is man in nature? A nothing, compared with the infinite; an all, compared with the nothing, a mean between nothing and all. As he is infinitely remote from comprehending the extremes, the end of things and their beginning must remain an impenetrable secret to him; he is equally incapable of seeing the Nothing from which he came and the Infinite in which he is engulfed. . . .

So let us take our measure. We are something, not everything. . . . Extremes elude us. . . . We are wafted about in a vast setting, drifting always in uncertainty, driven from one end to the other, every point which we would grasp and cling to wavers and leaves us, and if we follow it it escapes, slips by and vanishes for ever. Nothing stays for us. . . . We burn with longing for firm ground, some final solid basis for the tower we would build to the Infinite; but the foundation cracks, and the earth breaks open into chasms. . . .

Man, for instance, is related to all that he knows. His life requires space, time, movement, elements to compose him, warmth and food to nourish him, air to breathe. . . . He is in a dependent alliance with everything. . . . It is equally impossible to know the parts without knowing the whole, and to know the whole without knowing the parts in detail. . . .

Man is to himself the most astonishing thing in nature; for he cannot conceive what the body is, still less what the mind is, and least of all how a body can subsist with a mind. This is the climax of his perplexities yet it is his very being.'

Thus far, and Pascal will go much farther in this direction, he diminishes our human stature as ruthlessly as any modern cosmographer. He has to do so, for the facts compel him; and he can afford to, for he knows that this truth is not the whole truth.

Man's Feebleness

(127) 'Condition of man: inconstancy, ennui, inquietude.'

(110) 'Awareness of the falsity of present pleasures, ignorance of the emptiness of absent pleasures, cause our inconstancy.'

The Corruption of Human Nature

(100) '*Self-love.* The nature of self-love and of this human Ego is to love only the self and to consider only the self. But what can one do? This self that is loved is unavoidably full of faults and miseries; it wants to be great and knows itself little; it wants to be happy and knows itself wretched; it wants to be perfect and knows itself full of imperfections; it desires to be loved and esteemed of men, and knows that these faults only earn their aversion and scorn. From this perplexity arises the worst and most vile passion one can imagine; for a man conceives a mortal hatred against this truth which rebukes him and convicts him of his faults. He wants to get rid of it. Not being able to destroy it in itself he tries to obliterate the knowledge of it in himself and in others. . . .

There are different degrees in this hatred of truth, but all may perhaps be said to have it in some measure, since it is inseparable from self-love. . . .

No one speaks of us in our presence as he does of us in our absence. . . . Man is then only mask, falsehood, hypocrisy. He does not wish to be told the truth; he avoids telling others the truth; and all these dispositions, so contrary to reason and justice, have a natural root in his heart.'

Imagination

(82) '*Imagination.* This is that dominant faculty in man, mistress of error and falseness and all the more deceptive in that she is not always so, since we might infer the truth if we could rely on her always lying. . . .

I speak not of fools but of the wisest men; it is among them that imagination exercises the strongest sway. . . . She makes men happy and sad, healthy and ill, rich and poor; she forces the reason to believe, doubt, deny; she blunts or quickens the senses. . . .'

This long *Pensée* on imagination has a number of charming vignettes of which we quote the best known:

'Would you not assume that this magistrate, whose venerable age imposes the respect of all, is guided only by pure and tranquil reason, and that he judges things by their nature without distortion from the silly externals which bemuse the weak-minded? Very well; watch him, as he takes his place to listen to the sermon, absorbed in his devout zeal, reinforcing the solidity of his mind with the warmth of his charity. See him as he settles to listen with an exemplary respectfulness! Now let the preacher make his entrance; and suppose that nature has endowed him with a raucous voice or a ludicrous face, or the barber has made a mess of shaving him, or some chance has splashed his dress with dirt; then no matter what important truths he may enounce I will bet on our senator's loss of gravity.'

(88) 'Children who scare themselves by putting on beards. They are children, but—how to secure that what is so feeble because it is childish becomes strong as age increases? We only change our fantasy. All that is made perfect by progress perishes also by progress. Nothing that has been feeble can acquire absolute strength. It is all very well to say, *He has grown, he has changed*; he is also the same.'

(85) 'Things which have chief hold on us, such as hiding our poverty, amount to almost nothing. It is a trifle which our imagination magnifies to a mountain. Another turn of the imagination would reveal this to us without difficulty.'

The last-quoted sentence seems as far as Pascal can go in saying that the imagination, besides being deceptive and a sign of weakness, can have a positive function and value. He seems unaware of the fact that his own scientific discoveries, the Provincial Letters, and above all the project of convincing the mind and heart of the unbeliever made demands upon an exceptionally creative imagination.

Diversion

We have seen earlier (p. 109) that Pascal's attention was drawn to men's indulgence in occupations which seemed to have no better object than to pass the time. Many of the *Pensées* deal with this aspect of human character.

(171) 'The only thing that consoles us for our miseries is diversion, yet it is the greatest of our miseries. For it is that which chiefly prevents us from thinking of ourselves, and so insensibly destroys us. Without it we should suffer ennui, and this would goad us into seeking some more genuine way out. But diversion amuses us, and leads us insensibly to death.'

(170) '*Diversion.*—If man were happy he would be the more so the less diverted he were, like the saints and God.—Yes,

but is not this capacity to enjoy diversion a sign of happiness?—
No, for the enjoyment comes from elsewhere and from outside;
so it is contingent, subject to a thousand accidents, which bring
inevitable afflictions.'

Pascal's treatment of the subject of diversion may have particular interest for the present age, in which the provision of enter-
tainment has become a major industry. His most immediate
reaction to the spectacle of time being 'killed' was one of distress
amounting sometimes to horror; an exclamation in the margin of
one of the *Pensées* (194) in which he declares the indifference of
men to their eternal welfare to be unnatural, reads, 'Are they so
hardy that they care not about *anything* that touches them? Would
they behave like this on any question of their honour or their
property? What? It must be a sort of enchantment!'
Investigation showed him that play, of any sort, was not the
simple frivolity that it might seem. Men who were quite content
to spend their days gaming for small stakes would find no pleasure
in the stake without the game, or in the game without the stake.
What, then, was the nature of their pleasure? It lay in the excitement of passions aroused by some artificially created object of
passion, in default of, or in fear of, the contemplation of real
objects.
Such men, he concluded, were 'wise in their generation', for
anything was better than the blackness of ennui (of which he had
experience); yet such wisdom was folly in the long run.

'They have a secret instinct which forces them to seek external distraction, and which arises from their habitual unhappiness. They have another secret instinct, left over from the
greatness of our original nature, which gives them to under-
stand that happiness is really only found in repose, not in
tumult; and from these two instincts arises a confused idea,
hidden in the very depths of their soul, prompting them to aim
at repose through agitation and to suppose that the satisfaction
they lack will come to them if by surmounting all the difficulties

that face them they can by such means open the door to rest'
(139).

Pride

Pride in its worst sense, the sense in which it is the worst of the
seven deadly sins is, for Pascal, a feature not so much of average
human nature as of the types of philosophy which encourage man
to imagine that his redemption is within his own capacity.

(430) 'C'est en vain ô hommes, que vous cherchez dans
vous-mêmes le remède à vos misères. . . . Les philosophes vous
l'ont promis, et ils n'ont pu le faire. . . .'

(434) '. . . Connaissez-vous donc, superbe, quel paradoxe
vous êtes à vous-mêmes! Humiliez-vous, raison impuissante!
Taisez-vous, nature imbécile! Apprenez que l'homme passe in-
finiment l'homme, et entendez de votre Maître votre condition
véritable que vous ignorez! Écoutez Dieu!'

But pride in its more venial form, as self-conceit (which was
his own besetting weakness), is prominent in his portrait of the
ordinary man.

(148) 'We are presumptuous enough to wish to be known by
everybody, even by people born after we no longer exist; and
we are so vain that the esteem of five or six acquaintances
entertains us and keeps us happy.'

(150) 'Vanity is so anchored in the heart of man that a
soldier, a day-labourer, a cook, a porter swaggers and likes to
have his admirers. Writers who condemn vanity enjoy the
glory of having written well on the subject; and their readers
like it to be known that they have read them; and I who write
this perhaps have this disposition, and possibly those who read
it. . . .'

Egoism

(457) 'Each man is a whole to himself; for him when dead,
all else is dead. Whence it comes that each man believes himself

a totality to everyone. We should judge nature by itself, not by ourselves.'

The *Pensée* which we have quoted earlier, which begins 'Le moi est haïssable' and continues by rebuking Miton for his self-centred life, continues:

(455) '. . . In a word, the *moi* has two qualities; it is unjust, because it makes itself the centre of all; it is unfair to others, in wishing to be served by them; for each *moi* is the enemy, and would like to be the tyrant, of others. You (Miton) manage to be an egoist without injury to others, but you do not succeed in removing its wrongness, and to those who hate wrongness you do not manage to make it acceptable, but only to unjust people. So, after all, you remain in the wrong, and can only please those who are in the wrong.'

Such are the main 'deceptive faculties' with which Pascal fills in his picture of the misery of man without God, which is of course only one aspect of his complete picture. He seems to round it off with the brief but graphic *Pensée* (183):

'Nous courons sans souci dans le précipice, après que nous avons mis quelque chose devant nous pour nous empêcher de la voir.'

But as we turn to the other side of the picture it is important to recognize that Pascal is not presenting man to us as a simple mixture of qualities, some good and some bad. Man's *misère* is so blended with his *grandeur* that human faults are, in many cases, distorted and misdirected indications of his greatness.

The Greatness of Man

(409) 'Man's greatness is so visible that one can infer it even from his misery. For what is natural in animals is just what we call misery in men; whence we recognize that his nature, now

being reduced to the animal level, is fallen from a higher nature which was once his own. For who is afflicted at not being a king, except a dispossessed king?'

(411) 'In spite of the vision of all our miseries which touch us and grip us by the throat, we have an instinct which we cannot repress, which raises us up.'

(398) 'Man's greatness is indeed proved by these miseries. They are the miseries of a great lord, of a dispossessed king.'

The Thinking Reed

(146) 'Man is visibly made to think; that is his whole dignity and his whole merit; and his whole duty is to think rightly. . . .'

(347) 'Man is only a reed, the feeblest thing in nature; but he is a thinking reed. There is no need for the whole universe to arm itself to crush him; one vapour, one drop of water, will suffice to kill him. But when the universe crushes him, man is still nobler than that which kills him, because he recognizes what kills him, and he knows the advantage the universe has over him; the universe knows nothing of this. . . .'

Longing for the True Goal of Life

Pascal came to regard the most trivial occupations of men as giving some indication of a reaching out for a forgotten or lost ideal.

(154) *The search for the true good.* Most men look for the end of life in fortune or in external benefits, or at least in amusement. Philosophers have shown the vanity of all that, and have placed the ideal as best they could.'

(422) 'It is good to be tired and fatigued by the fruitless search for the true good, so that we stretch out our arms to the Liberator.'

Here Pascal exactly echoes the thought in George Herbert's poem 'The Pulley', which ends thus:

Yet let him keep the rest,
But keep them with increasing restlessness;
Let him be rich and weary, that at least,
If goodness lead him not, yet weariness
May toss him to My breast.

(397) 'A tree does not know itself to be miserable. To know oneself to be miserable is therefore a miserable condition but also it is a sign of greatness.'

Even pride in its various forms bears testimony to man's sense of the high rank he was intended to assume in the scheme of things.

(400) '*Greatness of man.* We have so great an idea of the soul of man that we cannot bear being scorned, or that any one soul should fail to esteem us; the whole happiness of men consists in this esteem.' (404) 'The pursuit of glory is man's worse baseness, yet it is also the chief mark of his excellence. . . .'

Man's whole nature, for Pascal, bears this character of mixture and fragmentation, like some ancient stained glass window which has been broken and clumsily reassembled, with the remaining pieces all in the wrong places, giving only dim hints of the original design, but retaining evidence of its splendour. Both the naturalistic and the idealistic account of man would be equally wide of the facts:

(358) 'Man is neither angel nor brute, and the pity of it is that in trying to behave like an angel he behaves like a brute.'

Man's essential mystery and bewilderment lead Pascal to that famous passage which Pope borrowed almost as it stands for his *Essay on Man*:

(434) '. . . What then can man do? Ought he to doubt everything? Doubt whether he is awake, whether he is being pinched or being burned? Doubt whether he doubts? Doubt his own

existence? In fact no one goes as far as that, Nature sustains our feeble reason and prevents us from raving to that extent. What then? Shall a man claim that he possesses certain truth, when the slightest pressure forces him to let go his hold on it?

Quelle chimère est donc que l'homme! Quelle nouveauté, quel monstre, quel chaos, quel sujet de contradiction, quel prodige! Juge de toutes choses, imbécile ver de terre; dépositaire du vrai, cloaque d'incertitude et d'erreur; gloire et rebut de l'univers.'

Pope's version of this is familiar:

> *Chaos of thought and passion all confus'd;*
> *Still by himself abused or disabused;*
> *Created half to rise, and half to fall;*
> *Great lord of all things, yet a prey to all;*
> *Sole judge of truth, in endless error hurl'd;*
> *The glory, jest, and riddle of the world!*

As we know, Pascal found the answer to the riddle in the Christian religion as displayed over the whole range of Scripture and the history of the Church. Of the two characteristic doctrines of Augustinianism, the fall and predestination, he insisted on the first while feeling much less concerned about the second. His view on man's freedom of will is indicated in the very interesting *Pensée* on prayer (513). 'Why God has established prayer. 1. To communicate to His creatures the dignity of causality . . .' a highly un-Jansenist observation. But the fall of man was one of the two polar doctrines upon which the whole drama of man's redemption turned:

(556) '. . . The Christian religion, then, teaches men these two truths, that there is a God, of Whom men are capable, and that there is in our nature a corruption which renders them unworthy of Him. It is equally essential that men should know both these things; and it is equally dangerous to know God without knowing one's own misery, and to know one's own misery without knowing the Redeemer Who can set one free.

The one leads to the pride of the philosophers, the other to the despair of the atheists. . . . It is merciful of God to have given us knowledge of these two points. The Christian religion does this; that is what the Christian religion is.'

CHAPTER 13

GOD AND PASCAL

The main theme of this book was stated in the Introduction, as a study of Pascal's approach to truth. Pascal's spiritual experience and religious practice have come in to the extent that they throw light on this subject, but if these had been the writer's chief concern then this would have been a different book. In particular, the whole of the positive contribution to the defence of Christianity which occupies more than the second half of the *Pensées* has received here treatment which would have been rightly considered much too summary and scanty in that other book.

Yet if we ever see the real Pascal it is when we find him on his knees; and here we may leave him to speak for himself.

THE MEMORIAL

L'an de grâce 1654
lundi 23 novembre jour de St Clément pape et martyr
et autres au martyrologe
Veille de St Chrysogone martyr et autres
Depuis environ dix heures et demie du soir jusques
environ minuit et demi

Feu

Dieu d'Abraham, Dieu d'Isaac, Dieu de Jacob.
Non des philosophes et des savants
Certitude, certitude, sentiment, joie, paix.
Dieu de Jésus-Christ

Deum meum et deum vestrum
Ton Dieu sera mon Dieu.
Oubli du monde et de tout hormis Dieu
Il ne se trouve que par les voies enseignées
     dans l'évangile
     Grandeur de l'âme humaine.
Père juste le monde ne t'a point connu mais
     je t'ai connu.
Joie joie joie pleurs de joie
     Je m'en suis séparé
Dereliquerunt me fontem aquae vivae
     Mon Dieu me quitterez-vous?
Que je n'en sois pas séparé éternellement
Cette est la vie éternelle qu'ils te connaissent
Seul vrai Dieu et Celui que tu as envoyé, Jésus-Christ
     Jésus-Christ
     Jésus-Christ
Je m'en suis séparé; je l'ai fui, renoncé, crucifié,
     Que je n'en sois jamais séparé.
Il ne se conserve que par les voies enseignées dans l'Evangile
     Renonciation totale et douce etc.

LE MYSTÈRE DE JÉSUS

Jesus suffers in His Passion the pains which men inflict on Him; but in His Agony He suffers those that He inflicts upon Himself: *turbare semetipsum*. Not human but Almighty is the hand that brings this torture; He must needs be Almighty to bear it.

Jesus seeks some consolation at least from His three dear friends, and they sleep. He prays them to support Him if only a little while, and they leave Him with complete indifference, so slight is their pity that it does not rob them of a moment's sleep. So Jesus was abandoned alone to the wrath of God.

Jesus has no one on earth to feel and share His pain or even to know of it; only Heaven and He share that knowledge.

Jesus is in a garden; not of delights like the first Adam, where he lost himself and the human race, but in a garden of agony, where He saves Himself and the whole race. He suffers this anguish and this desertion in the horror of night.

I believe that Jesus never complained except this once, but then He complained as though He could not contain His weight of grief: 'My soul is sorrowful to death.'

Jesus seeks company and comfort from men. It seems to me that this is the one time. He does not receive them, for His disciples sleep.

Jesus will be in agony till the end of the world; we must not sleep during that time.

Deserted by all, even by the friends chosen to watch with Him, Jesus is anxious about the peril to which they expose not Him but themselves, and warns them for their own safety and their own welfare with a thoughtful tenderness amid their ingratitude and warns them that the spirit is willing but the flesh is weak.

Jesus, finding them still asleep undisturbed by care for Him or for themselves, has the kindness to refrain from waking them, and leaves them to their slumber.

Jesus prays, uncertain of the Father's will, and fears death; but when He knows it He goes forward to offer Himself to die: *Eamus. Processit* (Joannes).

Jesus has prayed to men and has not been heard.

While His disciples slept Jesus worked their salvation. Every saved soul has been saved in his sleep; the sleep of nothingness before he was born, and the sleep of sin after he was born.

He prays only once that the cup should pass, and even then with submission; and twice, that it should come if it ought.

Jesus in weariness.

Jesus, seeing all His friends sleeping, all his enemies awake, commits Himself utterly to the Father.

Jesus, regarding Judas, sees in him not his enmity but the

order of God which He loves, and admits, calling him friend.

To enter His agony Jesus tears Himself from His friends; we must tear ourselves from our nearest and dearest to be like Him.

Jesus in an agony and the sharpest pains, prays longer.

We implore the mercy of God, not that He may leave us at peace in our sins but that He may deliver us from them.

—'Be consoled; you would not seek Me if you had not found Me.'

—'I thought of you in My agony; I sweated such drops of blood for you.'

—'To wonder what you would do in some imaginary case, that is to tempt Me, not to test yourself; I would do it in you if it should happen.'

—'Give yourself up to be guided by My rules; see how well I have led the Virgin and the Saints who have let Me act in them.'

—'The Father loves all that I do.'

—'Would you that what costs the blood of My humanity should cost you no tears?'

'Your conversion is My affair; fear not, and pray with confidence as for Me.'

'I am present to you by My word in the Scriptures, by My Spirit in the Church and by inspiration, by My power in the priests, and by My prayer in the faithful.'

'Doctors will not cure you for you will die at last. But it is I Who cure and render the body immortal.'

'Endure the bonds and slavery of the flesh; as yet I deliver you only from spiritual bonds.'

'I am more a Friend to you than this man or that; for I have done more for you than they; they have not suffered for you as I have suffered; they have not died for you amidst all your infidelities and unkindnesses, as I have done, and as I am ready to do, and continue to do in My elect and in the Holy Sacrament.'

'If you knew your sins you would lose heart.'

—Then I do lose heart, Lord, for your word reveals to me their deadliness.

—'No, for I Who show them to you can cure you of them, and what I tell you signifies that I will heal you; and it will be said to you "Behold, thy sins are forgiven thee." Repent therefore for your hidden sins and for the veiled evil of your known sins.'

—Lord, I give You all.

—'I love you more than you have loved your defilements, *ut immundus pro luto.*'

—'To Me be the glory, not to thee, worm of earth.'

—'Inquire of your confessor, when My direct message to you may seem an occasion of ill or of vanity or curiosity.'

—I see my abyss of pride, curiosity, lust. There is no link between me and God or Jesus Christ the Just. But He has been made sin by me: all Thy lashes are upon Him; He is held in abhorrence more than I am, and far from scorning me He holds Himself honoured that I hasten to help Him.

—But He has healed Himself; still more will He heal me.

—I must add my wounds to His, and join myself to Him, and He will save me in saving Himself. But this must not be put off to the future.

—*Eritis sicut dii scientes bonum et malum.* Everyone behaves like God when judging 'This is good, or bad'; and men mourn or rejoice over-much at events.

—Do little things as though they were great, in view of the majesty of Jesus Christ Who does them in you and Who lives our life; and great things as though they were little and easy, because He is all-powerful.

THE SEPULCHRE OF JESUS CHRIST

On the Cross, Jesus Christ was dead, but seen. In the Sepulchre He is dead and hidden.

Jesus Christ was buried only by the Saints.

Jesus Christ worked no miracles in the Sepulchre.

Only the saints enter there.

It is there, not on the Cross, that Jesus takes a new life.

This is the last mystery of the Passion and of Redemption.

No other place of rest had Jesus on earth but the Sepulchre.

His enemies only ceased to persecute Him in the Sepulchre.

It seems to me that Jesus Christ allowed only His wounds to be touched after His resurrection: *Noli Me tangere.* We must unite ourselves only to His sufferings. He gave Himself, in the Last Supper, as mortal; to the disciples at Emmaus, as risen; to the whole Church, as ascended into Heaven.

THE WATERS OF BABYLON (459)

The rivers of Babylon roll and plunge and carry away. O holy Sion where all is firm and nothing falls!

We must rest upon the waters, not beneath them or in them, but upon them; and not standing but seated: being seated to be humble, and upon them to be secure. But in the porches of Jerusalem we shall stand.

This pleasure—let us see if it is stable or transitory; if it passes away it is a water of Babylon.

LETTER TO CHARLOTTE DE ROANNEZ
(Extract)

Those who forsake God for the world do so because they are drawn.... Those who quit the world to embrace the Cross of Jesus Christ do so because they are drawn.... The life of devotion is not a life of dejection; we forsake pleasures for others that are greater. The joy of having found God is the very principle of our sorrow for having offended Him. The world knows nothing of the joy of him that finds a treasure hid in a field. It is a joy the world cannot give, or take away. . . . The true devotion, perfected only in Heaven, is so full of satisfaction that it accompanies the whole way, the beginning, the progress, the arrival. Its light is shed on all around it; and if there be any sadness mixed with it, especially at the beginning, this comes not from virtue but from ourselves; not from the new devotion but from the attractions we are leaving and have not quite left.

SELECT BIBLIOGRAPHY

Pascalian research today is active, progressive and more factual, less tendentious, than at some previous periods. This book makes no claim to be a work of research though I hope it reflects the present stage of informed opinion. Had I 'but world enough and time' I should have worked upon Auguste Molinier's palaeographic edition of the *Pensées* (1877), Léon Brunschvicg's major edition and Jacques Chevalier's edition of the complete *Oeuvres* in the 'Bibliothèque de la Pléiade' (1941); and indeed many more books than those listed below, which have been read in the preparation of the present work.

TEXTS

LÉON BRUNSCHVICG: *Blaise Pascal: Pensées et Opuscules* (Classiques Hachette). Compact, complete and indispensable.

DR H. F. STEWART: *Les Lettres Provinciales de Blaise Pascal.* (Modern Languages Texts; Longmans, Green & Co., 1920.) Has the original orthography, and most informative introduction and notes.

Z. TOURNEUR: *Blaise Pascal, Pensées*, Édition Critique (Editions de Cluny). This clearly allows the reader to see Pascal's own erasures and alterations.

The Provincial Letters of Blaise Pascal: Ancient and Modern Library of Theological Literature (Griffith, Farran & Co.), the only version in English known to me.

Miscellaneous Writings of Pascal, translated from M. P. Faugère, Introduction and notes by George Pearce. (Longmans, Brown, Green & Longmans, 1849.) A very precious collection, especially of Pascal's correspondence.

Pascal's Pensées: Translated by W. F. Trotter, Introduction by T. S. Eliot. Everyman's Library (J. M. Dent & Sons). Since this is the most readily available English edition, I have used Brunschvicg's enumeration of the *Pensées,* which it follows.

DR H. F. STEWART: *The Heart of Pascal* and *Pascal's Apology for Religion.* (Cambridge University Press, 1942.) These two books give the whole text of the *Pensées* in the original French based upon Tourneur's readings of the manuscripts. All except the text is in English and includes two excellent introductions. The *Apology* gives all those *Pensées* which seem intended by Pascal as material for his defence of Christianity; *The Heart of Pascal* gives all those *Pensées* which were otherwise intended. Dr Stewart's great contribution is his rearrangement of the *Pensées* in an order which clarifies Pascal's apologetic plan. In 1950, Dr Stewart combined these into one book with an English translation, and this was published posthumously by Messrs Routledge, Kegan Paul, Ltd., as *Pascal's Pensées, Bilingual Edition.*

ERNEST HAVET: *Les Pensées de Pascal,* Paris, 1891, has very revealing and scholarly notes.

VICTOR GIRAUD: *Les Pensées de Pascal* (Bonne Presse). This is the second volume of Giraud's *Pascal.* It is an arranged selection, with a number of very 'pascalian' notes *en marge.*

The Essays of Michael, Lord of Montaigne, translated by John Florio, three vols., Everyman's Library (Dent). Pascal steeped his mind in Montaigne, especially in the *Apology* of Raymond Sebonde (II, xii) but also in I, iii, xii, xx, xxii, xxv, xxvi, xxvii, xl; III, iv, viii.

Les Provinciales ou Les Lettres Escrites par Louis de Montalte à un Provincial . . . avec La Théologie Morale des Rev P. P. Jésuites: À Cologne 1659.

CORNELII JANSENII EPISCOPI IPRENSIS: *Augustinus,* Lovanii 1640.

BOOKS ABOUT PASCAL AND HIS WORKS

SAINTE-BEUVE: *Port-Royal,* in the three-tome *Pléiade* edition. Of this epic, the third volume and much of the fourth are devoted to a marvellously evocative picture of Pascal, romantic in tone but with a solid basis of critical judgment.

ALEXANDRE VINET: *Études Sur Blaise Pascal,* Paris, 1876. A searching analysis of the *Pensées* and their penseur, distinguished by a close correspondence of nature between the writer and his subject.

FORTUNAT STROWSKI: *Pascal et Son Temps,* three volumes (Paris, Plon-Nourrit, 1921), a work of true erudition and great charm, to which I am heavily indebted.

FORTUNAT STROWSKI: *Pensées de Pascal: Étude et Analyse* (Melotté, Paris), devotes the qualities shown in Strowski's earlier book to the exposition of Pascal's main thoughts.

A. LA HAYE: *Discours sur la Vie de Pascal* (Paris, 1781).

VICTOR GIRAUD: *Pascal, L'Homme, L'Oeuvre, L'Influence* (Paris, 1905). Notes for a course of Lectures given at the University of Freiburg.

VICTOR GIRAUD: *Pascal: Essai de Biographie Psychologique* (Bonne Presse), has been particularly helpful to my theme.

ÉMILE BOUTROUX: *Pascal* (Librairie Hachette; Les Grands Écrivains Français), a deservedly standard work.

LÉON BRUNSCHVICG: *Descartes et Pascal, Lecteurs de Montaigne.* (Être et Penser; Cahiers de Philosophie, Neuchâtel, 1945.) This last work of Brunschvicg's includes a deep comparative study of the philosophies of Descartes and Pascal.

JEAN GUITTON: *Entretien avec M. de Saci* (Aix, 1946), a small but authoritative study of this document.

GILBERT CHINARD: *En Lisant Pascal* (Lille et Genève, 1948). A stimulating critique especially of Pascal's political ideas.

ANDRÉ CRESSON: *Pascal, Sa Vie, Son Oeuvre* (Paris, 1947).

ANDRÉ SUARÈS: Puissances de Pascal (Emile-Paul Frères, Paris, 1923).

Études sur Pascal. This is the Pascal Tercentenary number of the *Revue de Metaphysique et de Morale*, Avril–Juin, 1923, and contains a remarkable series of studies of Pascal's importance for the twentieth century, by Maurice Blondel, Léon Brunschvicg, Jacques Chevalier, Harald Hoffding, Jean Laporte, Frédéric Rauh and Miguel de Unamuno.

VISCOUNT ST CYRES: *Pascal* (Smith, Elder & Co., 1909).

DR H. F. STEWART: *The Holiness of Pascal* (Cambridge University Press, 1915). Hulsean Lectures: and *The Secret of Pascal* (Cambridge University Press, 1941). Everything the late Dr Stewart wrote about Pascal is exact and illuminating.

FRANÇOIS MAURIAC: *Pascal* (Living Thoughts Series, Cassell & Co. Ltd., 1941) a useful anthology.

MGR. R. A. KNOX: *Enthusiasm* (Oxford, Clarendon Press) contains an over severe but brilliant assessment of Port Royal and Jansenism. The broad sympathy which distinguishes this great book seems at an ebb throughout the section on Jansenism and I have felt the lack notably in the writer's account of Pascal, which nevertheless has contributed some features to my own picture.

EMILE CAILLIET: *The Clue to Pascal* (S.C.M. Press Ltd., 1944). A study of Pascal's debt to the Bible, which perhaps rides too hard the Protestant thesis.

MARGARET TROUNCER: *The Reluctant Abbess* (Hutchinson, 1957), a fascinating novel which throws a clear light on Mère Angélique and a rather spectral light on Saint-Cyran.

DENZIL G. M. PATRICK: *Pascal and Kierkegaard: A Study in the Strategy of Evangelism*, two volumes (Lutterworth Press, 1947). A weighty study of Pascal's anticipation of Christian existentialism.

DR C. C. J. WEBB: *Pascal's Philosophy of Religion* (Oxford University Press, 1929).

PROFESSOR WILLIAM CLARK: *Pascal and the Port Royalists.* (Edinburgh, T. & T. Clark, 1902.)

LOUIS LAFUMA: *Recherches Pascaliennes.* (Delmas, Paris, 1949.) Opened a new chapter in the study of the Pascal manuscripts, showing that they retain much of Pascal's own arrangement of them.

JEAN MESNARD: *Pascal: His Life and Works*, translated by G.S. Fraser (Harvill Press, 1952), with introduction by Mgr Knox. This admirable book came my way too late to allow the raids I should have been tempted to make on it. I have used it to correct some statements and to re-cast the section on the manuscripts of the *Pensées*.

APPENDIX

The following are translations of most of the foreign language passages in the text.

p. 35   'By good fortune for which I cannot be too grateful, I was taught on a peculiar plan and with more than fatherly care.'

p. 55   'There was some mystery in Saint-Cyran. There was more than a hint of the prophet and of strange inspiration. His words came from beyond himself; he would delay utterance until they were dictated from elsewhere. He was imperious and absolute, yet tender and full of pity; this dualism set up no disharmony in him. He had what a man of inspiration needs to command and to decide, but he knew how to stir feeling and attraction and tears. His chosen were not very numerous. They were an *élite;* they formed a sort of general staff; in fact they were his fanatics.'

p. 67   'People don't know what this natural model is, which one is supposed to follow; and in default of this knowledge they invent extravagant terms: the Golden Age, the wonder of our times, fatal, etc.; and they describe this jargon as poetic beauty' (33).

'"Quench the torch of sedition," too luxuriant. "The inquietude of his genius," two excessively vigorous words' (59).

p. 70   *'Whatever evils, Fate, you bring,*
I know the way to draw their sting.'

p. 75   [This is given as an example of Pascal's style. It is Isaiah, ch. 49, verses 14-16.]

237

p. 84   [Latin] 'It is most unseemly and not to be tolerated that the doctrines of the Faith should be subject to the puerile principles of logic or the little guesses of the human mind.'

p. 90   'Do not rob me of that which you could not give me. For though God did use you to bring me the first movements of His grace, you know well that all the love, all the joy, that we find in goodness comes only from Him. So you might indeed disturb my joy but you could not restore it if once it should be lost through you. . . . If you lack the strength to follow me, at least do not hold me back. . . . Do by virtue that which thou must do by necessity; make a gift of what God is taking . . . from thee above all I ask this sign of affection.'

p. 91   'I am well aware, Monsieur, that among many so learned ones who have searched the last recesses of mathematics there must be some who regard my action as presumptuous, in view of my youth and my weakness, and my daring to find a new way in a region so full of briars, and without a guide. . . .'

p. 94   'See, Monsieur, we learnt from M. de Saint-Cyran to accept nothing for God's house except from God's hand.'

p. 95   'Man is born to think' (cf. 'Man visibly is born to think' (146)).

p. 96   'The greater the mind, the greater the passions . . . in a great soul all is great.' 'In proportion as a man has more intellect he discovers more original things of beauty.' . . . 'There is an eloquence of silence more penetrating than the tongue can utter' (cf. 'The heart has its reasons which the reason cannot know'). 'All the same, one must guess, but it must be good guessing' (cf. ' —it is only a question of having good sight, but it must be good' (1)). '. . . of which he feels in his heart the sources, so vital and so deep' . . .

p. 97   '*Summum jus, summum injuria* [The strongest law is the worst injury] . . . thus one calls just whatever one has to do. From this arises the right of the sword, for the sword does give a right. . . . From this arises the injustice of the Fronde, which raises its pretensions to justice against force' (878). 'In order that the members should be happy they must have one will, and they must conform to the whole body' (480).

p. 99   'Once involved in this duplicity, Jansenism is lost; and I must add, it deserves it. Saint-Cyran where art thou?'

p. 111   'As for me, I have never been prevented from doing what I will, or compelled in spite of myself to do what I do not will.'

'the numerous thoughts on the vanity, weakness and contradiction of man, which Pascal commandeers and reproduces, *while crowning them, like (captured) minarets, with the Cross.* What should strike us more than the resemblance . . . is the difference of [Pascal's] tone and his seriousness of purpose in contrast to [Montaigne's] fencing bout'.

p. 113   'You observe only the policing of this little cave where you are stuck, even if you see that much. This scrap is nothing compared to the whole. . . . What you are appealing to is a municipal law; you must not assume that it is universal.'

p. 117   *Your pencil, young and charming hostess, drew*
    This dainty sketch,
And I have coveted your art to etch
    The lovely view.
Gods throng my sky, and goddesses, yet still
To show one goddess fair I lack the skill —
    To make her you!

p. 119   *Nothing is so intolerable*
  For man as to be
  In complete repose;
 Without passion, without occupation,
  Without diversion, without study.
   He then feels
 His nothingness, his desolation,
 His insufficiency, his dependence,
  His weakness, his emptiness,
 Instantly from the depths of his soul
  will arise tedium,
 Gloom, dejection, woe, misery,
   Despair.

p. 121   [Greek] . . . unless a man might sail upon some surer and stronger vessel (than human reason), some word of God, and so come safe to shore.

p. 122   'Open my heart, Lord . . . the image of the world is so deeply graven there that thine can no longer be traced. . . . Let me find thee within myself since I lack the strength to find thee in the world around. . . . Enter my heart and my soul. . . .'

p. 128   'Behold, Monsieur, the message of this great mind who knew so well the duty of man. I venture to assert that he would have deserved profound regard if he had been equally aware of the weakness of man'.

p. 129   'All his opinion is distilled in this doubt which even doubts itself, this ignorance ignorant of itself. . . . Unwilling to say "I do not know," he says "What know I?" All the Essays move on these lines.'

'leaving it no power to act without confessing humbly its own feebleness'.

'and I should have loved with all my heart the minister of so great a vengeance'.

p. 130   'It teaches . . . these two truths: both that there is a

God, of Whom men are capable, and that there is a corruption in man's nature making him unworthy of God' (556).

p. 131   'Custom is our nature. Who accustoms himself to the faith believes it, and is unable to avoid fearing hell' (89). 'The exterior has to be joined to the interior; that is, one has to get down on one's knees, pray with the lips, etc.' (250).

p. 143   'but the movement of the argument, the vitality of the style, are Pascal's and are most admirable. Genius saves everything!'

p. 148   'The first work of genius in prose to be recognized is the collected edition of the Provincial Letters. All kinds of eloquence are exhibited in them. One must attribute to this work the moment when our language takes its form.'

p. 150   [This is only an example of Pascal's French . . . translated in next paragraph.]

p. 179   'and thus he held to the sentiment of the Church on these great questions and wished to show perfect submission to the vicar of Jesus Christ, who is the Sovereign Pontiff . . .'

p. 189   'Cleopatra's nose: had it been shorter, the whole face of the earth would have been altered.'

p. 190   'Man doesn't know what rank to claim for himself. He is visibly adrift, and fallen from his true place without being able to get back. He seeks it restlessly and vainly in impenetrable shades' (427).

'The final act is brutal, however charming the comedy which led to it. Earth is thrown on the head; that is all, for ever' (210).

'All these same miseries prove his greatness. They are miseries of a great lord, a dispossessed king' (398).

'The eternal silence of these infinite spaces appals me' (206).

'Then let man contemplate all nature in her high and full majesty; let him lift his eyes from the low objects which surround him. Let him gaze upon this blazing light, set like an eternal lamp to lighten the universe, and let the Earth seem to him a mere point compared with the path which that star describes . . .' (72).

p. 194   'What constitutes the eternal force of Pascal. . . . is that there are as many Pascals as there are men who, while they read him, feel him, not limiting themselves to understanding him.'

p. 200   'He (Descartes) has reduced knowledge to an abyss of uncertainty by classifying human thought along with angelic thought' (p. 78). 'This knowledge becomes inhuman through trying to be superhuman. That is the ground, not only of Descartes' brutal disregard for the humanities . . . it is the principle and origin of the profound *inhumanity* of our modern science' (pp. 92-3). 'We see today the delightful outcome of this materialization of science, and the dismaying intellectual poverty characteristic of a progress (wonderful in its own way) of technical specialization and mechanical process' (p. 94).

p. 204   'Nature imitates herself. A seed, thrown into good soil, produces; an idea, thrown into a good brain, produces. Numbers imitate space, though they are so different from it. One Master makes and guides all things; roots, branches, fruits; principles, consequences' (119).

p. 218   (430) 'Vainly, O men, do you seek within yourselves the remedy for your pains. Philosophers have promised you this, but they could not bring it. . . .'

(434) 'See then, proud men, what a paradox you are to yourselves! Humble yourself, impotent reason! Be silent, foolish nature! Learn that man transcends man beyond limit, and learn from your Master your real state, of which you are ignorant! Hear God!'

p. 219   'We run carelessly to the precipice after putting something in front to hide it from us.'

p. 224   [The Memorial—translated on pp. 123-4.]

INDEX

INDEX